Hui Muslims in China

Hui Muslims in China

Edited by

Gui Rong, Hacer Zekiye Gönül, Zhang Xiaoyan

LEUVEN UNIVERSITY PRESS

© 2016 by Leuven University Press / Presses Universitaires de Louvain / Universitaire Pers Leuven
Minderbroedersstraat 4, B-3000 Leuven (Belgium)

ISBN 978 94 6270 066 6
D / 2016 / 1869 / 40
NUR: 741/761

Layout: CO2 Premedia
Cover design: Paul Verrept

GPRC
Guaranteed
Peer Reviewed
Content
www.gprc.be

Table of Contents

Introduction

CHAPTER I

Identity, Interaction and Islamic Practice: Hui Muslims in China

Gui Rong

Yunnan University

For nearly a century, some western scholars who studied Chinese Muslims, from Marshall Broomhall (1910), Dru C. Gladney (1991, 1998), Raphael Israeli (1994, 2002), Jonathan N. Lipman (1997), Michael Dillon (1996, 1999), David Atwill (2005), Maris Boyd Gillette (2000), Barbara Pillsbury (1981), Sachiko Murata (2000), Donald Daniel Leslie (2006), Zvi Ben-DorBenite (2005), and James D. Frankel (2011) conducted their research from multiple perspectives, disciplines and fields. They paid more attention to the specific historical and geographical context, as well as the local knowledge of Chinese Muslims, which all enlightened Chinese scholars with much theoretical and methodological inspiration. Probably due to the limitations in translation and the international academic exchanges, not much research done by Chinese scholars on Chinese Muslims is translated into English, in spite of their fruitful achievements. This inequality in the dissemination of knowledge and information between the East and the West is surely unfavorable to the sharing of knowledge, as well as the dialogue of civilizations all over the world. In order to promote cooperation and exchange in Muslim research between China and Europe, in May 2014, Gülen Chair for Intercultural Studies in KU Leuven and the National Research Institute of Yunnan university (Centre for Studies of Chinese South-Western Borderland Ethnic Minorities) in China jointly held an international conference on the topic of 'Developing A Sense of Belonging in Diverse Societies: Hui-Muslims in China and Muslims in Europe'. The papers that are offered in this volume are based on the speeches at this conference. For this reason, most of the papers from Chinese scholars (from Yunnan University) focused on Hui Muslims in Yunnan. We hope that this volume in English, to some extent, can shed light on the local characteristics and local cultural diversities of Hui Muslims in China, and illustrate Chinese and the Western research perspectives. We also expect this volume to be helpful in encouraging thoughts on how to promote social integration of the different countries' Muslims, as well as successful dialogues between Muslim countries and non-Muslim countries, and between Islamic civilization and other civilizations.

Islam and Hui Muslims in China

According to Chinese historical records, in the second year of Yonghui, Tang Dynasty (651 AD), the Arabian empire sent an envoy to establish contact with China. Since the Tang and Song Dynasty, a large number of Arabian and Persian merchants did business in China, importing Islamic teachings and lifestyle. At the beginning, these Muslims often gathered and lived in important cities and ports in China so as to maintain their religious beliefs and unique lifestyle. This was the origin of 'foreigners' quarters' (*bofang* 蕃坊). Throughout the Tang Dynasty, Five Dynasties, Song Dynasty, Yuan Dynasty, Ming Dynasty, Qing Dynasty and the Republic of China, Islam had gradually become the religion of the majority of the following ten peoples in China: Hui, Uyghur, Dongxiang, Salar, Kazak, Uzbek, Kirgiz, Tajik, Bao'an, and Tatar. Consequently, Islamic culture in China shows different national characteristics and regional characteristics. Islam gradually developed into two different systems in China. Six Muslim minorities, including Uyghur, Kazak, Uzbek, Tajik, Kirgiz and Tatar, mainly inhabiting the Xinjiang Autonomous Region, where the land was vast and near to some Islamic countries in Central Asia, explains the complex religious environment, which evolved during the succeeding dynasties since ancient times. Xinjiang Autonomous Region maintains close ethnic, religious, economic and cultural exchanges with the neighboring Islamic countries since ancient times, while it has political, economic and military ties to the Chinese central government. Indeed, it never really broke away from the control of the central government. Most of the ancestors of the Hui, Salar, Dongxiang, and Bao'an were merchants who came into China via the 'Sea Silk Road' and the 'Land Silk Road', soldiers and craftsmen who moved into the Central Plains with Mongol forces, and Muslims of the Western Regions, submitted to the authority of central government. They went on expeditions, opened up wastelands, or ran businesses. They reproduced by marrying with other ethnic groups and rarely ran into conflicts with central or local authorities. These two systems of Islam had different conditions, contents and forms of development (Mi and You, 2001: 132-136).

The Hui people developed into a distinct ethnic group during the Ming Dynasty (Bai, 1984: 15-28). Hui people mainly descend from ethnic groups of Central Asia, Persians and Arabs who migrated in the 13th century, including descendents of Arabs and Persians who settled in coastal merchant ports in the South East of China and Hui Muslim ancestors who moved to the Central Plains during the Ming Dynasty. While these immigrants gradually developed the Hui Muslim culture and identity, they also absorbed ingredients of the Han, the Mongolian, Uyghur and other ethnic groups' culture (Hu 1993: 1-2). Hui people are distributed in most of the Chinese counties and cities and mostly live around mosques; they form highly scattered religious communities but do share their common Islamic beliefs and cultural system. Historically, while maintaining their Islamic beliefs, Hui Muslim ancestors also tried to look for common ground with traditional Chinese culture and Confucian culture, for mere survival. They absorbed elements of traditional Chinese culture whose core was Confucian culture in philosophical, moral and ethical realms. They learned Chinese language varieties and made adjustments in houses and clothing in order to adapt to the traditional Chinese society. With the flourishing of mosque education, development of Chinese translation activities, and formulation of religious sects and the Menhuan system (*menhuan zhidu* 门宦制度) since the Ming and Qing Dynasty, the Hui people gradually developed their distinct ethnic and religious cultural systems.

Most of the Muslims in China are Sunni, but they generally follow the Islamic law of the 'Hanafi' school. In late Ming Dynasty and early Qing Dynasty, with the introduction of Sufism, independent Islamic schools and Menhuan (门宦) of different sizes appeared in the Northwest China and developed rapidly. The Hui Muslims adhere to orthodox Hanafi, but have many and complicated Islamic schools. They were generally classified into four kinds: Qadim, Ikhwan, the Han-school's sect or Xidaotang (西道堂) and Sufiyyah. Sufiyyah is further classified into al-Khufiyyah, al-Jahriyyah, al-Qādiriyyah, and al-Kubrawiyyah, as well as more than 40 Menhuan derived from it (Ma 2000: 78). Qadim was an Arabic transliteration, meaning 'old' or 'old religion'. It was an Islamic school that spread as the earliest and most widely in the Chinese Muslim world, which also has the largest number of followers. Al-Sufiyyah and Menhuan mainly existed in Xinjiang Autonomous Region, Gansu, Qinghai, and Ningxia. In recent years, some scholars have suggested that the Islamic schools in China can hardly be summarized as 'Three Islamic Schools and Four Menhuan' (*San Da Jiaopai, Si Da Menhuan* 三大教派、四大门宦). A more scientific and rigorous classification should be 'Three Sufi Orders and Four Islamic Schools' (*San Da Jiaotuan, Si Da Jiaopa i* 三大教团、四大教派). The Three Sufi Orders are the current three major branches: Naqshbandiyyah, Qādiriyyah and Kubrawiyyah; the Four Islamic Schools are Qadim, Menhuan, Ikhwan, and Salafiyyah (Ding 2014: 246-255).

According to the sixth national census published on the website of the National Bureau of Statistics, the Muslim population in 2010 was 23.1421 million, of which the populations of Hui and Uyghur were both more than 10 million, measuring respectively at 10.586 million and 10.69 million, accounting for 45.74% and 43.51% of the total Muslim population. Together they accounted for nearly 90% of the total Muslim population (Liu 2014: 70-76). The Hui nationality is one of the ethnic minorities that is most extensively distributed, second only to the Han nationality (Hu 1993: 3). Hui people are distributed in all the provinces, especially Ningxia, Gansu, Xinjiang, Henan, Qinghai, Yunnan, Hebei and Shandong. The Hui population in each of the above mentioned provinces was more than 500,000 (Ding and Yang 2011: 48- 56). The Hui population in the Northwest (Xinjiang, Gansu, Qinghai and Ningxia) was about 5.25 million, accounting for 49.6% of the total population of Hui Muslims. Hui Muslims are scattered in most regions, except in Henan (about 960,000), Yunnan (about 700,000), Hebei (about 570,000) and Shandong (about 540,000)[1], presenting a pattern of 'living compactly in small communities'.

Since these collected papers are mainly about Hui Muslims in Yunnan, here is a brief introduction to Hui Muslims and Islam in this province. Hui Muslims in Yunnan share basically the same religious life as Hui Muslims across the country. However, they also show local cultural differences due to natural conditions, historical traditions, social and economic life as well as religious fractions. Compared with the Hui Muslims in the northwest, the Hui Muslims in Yunnan demonstrate several obvious local characteristics. First, the main ancestors of Hui Muslims in Yunnan were related to the history of military conquest, the opening up of wasteland by stationed troops, and immigration to frontiers during Yuan, Ming and Qing dynasties. The formation of large families of Hui Muslims in Yunnan were from Sayyid Ajjal Shams al-Din Omar and Nestardin, who were local officials in Yuan Dynasty, and Mu Ying, Ha Yuansheng and

Ye Daxiong, who were generals stationed in Yunnan during Ming and Qing Dynasties. Located at the southwest frontier of China, Yunnan boarders on Thailand and Myanmar. Historically, the caravan trade of the Hui Muslims in Yunnan flourished and played an important role in the modern border trade in Yunnan. Second, there were special cross-ethnic cultural phenomena among the Hui Muslims in Yunnan. Historically, a small number of Hui Muslims in Yunnan came to the communities of other ethnic minorities for trade, and there were escapees from violent repression under the Qing government. These migrants gradually adapted to local mainstream cultures while maintaining their own Islamic religion and religious practices, and they were called 'Hui of Dai Nationality' (Dai Hui 傣回), 'Hui of Tibetan Nationality' (Zang Hui 藏回), 'Hui of Zhuang Nationality' (壮回), and 'Hui of Yi Nationality' (Yi Hui 彝回). Third, the Islamic schools in Yunnan were not as complicated as those in the Northwest. There are mainly three: Qadim, al-Jahriyyah, and Ikhwan. More than 90% of the Muslim population in the province belonged to Qadim. Ikhwan was considered as a new religious school in the northwest, while Qadim, Menhuan and Xidaotang, as old religious schools. However, al-Jahriyyah was considered as a new religious school in Yunnan, while Qadim and Ikhwan as old religious schools.

State Policies and Muslims

From the history of state management over the Hui and Islamic affairs, the Hui community has been the basic unit of Hui society and enjoyed partial autonomy during certain historical stages. During the Tang and Song Dynasty, the Hui Muslim ancestors were foreign residents in China and their affairs were managed by leaders of foreigners' quarters (*bofang* 蕃坊) delegated by the government. In the Yuan Dynasty, the Hui ancestors were called the Huihui (回回), as part of the Semu people (Semuren 色目人) whose social status was second only to the Mongol ruling rank. The government set up an official institute to manage the affairs of Huihui communities. Since the Ming and Qing Dynasty, *xianglao* (乡老) and *shetou* (社头) were appointed to work with Imams in dealing with Hui Muslim religious and community affairs. In the Ming Dynasty, the government implemented limitation and assimilation policies, such as installing garrison troops or peasants to open up wastelands and grow crops, incorporating all the people into household registration, forced migration, and prohibiting marriage with people of the same ethnic origin. The government strengthened the management and control of mosques, Imam's judicial power was canceled (Yu 2012:109-110). In the Qing Dynasty, the state government took a series of policies to "oppress, relegate, and even eliminate the Hui people". Since the 1640 s, Hui people had suffered an unprecedented greater oppression (Bai 2003: 130). During the Republic of China, the mosques in different places organized boards of directors for self-management (Bai 1942: 4). After the founding of People's Republic of China, the mosque management committees continued their board of directors in the Republic of China.

For a multi-ethnic nation, eliminating the tension between the ethnic heterogeneity and the national unity inside a country, and the tension between the egalitarian law community and the historical destiny community, and so uniting all ethnic minorities are the core issues in the integration of a multi-ethnic nation (Habermas 2002: 135; Jun and Gao 2009: 17-21). After the founding of People's Republic of China, in order to achieve the integration of all the nationalities, the government chose the third development road of implementing regional autonomy of ethnic minorities, other than the two development possibilities of accepting cultural assimilation according to environment or building a 'nation-state' in the position of nationalism suggested by Ernest Gellner (Ma 2005: 245-246). In order to show national equality in all levels of authorities, the number of representatives of different nationalities in people's congresses at all levels was set, and the regional autonomy of ethnic minorities (Minzu quyu zizhi 民族区域自治) in concentrated areas of nationalities was implemented (Fei 1980: 147-162), a large-scale ethnic identification campaign was launched in the 1950s. The realistic basis and the principle for the ethnic identification in China were to facilitate national unity and national self-development, respecting national characteristics and geographic closeness (Wang 2010: 1-15). To resolve the contradiction between minority identity and national identity theoretically, Fei Xiaotong, a famous Chinese scholar, proposed 'the Pattern of Diversity in Unity of the Chinese Nation' (Zhonghua minzu duoyuanyiti gejiu 中华民族多元一体格局), stressing that the Chinese national identity was at a higher level than the ethnic identity for members of the Chinese nation (Fei 2004: 163). Although the implementation of these national policies was influenced by the Marxist ethnic theory to some extent, it was also a positive exploration and innovation of the Chinese Communist Party based on the reality of China, and ensured the political interests of "allowing all nationalities to be the masters of their own affairs" (ge minzu dangjia zuozhu 各民族当家作主).

In the area of social life, by developing ethnic and religious policies that are in line with national conditions and current situation of minorities, the state provides an institutional guarantee for equality, unity and common prosperity of all nationalities in China. Article 36 of the Constitution in China (中国《宪法》第 36 条) states: "All the Citizens of the People's Republic of China have freedom in religious beliefs." With the symbol of the Third Plenary Session of the 11ᵗʰ Central Committee in 1978, the Chinese government resumed the implementation of the religious freedom policy; the CPC formulated the *Basic Opinions and Basic Policies on Religious Affairs in Socialist China* (《关于我国社会主义时期宗教问题的基本观点和基本政策》) (No. 9 document issued in 1982) (发 1982 年 9 号文件). This framework document marked the significant achievements that the CPC made in socialist religious theory and issues (Chen and Chen 2002: 479-510). The Sixth Plenary Session of the 16ᵗʰ Central Committee of the Communist Party of China urged to "actively guide religions to adapt to Socialism" and "exploit the positive role of religions in promoting social harmony". The 17th National People's Congress of the Communist Party of China took "making religious people play the positive role in the overall economic and social development" as one of the Party's guiding principle. The mosques across the country fully implement the religious policies of the Party and manage religious affairs according to *Regulations on Religious Affairs of the State Council* (《国务院宗教事务条例》) and the local *Democratic Management Methods of Mosques* (《清真寺民主管理办法》). In terms of social development, the Fourth Plenary Session of the Sixteenth CPC Central Committee proposed to build a socialist harmonious society, and the Fifth Plenary Session proposed the new rural construction. Meanwhile, a series of preferential policies for ethnic minorities, such as the construction of small towns, the development of the West, and the new rural construction, in particular the modernization course for half a century, have greatly promoted the overall social, economic, educational and cultural development of minorities. From the time of the reform and opening up in China, confronted with the impact of globalization, modernization and introduction of free market mechanisms, there have been measures that are essential for the minorities, in their call for institutional, legal and policy preferences, and the demand for more allocation of rare resources (Zhang and Liu 2005: 98-101). Thus, their reliance on the state and national identity is also enhanced (Chapter 4).

As one of two nationalities with larger populations of Muslims in China, the Hui are generally considered as representative of Muslims who speak Chinese and the Uyghur are considered as representative of Muslims who don't speak Chinese. Thus they have become two major comparable research objects for domestic and foreign scholars to analyze Islam and Muslims in China. The interaction between Muslims and the state power is naturally an important topic to examine Islam in China. By comparing and analysing the different influences of the national and ethnic policies on the Hui and the Uyghur Muslims, Ross Holder expected to offer a model that can be applied to the Uyghur in Xinjiang, based on the harmonious interactive relationship between Hui society and the state (Chapter 2). Aaron Glasserman examined the reform and regulations of the China Islamic Association (Zhongguo Yixie 中国伊协) on the courses of Islamic schools and argued that ZGYX's actions to discover and promote the inner ethnic harmony and patriotic traditions of Islam were in line with the national policy of ethnic harmony. However, there is a heavy reliance on the discourse and history of the Hui and the experience of Hui intellectuals which is to be taken into account given the difference between the Uyghur Muslims who are predominant in Xinjiang and the Hui Muslims who mainly inhabit other areas of Mainland China. Thus, he studied and reflected on the tension between interethnic harmony as a state policy and the Hui and 'Interior China' bias as a pervasive element of the CIA's textbooks and larger Islamic discourse (Chapter 3).

Muslim ethnic groups are culturally different due to the living areas and surrounding environments. Compared with Hui Muslims, historically, the Uyghur and other Muslim minorities in Xinjiang generally inhabit the same region, with common ethnic areas, common ethnic economic life, and common ethnic language. They also do show distinctive ethnic cultural characteristics. Early before Islam was introduced into China, Uyghur and other native ethnic minorities had already established themselves in the area. They were far from the center of Chinese Confucian culture, which made them less influenced by the traditional Chinese culture (Mi and Jia 2001: 150-169). However, the Hui Muslims showed special features in their formation and development in China, including long time span of formation, diverse ethnic origins, wide distribution of Hui ancestors, and strong mobility. As a result, the Hui Muslims in China were closely related with the mainstream of the Han ethnic group in China. Due to the strong cohesion and attractiveness of Han culture and the national assimilation policy, Han culture became an important part of the cultural identity during the course of development of the Hui Muslim population. During the identification of Hui Muslims, they were even considered 'Han Hui' (汉回), which made them different from other groups that believed in Islam in Xinjiang (Li and Peng 2009: 20-33). However, other Muslim ethnic groups that live in Xinjiang do not speak Chinese, including Uyghur, Kazak, Kirgiz, Ozbek and Tatar, their languages all belong to the Turkic language system (except Tajiks). Their adaptation to and interaction with the mainstream Han culture is far less intense than the Muslims speaking Chinese. Their geographical closeness to Central Asia also leaves them deeply influenced not only by Central Asia, but also by the international pan-Islamism (*fan yisilanzhuyi* 泛伊斯兰主义) and pan-Turkism (*fan tujuezhuyi* 泛突厥主义) (Qi 2002: 54-58). However, some of relevant research findings abroad, such as *Islam in China: religion, ethnicity, culture, and politics*, exaggerated the Chinese Muslims' identity for the universal Islamic concept, 'Ummah' and ignored the social, cultural, environmental and historical differences between the Muslims who speak Chinese and the Muslims who do not speak Chinese, and the differences within the Hui Muslim population (Israeli 2002: 16). Those research findings did not realize that the Hui Muslims have developed an identity deeply linked to the Chinese culture by successfully reconciling the relationship between traditional Chinese culture and Islamic culture.

From the perspective of the interaction between Muslims and the state power (the Chinese Confucian cultural tradition), the integration of Hui Muslims in the Chinese nation is of a much higher degree than the Uyghur. However, it should be noted that the relationship between Chinese Muslims and the state is a dynamic historical process. On the one hand, different ethnic-religious policies of the state in different historical periods have different social effects. The state power in the Ming and Qing Dynasties emphasized forced assimilation, while after the Cultural Revolution in the People's Republic of China, especially since the 1980s, the national policies have shifted to supporting self-development of the Muslims. On the other hand, the long-term harmonious relationship between the state and Muslim society has been a two-way interactive process. Since the 1980s, the cultural consciousness of Hui Muslims and their initiative in cultural adaptation have been increasingly highlighted. Thus, the understanding of the Chinese Hui Muslim population and other Muslim ethnic groups should discard the orientation of Han culture versus Islamic culture and focus on the interaction between the Muslim minority and the state power and other ethnic groups (Hu 2005: 47-56).

Relations between Hui and non-Muslims

In the long history before the establishment of the People's Republic of China, the Hui people had not been recognized by the state power. After the Ming Dynasty, under the assimilation policy of the rulers, the Hui scholars have developed the Islamic cultural and ideological system of Hui Muslims with Chinese characteristics by translating Islamic scriptures into Chinese, an activity that has been done for several centuries. Particularly, they suggested the concept of 'dual loyalties': the loyalty to Allah and the loyalty to the Emperor, which was the biggest step in sinicization of Islam to adapt to the Chinese society. Due to the dual cultural identities, the Hui people demonstrated obvious flexibility and adaptability (Hong 2005:69-77). During the Republic of China, the Hui people were considered a religious group and called as 'Han people' believing in Islam, moreover, the elites among the Hui people used the term Hui religion (回教) or Hui religion believers (回教人) (Yang 2000: 4-8). To this day, Hui society passes down its ethnic and religious culture and explores cultural adaptation to the state through mosque education in their communities. Clearly, the Hui people still maintain a close and deep inner connection and cultural similarities with the Han people.

Frauke Drewes explored and summarized the relationship between the modern Hui people, the Han nationality, and the state through interviews with Hui respondents, non-Muslim respondents and an analysis of the media. She discovered that the Hui respondents and the non-Muslim respondents had a greatly different perception and understanding of the Hui people, Islam, the relationship between the Hui people and the Han nationality, and the actual effects of national ethnic and religious policies. The media held a positive attitude towards the descriptions of the Hui respondents and stressed the traditional characteristics of the Hui cultural religion (as in contrast with the modernization of the Han people), of the Arabization of Hui Islamic culture, and of the influence of cultural features of Middle East. The final conclusion was that among all the Muslim nationalities in China, the Hui Muslims are the closest to the Han people (Chapter 6).

Islam played an important role in uniting the Hui people in their long history, and such a binding role was partially reflected in the settlement of Hui Muslims around mosques. This settlement form started from the large-scale distribution of Hui ancestors in China during the Yuan and Ming Dynasties. As the most widely distributed Muslim ethnic group, the Hui Muslims' interaction with non-Muslims inevitably led to special cross-nationality ethnic groups. These special ethnic groups, on the one hand, maintained traditional Islamic cultural characteristics. On the other hand, they gradually accepted the cultures of neighboring nationalities, including food, clothing, language and mindset, because they had lived and married with them. Examples in this regard included the Mongolian Hui living in Alxa Left Banner of Inner Mongolia, Tibetan Hui living in Kaligang in Hualong Hui Autonomous County in Qinghai and Diqing Tibetan Autonomous Prefecture in Yunnan, Pashi Dai (Dai Hui) living in Menghai County in Sishuangbanna in Yunnan, and Yi Hui living in Bazhili in Xinping County in Yunnan. By investigating and comparing the special ethnic groups, Ding Mingjun suggested that religion was the core of ethnic identity and played an important role for determining ethnic boundaries. Changes in religious belief determine the changes in ethnic attributes. Ethnic intermarriage was the main reason for the formation of those special Muslim ethnic groups. The boundaries and ethnic identities of those special Muslim ethnic groups were dual. The Islamic belief and food taboos originating from the Islamic *Shariah* constituted the first ethnic boundary within which the Muslim identity was relatively stable. If any Muslim member went beyond this boundary, they were likely to be denied by the mainstream of Muslim society. Language, clothing and lifestyle constituted the second boundary which could change anytime with the migration of ethnic groups and the people they interacted with. This changeable boundary made Muslim culture diverse (Ding 2006: 8-16).

In his book *Ethnic Group and Boundaries: The Social Organization of Cultural Difference* published in 1969, Barth treated the ethnic group as a social organization and argued that observing ethnic boundaries was more important than describing the cultures of ethnic groups objectively. He thought that the ethnic consciousness developed when the ethnic group was able to distinguish the boundaries between them and others subjectively. Ethnic identity, according to Barth, was the most basic ethnic characteristic. Barth's boundary theory recognized the mobility of different relations between ethnic groups in a pluralistic society, challenged the argument that interactions between ethnic groups often led to assimilation, and emphasized that the formation of ethnic groups was the result of social interaction (Barth 1969: 9-38). For the identities of special ethnic groups believing in Islam, attention should be paid to the subjective ethnic identity and its influence on the ethnic boundaries. Bai Zhihong's study on the 'Tibetan Hui' in Shangri-La County of Dingqing Tibetan Autonomous Prefecture in Yunnan Province showed that the boundaries between the

Tibetans and the Hui in Diqing were blurred and changeable. Superficially, the formation of 'Tibetan Hui' was the intermediate result of two ethnic groups living together and intermarrying, but it did not necessarily lead to changes in the subjective ethnic identities or ethnic attributes. The national state that allows children to define their ethnic identity with any of their parents provides the policy guarantee for independent ethnic identities. The commemoration of ancestors drive them to preserve the Hui identity and maintain the ideological and psychological boundaries that separate them from Tibetans and other ethnic groups, while the expectations for realistic interests and the uncertainties about the future lead them to register their offsprings as Tibetans (Bai 2008: 58-65). Ma Chuang and Feng Yu studied the Pashi Dai in Yunnan and discussed the identity of this special ethnic group from different angles. Ma Chuang stressed that the formation and identity of this special ethnic group was closely related to their intermarriage circle (Chapter 5). Feng Yu stressed that the identity of this ethnic group was dynamic in different historical stages and the multiple identities that ran through daily life competing and negotiating with each other, show the diversity of Muslim identities in China. Feng Yu thus challenged the common theory about separation and assimilation of the interaction between Hui Muslims and non-Muslims (Chapter 7).

Hui Identity and Islam

In fact, Hui people are not always practicing Muslims. In contemporary China, the Hui identity and the Muslim identity corresponding to Islamic religion are not entirely matched, although ethnic identity has the essential characteristics and despite the homogenization tendency of the given identification symbols in the national system and ethnic cultural tradition. In the acquired social lives, the construction process of the Hui identity was multi-level, contextualized and diverse. As an identity attribution, the Hui identity was closely related to Islam and religious identity. After the Ming Dynasty, the Hui ethnic group was internally divided. Some (especially those living in the southeast coastal areas) began to maintain Confucianism partly due to the circumstances and changes in their status and thoughts. They gradually drifted away from Islamic beliefs and even hid their Muslim identities. Others (especially those living in the concentrated settlements of Hui people in the Northwest) strongly manifested Islamic culture and regarded it as a tool to resist assimilation and maintain their ethnic characteristics. Such division further led to the differences of cultural identity between different regions and among individual Hui people, and these differences had the tendency to intensify (Hong 2005: 69-77). If the Hui people in different regions were evaluated by how much they stuck to the Islamic religion and the degree of religiosity, they would diverge from each other in many aspects as an ethnic group (Fan 2009: 69-76). For example, Dru C. Gladney found that the Hui people in the southeast coastal areas of Fujian almost lost all contact with Islam in their daily life, except when they stressed they were descendants of Arabians and thus admitted that they were Huis (Gladney 1998). The varying degrees of internal differentiation in religious beliefs and Islamic practices were mainly reflected in three levels. The most widely recognized Hui identity was expressed by symbols of ethnic identification. This was reflected in registration and inheritance of identification in the national household registration system that had no connection with Islamic practices. The second level was the recognition of lifestyles and eating habits. This was reflected in the food taboo of not eating pork. The deeper level of ethnic identity was reflected in the unity of Islamic knowledge, the practice and the existence of the sense of belonging to Islam. The Hui people who grew up in traditional Hui Muslim communities mostly followed an internalized process of religion to gain religious identities, especially from the socialization of religion in families and communities. However, the Hui people who lived in cities were not surrounded by a thick religious atmosphere and mostly maintained close contacts with the mainstream culture of the Han people. Thus, they did not have the faith and religious experience of Islam and their family lives were more inclined to the Han culture, although they might still keep some life habits and ethnic affection of Hui Muslims. However, a considerable number of them returned to Islam, learning religious knowledge and worshiping in mosques when they grew old or after they retired. Clearly, Hui identity and religious identity of Islam are two major separated but related concepts. The Hui identity is not necessarily related with the religious identity and Islamic practice, but the religious faith and the identity practice based on Islam usually become important signs and symbols to maintain the ethnic boundaries of the Hui.

After the Third Plenary Session of the 11th CPC Committee, China began the reconstruction of social undertakings. With the social and economic development and the improvement of economic conditions of Hui Muslims, more and more investments were made for religious development. Specifically, in many places private funds were raised for renovation and expansion of mosques and mosque education. There was an increasing number of Muslims who went abroad for further studies and performed the *hajj* in Saudi Arabia. Great improvements were found in both religious faith and religious atmosphere in the communities of Hui Muslims. Such religious and cultural phenomena aroused concerns among some Chinese people: would the growing Islamic culture or Arabic Muslim culture completely dispel the original Chinese culture of the Hui Muslims? Foreign cultural observers found that Chinese Muslims still largely maintained local Chinese characteristics in the architectural style of mosques, the religious practices in their daily life, and female clothing, which was a great difference from the cases in the Middle East and other Islamic countries. In this regard, the authors have paid attention to the views of local officials, religious elites, ordinary believers and scholars from both subjective and objective perspectives during several years of fieldwork. Considering the general views, the authors believe that the unique cultural characteristics of Hui Muslims in China were shown in symbols of the nationality, such as mosque buildings, national costumes and religious rites. The Hui nationality itself was a product and a carrier for communication and development of Islam in China for more than a thousand years and was closely related to the Han nationality in terms of ethnic origins, cultures and social environments. Thus, it was impossible to completely remove the influence of Han culture, which had been rooted for more than a thousand years, from Hui culture. Although Islamic culture is developing continuously, it is the core and a necessary component, but not all-defining for Hui Muslim culture. The Hui Muslims have gone through class oppressions during several dynasties, especially in the Qing dynasty. Only in the modern times they can enjoy equal opportunities and development and have more and deeper cultural contacts with foreign Muslims abroad through studying abroad, performing the *hajj*, etc. The awareness of the Hui Muslims as Chinese people and their national consciousness have to some extent been enhanced (Gui 2011: 100-105). It can be said that such complex ethnic and religious cultural phenomenon of Hui Muslims will perpetuate.

By studying the modernization and consumption of urban Chinese Muslims in the Hui Community of Xi'an, Maris Boyd Gillette argued that the Muslims were in the process of Arabization as they built Arabian buildings, learnt the Arabic language and received Islamic religious education. She believed that Arabization offered an optional ideology and modern development model different from the one provided by the state, allowing the residents to get involved in a series of concepts and practices associated with the international Islamic revival (Gillette

2000: 77). By examining the religious practice of Muslims in Shadian, a famous Hui community in Yunnan, Lesley Turnbull found that Shadian maintained the modern Islamic tradition and the Chinese localized characteristics of Islamic practice, which was reflected in the utilization of Arabian buildings and development of Islamic religious education in the Hui community. She thought that they were influenced by Arab or other Muslim ethnic groups but not Arabized. Her investgation indicated those were the cultural expressions of Hui Muslims based on their studies of *Koran* and sublimation of their Islamic faith. Although Gillette argued that the Arabization in Xi'an was somehow the result of the increasing contacts between China and the Middle East since the 1980s, Lesley Turnbull found that the Hui Muslims in Shadian stressed that they were not influenced by the increasing contacts with international Islam, and that the enhanced Islamic features of Shadian (in terms of architecture and clothing) originated from the learning and communication of the Chinese version of *Koran* in 1981. In other words, the Islamic practice of Muslims in Shadian is to observe and practice the doctrines and laws of Islam by carefully studying *Koran* instead of by simply following the ethnic customs of Arabs in the birthplace of Islam. Lesley Turnbull thus concluded that stressing the true Islamic practice required in *Koran* was the core element of religious identity of Hui Muslims in Shadian (Chapter 8).

In China, there was no appropriately recognized translation of the term Islam during the Song and Yuan Dynasties. Only in the Ming and Qing Dynasties did the name 'Qingzhen Religion' gradually become the recognized appellation for Islam. Therefore, *qingzhen* could be argued as being a free translation of Islam in China (Bai 2003: 322). The term *qingzhen* has now been widely disseminated in the Chinese communities, and the Muslim living practice and culture based on the religious beliefs of Islam is called qingzhen culture. The Chinese Muslims call 'chanting' one of the five pillars of Islam, as chanting *qingzhenyan* (*shahada*), the place of worship is called *qingzhensi* (mosque), and the food made by Muslims is called *qingzhen* food. Therefore, the examination of the *qingzhen* living practices and culture of Hui Muslims is imporant for us to understand the Hui people and their identities in China.

What role do the *qingzhen* lifestyle and Islamic faith play in Hui identity? Dru C. Gladney and Jonathan N.Lipman were two foreign scholars who paid more attention to the lifestyle and the culture of Qingzhen of Hui Muslims. Dru C. Gladney noticed that the Hui people in different Hui communities such as Niujie, Chen Dai, Najiahu, and Changying had different understandings of *qingzhen*, which led to profound insights about the identity symbols of Hui people. He urged that members of the Hui ethnic group believed that they shared something in common in spite of the diverse identities and great differences within the ethnic group, and it was through the interaction between self-identity and national recognition, and through the institutionalization of national recognition that the Hui people developed into a nationality or *minzu* (民族). Thus, he came to the conclusion that the Hui ethnic group was the result of ongoing negotiating and making (Ma, 1998: 77-88; Zhou 2005: 97-106; Kejia and Xuefeng 2008: 71). Lipman was concerned about the cultural uniqueness of endogamy, the residential structure of living around mosques, and the special dieting style of Sino-Muslims in Northwest China. He thought that the Sino-Muslims shared a common mosque education, communicant internal religion and ritual knowledge, which allowed them to find Muslim food, familiar discourse and common places of worship in other Muslim communities when they were away from home. This distinguished them from non-Muslim neighbors. To the Chinese in non-Muslim communities in China, Muslims were both familiar and unfamiliar. 'Familiar strangers' implied a unique interactive form for Muslims and the wider Chinese society. They lived in a 'middle ground' and created a new intergrated culture that has adapted to Chinese society (Lipman 1997: 212, 224; Ma 2000: 95-103).

Zhang Liang and Hacer Z. Gönül illustrated the realistic significance of *qingzhen* lifestyle for the survival of urban Hui residents and students in different fields of communities and Islamic schools. Through a case study on the community in Tongliao Street of Hohhot in Inner Mongolia, Zhang Liang found that the *qingzhen* lifestyle offered a path to interpret Hui identity and the Islamic life practices. It was also key to understand the integration of social cultures in a multi-ethnic country and help understand the local interactive relationships of nationalities and the interactive mechanism of social cultures (Chapter 9). Through an investigation on Hui minority college students, Hacer Z. Gönül concluded that the *qingzhensi* (mosque) and *qingzhen* canteens were important for Hui college students to maintain their identity and culture while studying, as significant factors to express their identity and preserve self-confidence (Chapter 10).

Conclusion

In this volume, the authors are providing an analysis of ethnic identity and Islamic life practice of Hui Muslims, and the interaction between Hui Muslims, non-Muslims and the state, which was based on three aspects: State Policies and Muslims, Relations between Hui and non-Muslims, and Hui Identity and Islam, with the focus on the important relationships between identity, interaction and Islamic practice. Religious identity, ethnic identity, and national identity are the most important identities for Hui Muslims and the three identities have dynamic and complicated relationships. As a member of the 56 official ethnic groups and 10 Muslim ethnic groups in China, the Chinese Hui Muslims show different religious, collective and ethnic cultrural expressions and practical significance by interacting with the state power, non-Muslims, other Muslim groups, and even with different local communities of the same nationality. The basis for identity and interaction is the life practice of Islam, and Islamic practice is a symbolic behavior of identity and interaction. On this basis, we may further reflect and explore the complex feature of the diverse, fluid and dynamic identity of Hui Muslims.

This book also demonstrates the different perspectives and focuses of Chinese and foreign researchers. Most of the Chinese authors of this book are Hui Muslims and they were mainly concerned about the survival, the social and cultural adaptation, the subjective initiative and social development of Hui Muslims in a multi-ethnic country like China. Compared with Western scholars, they may be short of theories; however, with their convenient and effective interactions with the research subjects, it is reasonable to believe in the authenticity and empirical value of the ethnographic materials they present. Foreign researchers pay more attention to the state policy environment of China, the comparison of the influence of the state policies on the Hui Muslims and the Uyghur Muslims, and the interaction between Hui Muslims and non-Muslims. These researchers were highly question-oriented and mostly collected the data based on observations, results of previous studies and a variety of media (including the Internet). However, the cultural politics and power discourse implied in the media channel would inevitably influence the knowledge construction of the authors and readers, and then may negatively influence the correct understanding of the Hui Muslims as a complex ethnic group. In any case, the study on Chinese Muslims is an integral part of the study on Muslims around the world. The collection and demonstration of research findings provide rich angles for readers to understand Chinese Muslims and offer a chance for dialogue and mutual reflection between Chinese scholars and international scholars from multiple perspectives, ranging from theoretical methods, ethnography styles, and the stance of researchers as insiders or outsiders.

Notes

1 National Bureau of Statistics: http://www.stats.gov.cn/tjsj/pcsj/rkpc/6rp/indexch.htm.

References

Atwill, David G. (2005). *The Chinese Sultanate: Islam, Ethnicity, and the Panthay Rebellion in Southwest China, 1856-1873*. Stanford, CA: Stanford University Press.

Bai, Chongxi (1942). 'Islam in China and in the world', *Yue Hua (Guilin)*, 14(11-12), pp. 4. 白崇禧: 中国回教与世界回教, 《月华》(桂林)第 14 卷 11—12 期(合刊)第 4 页, 民国 31 年.

Bai, Shouyi (1984). 'Formation and primary development of Huihui nationality', in The History of Hui Nationality Team, eds, *Collected Essays on the History of Hui Nationality*, Yinchuan: Ningxia People's Publishing House, pp. 15-28. 白寿彝: 回回民族的形成与初步发展, 回族史组编《回族史论集》, 银川: 宁夏人民出版社, 1984 年, 第 15-28 页.

Bai, Shouyi (2003). *Nationality History of Huihui in China*. Beijing: China Book Company. 白寿彝: 《中国回回民族史》, 北京: 中华书局, 2003年, 第 130 页.

Bai, Zhihong (2008). 'The ethnic identity and subjectivity of Tibetan Muslims in the Tibetan-Yi Corridor – a case study of the Tibetan Muslims in Shangri-La County, Diqing Tibetan Autonomous Prefecture, Yunnan Province', *Journal of Studies on Nationalities*, 4, pp. 58-65. 白志红: 藏彝走廊中' 藏回' 的民族认同及其主体性——以云南省迪庆藏族自治州香格里拉县' 藏回' 为例, 《民族研究》2008 年第 4 期, 第 58-65 页.

Barth, Frederik (1969). *Ethnic group and boundaries: The Social organization of culture difference*. Boston: Little, Brown and Company, pp. 9-38.

Benite, Zvi Ben-Dor (2005). *The Dao of Muhammad: A Cultural History of Muslims in Late Imperial China*. Cambridge: Harvard University Asia Center.

Broomhall, Marshall (1987/1910). *Islam in China: A Neglected Problem*. London: DARF Publishers Limited.

Chen, Linshu and Chen, Xia (2002). *Principles for Religions*. Beijing: Religion and Culture Publishing House, pp. 479-510. 陈麟书、陈霞: 《宗教学原理》, 北京: 宗教文化出版社, 2002年, 第 479-510 页.

Dillon, Michael (1996). *China's Muslims*. Oxford: Oxford University Press.

Dillon, Michael (1999). *China's Muslim Hui Community: Migration, Settlement and Sects*. Richmond, Surrey: Curzon.

Ding, Hong (2005). 'Issue on mutual adaptation of islamic religion and China's society: from the perspective of cultural identy of Hui', *Journal of North West Nationalities Studies*, 2, pp. 69-77. 丁宏: 从回族的文化认同看伊斯兰教与中国社会相适应问题, 《西北民族研究》 2005 年第 2 期, 第 69-77 页.

Ding, Kejia and Ma, Xuefeng (2008). *The Hui Muslims in Vision of the World.* Yinchuan: Ningxia People's Publishing House, pp. 71. 丁克家、马雪峰: 《世界视野中的回族》, 银川: 宁夏人民出版社, 2008 年, 第 71 页.

Ding, Kejia and Yang, Jingqin (2011). 'A Population Analysis of the Hui and Other Muslim Ethnic Groups in Mainland China', *Journal of the Second Northwest University for Nationalities (Philosophy and Social Sciences),* 1, pp. 48-56. 丁克家, 杨景琴: 中国内地回族等四个穆斯林民族人口状况分析, 《北方民族大学学报》 (哲学社会科学版) 2011 年第 1 期, 第 48—56 页.

Ding, Mingjun (2006). *An Anthropological Investigation on the Chinese Marginalized Muslim Group.* Yinchuan: Ningxia People's Publishing House, pp. 8-16. 丁明俊: 《中国边缘穆斯林族群的人类学考察》, 银川: 宁夏人民出版社 2006, 8-16 页.

Ding, Shiren (2014). 'A new perspective on division of Islamic sects in China', *The Conference Proceedings of Study of Contemporary National Religious Issues in China,* 8, pp. 246-255. 丁士仁:中国伊斯兰教门派划分的新视角, 《当代中国民族宗教问题研究》 2014 年会议论文 (第 8 集), 第 246-255 页.

Fan, Ke (2009). 'National politics and Muslim identity of the Huis in Quanzhou', *Journal of Jiangsu Administration Institute,* 1, pp. 69-76. 范可: 国家政治与泉州回民的穆斯林认同, 《江苏行政学院学报》 2009 年第 1 期, 第 69-76 页.

Fei, Xiaotong (1980). 'Issues about ethnic identification in China', *Journal of Social Sciences in China,* 1, pp. 147-162. 费孝通: 关于我国民族的识别问题, 《中国社会科学》 1980 年第 1 期, 第 147-162 页.

Fei, Xiaotong (2004). *On Anthropology and Cultural Consciousness,* Beijing: Huaxia Publishing House, pp. 163. 费孝通: 《论人类学与文化自觉》, 北京: 华夏出版社, 2004 年, 第 163 页.

Frankel, James D. (2011). *Rectifying God's Name: Liu Zhi's Confucian Translation of Monotheism and Islamic Law.* Honolulu: University of Hawai'i Press.

Gillette, Maris Boyd (2000). *Between Mecca and Beijing: Modernization and Consumption among Urban Chinese Muslims.* Stanford, CA: Stanford University Press.

Gladney, Dru C. (1991). *Muslim Chinese: Ethnic Nationalism in the People's Republic.* Cambridge, MA: Harvard University Press.

Gladney, Dru C. (1998). *Ethnic Identity in China: the Making of a Muslim Minority Nationality.* Orlando, FL: Harcourt Brace & Company.

Gui, Rong (2011). 'Under the Background of Globalization: the Modernistic National Identity of Hui Ethnic Group', *Journal of Hui Muslim Minority Studies,* 2, pp. 100-105.

桂榕: 全球化背景: 回族国家认同的现代性, 《回族研究》 2011 年第 2 期, 第 100-105 页.

Habermas, Jürgen (2002). *Die Einbeziehung des Anderen: Studien zur politischen Theorie*, (Cao Weidong, trans). Shanghai: Shanghai People's Publishing House, pp. 135. 尤尔根·哈贝马斯: 《包容他者》, 曹卫东译, 上海: 上海人民出版社, 2002 年, 第 135 页.

Hu, Yunsheng (2005). 'The Hui's ethnic identity in the triple relationships', *Journal of Studies on Nationalities*, 1, pp. 47-56. 胡云生: 三重关系互动中的回族认同, 《民族研究》 2005 年第 1 期, 第 47-56 页.

Hu, Zhenhua (1993). *Chinese Hui Muslims*. Yinchuan: Ningxia People's Publishing House, pp. 1-2, 3. 胡振华: 《中国回族》, 银川: 宁夏人民出版社, 1993 年, 第 1-2 页、第 3 页.

Israeli, Raphael (2002). *Islam in China: Religion, Ethnicity, Culture, and Politics*. Lanham, MD: Lexington Books, p. 16.

Jun, Zhu and Gao, Yongjiu (2009). 'Segregation and integration: the logic of the ethnic integration in multinational country', *Journal of Guangxi Nationalities Studies*, 3, pp. 17-21. 朱军、高永久: '分' 与' 合' :多民族国家民族整合的逻辑, 《广西民族研究》 2009 年第 3 期, 第 17-21 页.

Leslie, Donald Daniel, Yang Daye, Ahmed Youssef (2006). *Islam in Traditional China: A Bibliographical Guide*. Sankt Augustin-Nettetal.

Lipman, Jonathan N. (1997). *Familiar strangers: A History of Muslim in Northwest China*. Seattle, WA: University of Washington Press.

Li, Shaoming and Peng, Wenbin (2009). 'Indigenized ethnic identification process in China – Li Shaoming Lecture at the University of Washington, Seattle, USA', *Journal of Southwest University for Nationalities (Humanities and Social Sciences)*, 12, pp. 20-33. 李绍明, 彭文斌: 本土化的中国民族识别——李绍明美国西雅图华盛顿大学讲座(一), 《西南民族大学学报》 (人文社科版) 2009 年第 12 期, 第 29-33 页.

Liu, Xiaochun (2014). 'Analysis on the Characteristics of Chinese Muslims Based on Population Census', *Journal of Hui Muslim Minority Studies*, 1, pp. 70-76. 刘晓春: 基于人口普查的中国穆斯林人口特征分析, 《回族研究》 2014 年第 1 期, 第 70-76 页.

Ma, Haiyun (1998). 'A new perspective on Hui studies: a methodological discussion and comments on Gladney's *Muslim Chinese*', *Journal of Hui Muslim Minority Studies*, 4, pp. 77-88. 马海云: 回族研究的新视野: 一个方法论的讨论——兼评杜磊《中国穆斯林》, 《回族研究》 1998 年第 4 期, 第 77-88 页.

Ma, Haiyun (2000). 'A familiar stranger: reading a history of Muslims in Northwest China,' *Journal of Hui Muslim Minority Studies*, 4, pp. 95-103. 马海云: 熟悉的陌生人——读一部西北穆斯林史, 《回族研究》 2000 年第 4 期, 第 95-103 页.

Ma, Rong (2005). *A Guide to Ethnosociology.* Beijing: Peking University Press, pp. 245-246. 马戎：《民族社会学导论》，北京：北京大学出版社，2005 年，第 245-246 页.

Ma, Tong (2000). *A Brief History of Chinese Islamic Sects and Menhuan System.* Yinchuan: Ningxia Publishing House, pp. 78. 马通：《中国伊斯兰教派与门宦制度史略》，银川：宁夏出版社，2000 年，第78页.

Mi, Shoujiang and You, Jia (2000). *Brief History of Islamic Religion in China.* Beijing: Religious Culture Press, pp. 132-136, pp. 150-169. 米寿江，尤佳：《中国伊斯兰教简史》，北京：宗教文化出版社，2001 年，第 150-169 页.

Murata, Sachiko (2000). *Chinese Gleams of Sufi Light: Wang Tai-yu's* Great Learning of the Pure *and Real and Liu Chih's* Displaying the Concealment of the Real Realm. Albany, NY: State University of New York Press.

Pillsbury, Barbara (1981). 'Muslim History in China: A 1300-Year Chronology', *Journal of Muslim Minority Affairs*, 3(2), pp. 10-29.

Qi, Qingshun (2002). 'The influence and representation of the contemporary international Islamic revival movement on Xinjiang', *Journal of China Communist Party School in Yili Prefecture*, 3, pp. 54-58. 齐清顺：当代国际伊斯兰复兴运动对新疆的影响及表现，《中共伊犁州委党校学报》 2002 年第 3 期，第 54-58 页.

Wang, Xi'en. (2010). 'Basis for ethnic identification in China', *Journal of Studies on Nationalities*, 5, pp. 1-15. 王希恩：中国民族识别的依据，《民族研究》 2010 年第 5 期，第 1-15 页.

Yang, Zhijuan (2000). 'Demarcation on ethnic identity and nationality: Taking an example of Hui Nationality', *Journal of Hui Muslim Minority studies*, 4, pp. 4-8. 杨志娟：族群认同与民族的界定——以回族为例，《回族研究》 2000 年第 4 期，第 4-8 页.

Yu, Zhengui (2012). *The Central Regime and Islamic Religion in China.* Yinchuan: Ningxia People's Publishing House, pp. 109-110. 余振贵：《中国历代政权与伊斯兰教》，银川：宁夏人民出版社，2012 年，第 109-110 页.

Zhang, Yonghong and Liu, Deyi (2005). 'On ethnic identification and national identification', *Journal of Guangxi Nationalities University (Philosophy and Social Science)*, 27(1), pp. 98-101. 张永红、刘德一：《论族群认同和国族认同》，《广西民族学院学报》(哲学社会科学版) 2005 年第 1 期，第 98-101 页.

Zhou, Chuanbin (2005). 'Remarks on the studies of Chinese Hui islam by western academic world', *Journal of North West Nationalities Studies*, 1, pp. 97-106. 周传斌：他山之石——西方学界对中国回族伊斯兰教的研究述评，《西北民族研究》 2005 年第 1 期，第 97-106 页.

Part I:
State Policies and Muslims

CHAPTER 2

Bridging Worlds: A Comparative Study on the Effects of Ethno-Religious Policies on China's Muslims

Ross Holder

Trinity College

Introduction

Islam occupies a unique position amongst the five different religions that are officially recognised within the People's Republic of China (PRC). The multivariate religious and cultural attributes that define the identities of China's Muslim minorities defies generalisation, and bears the diverse traits of a religion whose success has seen its spread throughout the world, expanding far past Arabia's eastern borders and crossing the breadth of China. This can be evidenced through an examination of the religious beliefs and cultural practices of China's two most populous Muslim ethnic minorities, the Hui and the Uyghur.

This paper will provide an overview of some of the Hui's defining characteristics, highlighting how some of these unique attributes have helped to distinguish the Hui from other Muslim minority groups such as the Uyghur, while also illustrating how these differences have manifested within government policy and its application, creating a dichotomy between how the state interacts with the Hui and the Uyghur on the basis of their religious and cultural identity.

The Hui – Cultural integration and ethno-religious resilience

The Hui exhibit a complex ethno-cultural identity that separates and distinguishes them from China's other minority nationalities. When compared with China's other nine Muslim minorities in particular, the Hui identity can be perceived at times to take on a sometimes amorphous quality, demonstrating an ethnographical diversity that transcends attributes that could otherwise be considered as core tenants of ethnic identity classification[1].

Indeed, this is borne out in an examination of Stalin's definition of a nation, which heavily influenced the CCP's ethnologists as a model for the PRC's nationality classification project, a system used to identify and prescribe nationality status (Gillette 2002: 9). On evaluation of the objective criteria that Stalin considers in his definition of nationality[2], it could be argued that the Hui's case for recognition as a minority nationality is rather ambiguous, with only religious identity clearly delineating the Hui from the Han Chinese.

Unlike the other nine Muslim minorities recognised in China (Mackerras 2003: 117 - 118), the Hui share no common language unique to their nationality. Instead, the Hui primarily speak Mandarin, with the acculturation of other minority languages also existing at a local level within certain regions (Gladney 1996: 32). This distinguishes the Hui from other Muslim minorities such as the Uyghur, whose unique Turkic based language forms a defining feature of their cultural identity, while its erosion through state policies often proves to be a source of tension that manifests in ethnic hostilities between Uyghur and Han Chinese communities in the Xinjiang Uyghur autonomous region (XUAR)[3], and increasingly throughout greater China[4].

Despite the predominant concentration of Hui residing in China's North-West in areas such as Ningxia Hui Autonomous Region (NHAR), Qinghai and Gansu, they are also the most widely dispersed of all China's ethnic minorities (Gladney 1996: 27), with Hui communities existing in urban centres and rural townships throughout the breadth of China, far beyond the central plains. This is the result of the Hui's unique ethnographic history, having been descendants of successive waves of Muslim soldiers and merchants who arrived in China (Frankel 2009: 26; Jones-Leaning & Pratt 2012: 308; Gladney 2004: 293). Many Hui continued this mercantile way of life, shrewdly facilitating economic trade between China and Tibet during the Qing dynasty while the Ma clan administered de facto control over the Gansu region (Spengen 2013: 498; Lipman 1984: 291–296). As China's economy continued to evolve away from a reliance on agriculture, the role of merchants became increasingly important within Chinese society, with Colin Mackerras suggesting that the Hui's penchant for cross-border merchant trade helped to foster a commodity based economy within China (Mackerras 1994: 41–42). Consequently, it is not surprising to see the Hui also benefiting from a rise in public opinion during this period.

While generally keeping to their own communities within these areas, the broad distribution of Hui across China has increased the level of Hui-Han intermingling, perhaps contributing to increasing levels of mutual tolerance, and mitigating the perception of 'otherness' that may otherwise exist between the Hui and Han Chinese. This places the Hui in an advantageous position in some regards, allowing them to sidestep the often pejorative ethnic stereotypes that other Muslim Chinese ethnic minorities such as the Uyghur have been burdened with, while also avoiding some of the regionally implemented policies that disproportionately affect the Uyghur's ability to exercise religious belief (Davis 2008: 16).

The Hui's pragmatic ability to adapt to their environment, particularly with regards to their acculturation of the languages spoken by the more predominant nationality in their locale, has allowed the Hui to relatively successfully engage and integrate with that of contemporary Chinese society, while at the cost of distancing the Hui from the wider Muslim identity. This distance has manifested within Hui-Uyghur relations (Ben-Adam 2012: 204), with Joanne Smith Finley noting that Uyghur perception of the Hui as 'quasi-Han' (Smith Finley 2013: 336).

Partly in an effort to remedy some of the damage inflicted upon the Hui's religious identity during the excesses of the Cultural Revolution (FitzGerald 2012: 124-129; Yang 2006: 100-101), while also seeking to develop economic trade links with Muslim states (Dillon 1999: 178–181), throughout the 1980s the CCP orchestrated to increase the levels of exchange between Muslim Chinese (particularly the Hui) and other Islamic countries. This was achieved by organising Islamic training abroad, facilitating *hajj* pilgrimages, and allowing Islamic countries to directly donate funds for the construction of Mosques and Islamic schools (Gladney 1996: 326–327; Shichor 2005: 122). While the CCP may have had economic motivations behind such policies, leveraging Muslim Chinese in order to increase lucrative trade partnerships with neighbouring Islamic countries such as Pakistan, a perhaps unintended by-product of these policies has been a renewed interest in Islamic teachings among China's Muslim minorities. Maris Gillette refers to this Islamic revivalism as Arabization (Gillette 2002: 108–113), resulting in a renewed Islamic identity among China's Muslim minorities (Dillon 1999: 179). This revitalisation of religiosity among China's Muslim minorities, and the Hui in particular, is starkly at odds with the Marxist origins of the CCP's doctrinal philosophy, which posits that the pursuit socialism will naturally result in the demise of religion[5]. An increasing Islamic awareness amongst both the Hui and the Uyghur could be seen to be in conflict with the CCP's efforts to ultimately homogenise Chinese society into one that shares a unified cultural identity.

Much research has been made with regards to the accommodation of Hui identity within Han Chinese society, with some scholars emphasising how the Hui's identity has been broadly defined through the Hui's reconciliation of normative Islamic values with that of Chinese culture (Shichor 2003: 13; Sen 2009: 102–128; Chuah 2012: 272). More recently however this emphasis has been challenged by scholars such as Dru Gladney who instead emphasise the point that the complexity of Hui identity defies a cursory demarcation along religious lines. They instead observe that highly variable levels of acculturation can exist within Hui communities resulting from a wide range of factors (Zang 2007: 148 – 150; Gladney 1996; Veselič 2013: 104–106), making religiosity an overly essentialist marker for defining Hui identity. This is succinctly evidenced by the existence of those who do not actively adhere to Islamic doctrinal values or practices but still identify as Hui (Kaltman 2014: 40; Goossaert & Palmer 2011: 375).

The underlying ethnological complexity in defining the Hui identity further illustrates the challenges that emerge as a result of the CCP's nationality classification system itself. It also provides an understanding of the conflation that exists between the term 'Hui' both being used to define a discrete ethnic identity, and also in a broader sense in its traditional but persistent use as a synonym to define a person or group as 'Muslim Chinese' (Gillette 2002: 9; Sautman 2014: 91).

As the above examples illustrate concerning the Hui's experience within the PRC, the CCP's desire to portray China within the Muslim world as a tolerant, rights-based society that respects the ethno-religious identity of its Muslim minorities is hamstrung by its competing need to maintain an ideological primacy over its citizens' religious beliefs. This presents the CCP with the daunting challenge of having to reconcile these seemingly incompatible agendas, or risk straining its relatively harmonious relationship with its most populous Muslim minority.

The Uyghur – Cultural Dichotomies and Assimilative Policies

The Uyghur are China's second largest Muslim minority nationality, and unlike the Hui, the Uyghur population is heavily concentrated within the XUAR in

China's North-West. With a population of just over 10 million (Toops 2014: 65), the Uyghur are the majority nationality within Xinjiang. This is despite the efforts of the CCP, which has systematically diluted the Uyghurs' majority status in the region through the instigation of internal migration policies encouraging Han Chinese to migrate into Xinjiang (Lim 2010: 69; Smith Finley 2007: 641; Dillon 1995: 31; Howell & Fan 2011: 120; Hess 2009: 407). Evidence of this can be seen through the rapid change in Xinjiang's ethnic composition, particularly throughout the period between 1953 – 1982, where the Han population increased dramatically from 6.1% to 40.3% (Starr 2004: 246).

The primary funnel of Han Chinese migrants into the region has been the Xinjiang Production and Construction Corps (XPCC), a quasi-military unit that initially consisted largely of former People's Liberation Army members (State Council of the People's Republic of China 2003). Originally a military unit with a defensive mandate, upon the establishment of the XUAR the unit was demobilised with its troops remaining in Xinjiang to aid in the development of Xinjiang's infrastructure, in order to help ensure ethnic stability through economic development, and the consolidation Xinjiang's borders. The XPCC's establishment in Xinjiang provided the CCP with what is effectively an apparatus that facilitates the sinicization of Xinjiang (Becquelin 2004: 366–370). This source of frequent ire among the Uyghur is further compounded by the selection of the region as an appropriate location to house many of China's convicted criminals, a process dating back to the Qing Empire (Waley-Cohen 1991; Rowe 2010: 75). Lamentably, this policy has persisted following the establishment of the PRC, with the XPCC employing prisoners and convicts from the eastern provinces rather than employing and training Xinjiang's native Uyghur population of experienced farmers and agricultural labourers. Qian Guo provides an idea to the extent of this practice, asserting that during the 1950s as many as half of the XPCC agricultural labour force consisted of current and former convicts (Guo et al. 2009: 173). This underscores the negative perception held towards Uyghurs by XPCC officials, while also providing an historical context for the persistent Uyghur complaints of discrimination and employment inequality, with Anthony Howell's recent study finding that in Uyghurs in Ürümqi on average earn 39% lower income than Han inter-provincial migrants despite holding higher levels of education (Howell 2013: 18).

Xinjiang's regional migration policies are a considerable cause of ethnic tensions between Han Chinese and the Uyghur, and have added credence to the Uyghurs' long standing concerns over the ongoing sinicization of minority culture throughout the region. This further highlights the failures of the state in addressing the underlying issues behind the ethnic tensions between the Uyghur and Han Chinese. The CCP has mistakenly created these policies under the incorrect assumption that rapid economic development spurred by the XPCC would help address the fissures of ethnic inequality, stabilising the region.

This is in stark contrast to other areas where there are larger proportions of Hui such as Qinghai, where it is noted that mass migration policies have not been implemented. This can be evidenced by the fact that the Hui have consistently represented around 15.5% of the region's population since the CCP commenced its first population census in 1949 until 2010 (Cooke 2008: 412). While the dichotomy in mass migration policies between Xinjiang and Qinghai may be attributed to the CCP's desire to shore up Xinjiang's outer borders, the negative effect that such policies have on the preservation of Uyghur culture and traditions is considerable.

As outlined previously, another distinguishing characteristic that differentiates the Uyghur from the Hui is the Uyghur language, which bears a stronger resemblance to the Turkic languages used throughout much of Central Asia. It is spoken by the vast majority of Uyghur within Xinjiang, and also amongst much of the Uyghur diaspora who reside throughout several of China's neighbouring central Asian states including Kazakhstan, Kyrgyzstan and Uzbekistan. The distinct characteristics of the Uyghur language illustrates some of the significant cultural differences that exist between Uyghur and Han, and positions the Uyghurs' cultural identity closer to their Turkic speaking Muslim counterparts.

These linguistic differences have resulted in the Uyghurs' exposure to additional policies which effectively serve as means of Sino-centric acculturation through the promotion of Mandarin as China's primary language. While there is certainly merit to the advancement of a common vernacular amongst China's citizens, the CCP has moved from initially adopting a bilingual approach of promoting of Mandarin as a lingua franca in conjunction with maintaining the viability of minority languages (Wang 2013: 43), to a more assimilatory stance which instead has had a discriminatory impact on minority languages in favour of Mandarin (Bewicke 2009: 167; Dwyer 2005: 29–40).

The negative effects of China's assimilatory language policies on the Uyghur can be seen within the educational sphere in Xinjiang, where the Uyghur are still lagging behind in enrolment in higher level education when compared to their Mandarin speaking peers (Zhou 2001, p. 129). The causes of this disparity are the result of a number of socio-economic factors which have been noted by Timothy Grose, among which is his observation that the promotion of Mandarin language education by the CCP has been at the expense of an effective bilingual education (Grose 2010: 98–101). This is further supported by Colin Mackerras, who observes that the efficacy of bilingual teaching of minorities in China is "spotty and inconsistent", and notes that the situation may be getting worse in some regions (Mackerras 2003: 131). The inefficacy of Xinjiang's system of bilingual education for minorities also extends to the university level, with Arienne Dwyer observing Xinjiang University's decision to cease teaching classes in Uyghur resulting from a lack of adequate academic texts available in Uyghur (Dwyer 2005: 40).

By limiting the third level education available in the Uyghurs' own language, it increases the difficulty faced by Uyghur in attaining the same level of upward social mobility that is available to Mandarin speaking Chinese. This places Uyghur in a compromising position where they may have to sacrifice their own language; a fundamental component of their minority identity, in order to compete in Mandarin dominated Chinese society. Xinjiang University's recent decision to educate only in Mandarin Chinese effectively facilitates the stagnation of the Uyghur language, with the best educated left with little recourse but to primarily use Mandarin Chinese. This has the knock on effect of mitigating the benefits of maintaining a command of the Uyghur language, resulting in the erosion of the presence of Uyghur language in the upper classes of society in Xinjiang, in effect ghettoising the Uyghurs' cultural identity.

The Uyghur also suffer greater regional restrictions with regards to their ability to exercise their religious beliefs than their Hui counterparts. In 1993, the Standing Committee of the Xinjiang Uyghur Autonomous Region's People's Congress, a municipal body tasked with the promulgation of laws and regulations specific to Xinjiang, issued a series of regulations titled 'Implementing Measures of the Law on the Protection of Minors'[6]. Contained within its body of regulations is Art. 14, which states that "Parents or other guardians minors may not permit to be engaged in religious activities"[7]. Evidence of the implementation of this regulation has since been observed by Jacqueline Armijo, who reported to the US Congressional-Executive Commission on China in 2003 that "there are signs on mosques refusing entry to anyone less than 18 years of age" (Armijo 2003). Later, in 2006 a report by Radio Free Asia provided an example demonstrating that such bans remained in place[8]. More recently, the blanket prohibition of minors from participating in religious activities has reappeared as Art. 37 in the 2015 Xinjiang Autonomous Regions' Regulations of Religious Affairs, which was promulgated in January 2015 (Xinjiang People's Congress Standing Committee 2015).

These restrictions also extend to third level education, with reports of Xinjiang university at times restricting religious activities amongst Uyghur students, even going so far as to prohibit students from fasting during the period of Ramadan (Bovingdon 2010: 71). Indeed, China's state media outlet the Global Times also alluded to the existence of such restrictions in a report published in 2014, noting that during the month of Ramadan that "CPC and League members, civil servants and students cannot take part in fasting and other religious activities. All CPC officials and civil servants should guide family members and friends to act in line with the law and fight against illegal religious activities"[9].

This brief selection of examples serves to highlight the troubled relationship that persists to this day between the authorities and the Uyghur as a result of government restrictions on religious activities, illustrating the dichotomy that exists between the Hui and the Uyghurs' interactions with the state through law and policy. Despite the existence of constitutional protections that ostensibly allow for a level of ethno-religious and cultural plurality among all China's nationalities, many Uyghur see their way of life continually being eroded due to what they perceive as the government forcibly attempting to integrate the Uyghur into a Han-centric Chinese society society. In spite of the withering effects of Xinjiang's assimilatory policies, many Uyghur still see their cultural and religious identity as a minority as wholly different from that of the Han Chinese identity.

To remedy this source of tension, the CCP needs to increase its efforts in supporting the education of the Uyghur and other minorities through their native languages. The state also needs to reassess its perception that the Uyghurs' religious identity poses a direct threat to its political authority. The CCP's attempts to assert its ideological orthodoxy by restricting outward manifestations of the Uyghurs' religiosity is evidence of this perceived vulnerability. By uniformly embracing a multicultural approach towards religious belief that would respect the Uyghurs' unique cultural and religious identity as it does for the Hui, the CCP could go a long way in alleviating what has been a long standing source of tension amongst the Uyghurs, while also improving the Party's legitimacy as a regime among one of its most vulnerable and disenfranchised minority nationalities.

Conclusion

The substantive differences between the CCP's relationship with the Hui and the Uyghurs is largely attributed to the extent with which either minority has managed to successfully integrate itself within a Party-centric view of contemporary Chinese society.

The Hui have emerged with a relatively amicable relationship with the state, and with varying degrees of success have ably negotiated the fine line between preserving their minority identity while cohabitating within Han Chinese society. This ethno-religious pragmatism has allowed the Hui to avoid some of the more discriminatory policies faced by Uyghurs in Xinjiang, while embracing many of the benefits that come from being a formally recognised minority nationality. A renewed interest in traditional Islamic values amongst Hui can be seen as both a by-product of the opening of China's borders, and as a result of the wider Islamic revival. While it may be a growing area of concern for a government keen to protect its position of ideological dominance, there is no evidence to suggest that an increased interest in Islam among Hui will pose a viable threat to the CCP's modernisation efforts.

In at times stark contrast, the Uyghurs' tumultuous relationship with the state is very much at odds with that of the Hui. The Uyghurs' ethno-geographic position at China's periphery combined with the refusal of some Uyghurs to integrate into contemporary Chinese society has served as a dramatic fault line within Uyghur-Han relations long before the CCP came to power. With the realisation of two separate republics in Xinjiang within the last century, some Uyghurs still actively call for increased levels of autonomy or separation from the PRC. Recent escalations in violence are a cause for significant concern and suggest that extremist groups are increasingly willing to resort to terrorism beyond Xinjiang's borders to achieve their goals.

Minority and religious policy in Xinjiang, despite genuine progress in some areas, has had a deleterious effect on the Uyghurs' religious and cultural identity, restricting their religious freedoms and curtailing their ability to maintain their unique cultural practices and traditions that help define their status as a minority. As a result, these policies have contributed to the increasing levels of unrest among the Uyghur population and have further deteriorated Uyghur-Han relations. In order to address this issue, the CCP must make an earnest effort to protect its minority's ethno-religious identities by strengthening the implementation of constitutional safeguards and reviewing Xinjiang's municipal policies that disproportionately and negatively affect the Uyghur population. The dichotomy that exists between national policy on religion and the municipal policy in Xinjiang is often jarring, and has done little to address the issue of Uyghur unrest. The CCP's reluctance to address this dichotomy may result in the Party having an unwitting hand in the continued emergence of increasingly organised terrorist groups capable of brazen acts of extremist violence, causing further internal instability throughout greater China.

By ensuring the consistent application of policies concerning religious minorities throughout China in accordance with its constitution, the CCP could do much to remedy the necrotic fissures that are damaging Uyghur-Han relations in Xinjiang, while at the same time further empowering its sizable Uyghur population to represent China, much like the Hui has done, as a culturally diverse, tolerant and harmonious society on the global stage.

Notes

1 For additional reading on ethnic identity and classification, see: Horowitz, Donald L. (1985). *Ethnic Groups in Conflict*. Berkeley, CA: University of California Press; Chandra, Kanchan (2006). 'What Is Ethnic Identity and Does It Matter?', *Annual Review of Political Science*, 9(1), pp. 397–424; Nagel, Joane (1994). 'Constructing Ethnicity: Creating and Recreating Ethnic Identity and Culture', *Social Problems*, 41(1), pp. 152–176; Mullaney, Thomas & Anderson, Benedict (2010). *Coming to Terms with the Nation: Ethnic Classification in Modern China*, Oakland, CA: University of California Press.

2 Stalin defined a nation as a "historically evolved, stable community of people, formed on the basis of a common language, territory, economic life, and psychological make-up manifested in a common culture". See: Stalin, Joseph (1947). *Marxism and the National and Colonial Question*. Lawrence & Wishart, p. 8.

3 For additional reading on the causes of the XUAR's ethnic tensions, see: Davis, Elizabeth, 2008. 'Uyghur Muslim Ethnic Separatism in Xinjiang, China', *Asian Affairs*, 35(1), pp. 15–30.; Dillon, Michael, 1997. 'Ethnic, Religious and Political Conflict on China's Northwestern Borders: The Background to the Violence in Xinjiang'. *IBRU Boundary and Security Bulletin*, 5(1), pp. 80–86.

4 For examples of Uyghur attacks outside of Xinjiang, see: Hatton, Celia (2014). 'China separatists blamed for Kunming knife rampage'. *BBC News*. Available at http://www.bbc.com/news/world-asia-china-26404566 [Accessed March 2, 2014]; Grammaticas, Damian (2013). 'Tiananmen crash: China police 'seek Xinjiang suspects'', *BBC News*. Available at http://www.bbc.com/news/world-asia-china-24722898 [Accessed November 2, 2013].

5　Document 19, a white paper published by the CCP which further establishes the Party's position on 'religion as a historical phenomenon', notes that "religion will eventually disappear from human history. But it will disappear naturally only through the long-term development of Socialism and Communism, when all objective requirements are met". See: Central Committee of the Communist Party in China, 1982. Document No. 19: The Basic Viewpoint and Policy on the Religious Question during Our Country's Socialist Period, Beijing. English translation can be found in appendix 2 in Spiegel, M., 1991. Freedom of Religion in China, London: Human Rights Watch/ Asia.

6　For original version of this document, see: Bayinguoleng Ruoqiang County People's Government Information Office (1993). 新疆维吾尔自治区实施《中华人民共和国未成年人保护法》办法 (Xinjiang Uyghur Autonomous Region implementation of the 'Protection of Minors Act'). Available at http://o.loulan.gov.cn/Htm/zhengcefagui/xjzzqzcfg/2007-8/24/200708241101340.htm.

7　Translation by the United States Congressional-Executive Commission on China, see: United States Congressional-Executive Commission on China (1993). Xinjiang Uyghur Autonomous Region Implementing Measures for the Law on the Protection of Minors (CECC Partial Translation). Xinjiang Uyghur Autonomous Region People's Congress Standing Committee. Available at http://www.cecc.gov/resources/legal-provisions/xinjiang-Uyghur-autonomous-region-implementing-measures-for-the-law-on#body-chinese.

8　Kamberi, Dolkun, Mudie, Luisetta & Jackson-Han, Sarah (2006). 'China Bans Officials, State Employees, Children from Mosques'. *Radio Free Asia*. Available at: http://www.rfa.org/english/uyghur/uyghur_religion-20060206.html.

9　Jie, Jiang (2014). 'No fast for CPC members during Ramadan', *Global Times*. Available at http://www.globaltimes.cn/content/868638.shtml.

References

Armijo, Jacqueline (2003). 'Statement by the Acting Assistant Professor, Religious Studies, Stanford University Dr. Jacqueline Armijo to the Congressional-Executive Commission on China'. Available at http://www.cecc.gov/events/hearings/will-religion-flourish-under-chinas-new-leadership.

Becquelin, Nicolas (2004). 'Staged Development in Xinjiang', *The China Quarterly*, 178, pp. 358–378.

Ben-Adam, Justin (2012). 'China', in Ingvar Svanberg and David Westerlund, eds, *Islam Outside the Arab World*. Richmond, Surrey: Curzon.

Bewicke, Aurora E. (2009). 'Silencing the Silk Road: China's Language Policy in the Xinjiang Uyghur autonomous region', *San Diego International Law Journal*, 11(1), pp. 135-170.

Bovingdon, Gardner (2010). *The Uyghurs: Strangers in Their Own Land*. New York: Columbia University Press.

Chuah, O.A. (2012). 'The Cultural and Social Interaction between Chinese Muslim Minorities and Chinese Non-Muslim Majority in China: A Sociological Analysis', *Asian Social Science*, 8(15), pp. 267–274.

Cooke, Susette (2008). 'Surviving State and Society in Northwest China: The Hui Experience in Qinghai Province under the PRC', *Journal of Muslim Minority Affairs*, 28(3), pp. 401-420.

Davis, E. Van Wie (2008). 'Uyghur Muslim Ethnic Separatism in Xinjiang, China', *Asian Affairs*, 35(1), pp. 15–30.

Dillon, Michael (1995). *Xinjiang: Ethnicity, Separatism and Control in Chinese Central Asia*. Department of East Asian Studies, University of Durham.

Dillon, Michael (1999). *China's Muslim Hui Community: Migration, Settlement and Sects*. Richmond, Surrey: Curzon.

Dwyer, Arienne M. (2005). 'The Xinjiang Conflict: Uyghur Identity, Language Policy, and Political Discourse', *Policy Studies*, 15, pp. 1–106.

FitzGerald, C.P. (2012). 'Religion and China's Cultural Revolution', *Pacific Affairs*, 40(1), pp. 124–129.

Frankel, James D. (2009). 'Benevolence for Obedience: and Policies on Muslims in Late Imperial and Modern China', *ASIANetwork Exchange*, 16(2), pp. 25–43.

Gillette, Maris Boyd (2002). *Between Mecca and Beijing: Modernization and Consumption Among Urban Chinese Muslims*. Stanford, CA: Stanford University Press.

Gladney, Dru C. (1996). *Muslim Chinese: Ethnic Nationalism in the People's Republic*. Cambridge, MA: Harvard University Press.

Gladney, Dru C. (2004). *Dislocating China: Muslims, Minorities and Other Subaltern Subjects*. Chicago, IL: The University of Chicago Press.

Goossaert, Vincent & Palmer, David A. (2011). *The Religious Question in Modern China*. Chicago, IL, The University of Chicago Press.

Grose, Timothy A. (2010). 'The Xinjiang Class: Education, Integration, and the Uyghurs', *Journal of Muslim Minority Affairs*, 30(1), pp. 97-109.

Guo, Baogang and Dennis V. Hickey, eds 2009. *Toward Better Governance in China: An Unconventional Pathway of Political Reform*. Lexington Books.

Hess, Steve (2009). 'Dividing and conquering the shop floor: Uyghur labour export and labour segmentation in China's industrial east', *Central Asian Survey*, 28(4), pp. 403-416.

Howell, Anthony & Fan, Cindy C. (2011). 'Migration and Inequality in Xinjiang: A Survey of Han and Uyghur Migrants in Urumqi', *Eurasian Geography and Economics*, 52(1), p. 119-139.

Howell, Anthony (2013). 'Chinese minority income disparity in the informal economy: A cross-sectoral analysis of Han-Uyghur labour market outcomes in Urumqi's formal and informal sectors using survey data', *China: An International Journal*, 11(3), pp. 1–23.

Jones-Leaning, Melanie and Pratt, Douglas (2012). 'Islam in China: From silk road to separatism', *Muslim World*, 102(2), 308–334.

Kaltman, Blaine (2014). *Under the Heel of the Dragon: Islam, Racism, Crime, and the Uighur in China*. Athens, OH: Ohio University Press.

Lim, Rosalyn (2010). 'China's Ethnic Policies in the Xinjiang Region', *Washington Journal of Modern China*, pp. 64-90.

Lipman, Jonathan N. (1984). 'Ethnicity and Politics in Republican China: The Ma Family Warlords of Gansu', *Modern China*, 10(3), pp. 285–316.

Mackerras, Colin (1994). *China's Minorities: Integration and Modernization in the Twentieth Century*. Oxford University Press (China) Limited.

Mackerras, Colin (2003). *China's Ethnic Minorities and Globalisation*. London and New York: Taylor & Francis.

Rowe, William T. (2010). *China's Last Empire: The Great Qing*. Cambridge, MA: Harvard University Press.

Sautman, Barry. (2014). 'A US/India Model for China's Ethnic Policies: Is the Cure Worse than the Disease?'. *East Asia Law Review*, 9, 89–159.

Sen, Tan Ta (2009). *Cheng Ho and Islam in Southeast Asia*. Singapore: Institute of Southeast Asian Studies.

Shichor, Yitzhak (2003). 'Ethno-diplomacy: The Uyghur hitch in Sino-Turkish relations', *Policy Studies*, 53. p. 13.

Shichor, Yitzhak (2005). 'Blow Up: Internal and external challenges of Uyghur separatism and Islamic radicalism to Chinese rule in Xinjiang', *Asian Affairs: An American Review*, 32(2), pp. 119-135.

Smith Finley, Joanne (2007). 'Chinese Oppression in Xinjiang, Middle Eastern Conflicts and Global Islamic Solidarities among the Uyghurs', *Journal of Contemporary China*, 16(53), pp. 627-654.

Smith Finley, Joanne (2013). *The Art of Symbolic Resistance: Uyghur Identities and Uyghur-Han Relations in Contemporary Xinjiang*. Leiden: Brill.

Spengen, Wim van (2013). 'The Geo-History of Long Distance Trade in Tibet, 1850-1950', in Gray Tuttle and Kurtis R. Schaeffer, eds, *The Tibetan History Reader*). New York: Columbia University Press, pp. 491–525.

Starr, S. Frederick (2004). *Xinjiang: China's Muslim Borderland*. New York: Routledge.

State Council of the People's Republic of China (2003). 'IX. Establishment, Development and Role of the Xinjiang Production and Construction Corps', *History and Development of Xinjiang.* Available at http://www.china.org.cn/e-white/20030526/9.htm [Accessed November 17, 2012].

Toops, S. (2014). 'Where inner Asia meets outer China: The Xinjiang Uyghur autonomous region', in S.M. Walcott & C. Johnson, (eds), *Eurasian Corridors of Interconnection: From the South China to the Caspian Sea.* New York, NY: Routledge.

Veselič, Maja (2013). 'Good Muslims, Good Chinese: State Modernisation Policies, Globalisation of Religious Networks and the Changing Hui Ethno-Religious Identifications', in Robert W. Hefner, John Hutchinson, Sara Mels and Christiane Timmerman, (eds), 2013. *Religions in Movement: The Local and the Global in Contemporary Faith Traditions.* Oxford: Taylor & Francis.

Waley-Cohen, Joanna (1991). *Exile in Mid-Qing China: Banishment to Xinjiang, 1758-1820.* New Haven, CT: Yale University Press.

Wang, Yuxiang (2013). *Language, Culture, and Identity among Minority Students in China: the case of the Hui.* New York: Taylor & Francis.

Xinjiang People's Congress Standing Committee (2015). 'Xinjiang Uyghur Autonomous Region Regulations on Religious Affairs' (新疆维吾尔自治区宗教事务条例). Available at http://news.ts.cn/content/2014-12/04/content_10789678_all.htm [Accessed December 20, 2014].

Yang, Fenggang (2006). 'The red, black, and gray markets of religion in China', *The Sociological Quarterly*, 47, pp. 93-122.

Zang, Xiaowei (2007). *Ethnicity and Urban Life in China: a Comparative Study of Hui Muslims and Han Chinese.* London: Routledge.

Zhou, Minglang (2001). 'The Politics of Bilingual Education and Educational Levels in Ethnic Minority Communities in China', *International Journal of Bilingual Education and Bilingualism*, 4(2), 125–149.

CHAPTER 3

Making Muslims Hui: Ethnic Bias in the New Curriculum of the China Islamic Association

Aaron Glasserman

Princeton University

Introduction

Muslims in China studying to become imams receive an education shaped largely by the political, security, and ideological priorities of the government and the Chinese Communist Party (CCP). These priorities, captured in the reigning ideology of constructing a 'harmonious society' (*hexie shehui* 和谐社会) and which include the promotion of patriotism, economic development, social stability, and interethnic harmony, define the parameters of lawful Islam in China — i.e., the religious tenets and practices that the government tolerates. Religious policy and legislation prohibit speech and action that violate these priorities, such as denigration of other sects and religions and religiously based opposition to the government. Given the perceived association between Islam and Uyghur unrest in Xinjiang, one of the most important criteria of lawful Islam is that it accept the official position of Xinjiang as an integral part of the Chinese 'ancestral country' (*zuguo* 祖国) and denounce the 'three forces' (*san fu shili* 三夫势力) of separatism, terrorism, and religious extremism.

In terms of containing the political and social influence of Islam, these parameters are intentionally porous: the state seeks not only to restrict Islam, but also to shape it. A salient feature of Chinese religious policy since 1993 and especially after 2001 has been the requirement that religious citizens reinterpret and elaborate their beliefs to 'mutually adapt' (*xiang sheying* 相适应) with contemporary Chinese society and to articulate their relationship to it according to their tradition. At a major conference on religious work in 1993, then-president Jiang Zemin introduced the 'Three Sentences' (*san juhua* 三句话), which would become pillars of religious policy: the government must "first, comprehensively and correctly implement and carry out the party's religious policy; second, strengthen the administration of religious affairs through law; and third, actively guide the mutual adaptation of religion and socialist society." (Jiang 1995: 253). The government and Party's priorities thus do not only confine legal Islam in China — they are also supposed to guide its interpretation.

The China Islamic Association (*Zhongguo Yisilajiao Xiehui* 中国伊斯兰教协会, CIA), the organization responsible for communicating government policy to China's Muslim population and for representing Chinese Muslim interests to the government, directs Islamic education in China. In 2001, responding to Jiang's 'third sentence,' the CIA established the Religious Affairs Guidance Committee (*Jiaowu Zhidao Weiyuanhui* 教务指导委员会) to conduct and publish interpretations of Islamic scripture, belief and law in accordance with state policy and Chinese socialism. This new exegetical project, known as *Jiejing* (解经, 'interpreting scripture' or 'exegesis'), encompasses two main endeavors: the compilation and distribution of state-sanctioned religious opinions in the form of sermons; and the revision and standardization of the curriculum and textbooks at the CIA-run Islamic Scripture Academies (*Yisilanjiaojing Xueyuan* 伊斯兰教经学院), where legally practicing imams are trained and licensed.[1]

For those observers who view the CIA and its equivalent institutions for other religions as merely the state's 'instruments of control,' (Spiegel 2000) the *Jiejing* project is simply a further intrusion by the government into what should be Chinese Muslims' internal affairs, based on the constitutionally guaranteed freedom of religious belief. The government does exercise ultimate control in tolerating or suppressing certain religious activities and permitting or banning certain religious literature. But profitable cooperation with the government does not imply, let alone prove, that the CIA simply executes the government's religious policy vis-à-vis Islam and lacks its own set of interests. As I will argue, although the CIA claims for political reasons to represent all Muslims in China, the Hui (one of the ten recognized Muslim ethnicities in China[2]) dominate its leadership. The CIA leadership does not necessarily aim to promote the Hui over the other nine groups out of a belief that the Hui, as an ethnicity, are somehow superior. Rather, the Hui bias surfaces as the CIA attempts to justify *Jiejing*, a project which itself represents a particular understanding of Islam not shared by all Chinese Muslims. Beginning in the late Qing (1644-1912) and early Republican (1912-1949) periods, certain reformist Huis began advocating pedagogical modernization and religious revitalization. These processes were intertwined: by teaching young Chinese Muslims both Chinese and Arabic and secular and religious subjects, these reformers believed they could simultaneously modernize their country and energize their religion, which they saw as crippled by the backward Sufi orders and widespread ignorance of the *Qur'an* and *Hadith*. In both their patriotism and their call for a return to the central texts of Islam, these scriptural modernists were well suited to organize themselves into a large national organization dedicated to publication, education, managing the *hajj*, and other fundamental Islamic affairs. The establishment of a central body for interpreting Islam in accordance with contemporary society similarly reflected the views of the scriptural modernists, who rejected the notion, popular among the Sufi orders, that certain individuals (e.g. particularly charismatic shaykhs or alleged descendants of the Prophet Muhammad) enjoyed special religious authority.

The CIA is a principally scriptural modernist organization, not a principally Hui one. The Uyghurs are not without their own modernists — indeed, Bao Erhan (包尔汉), one of the founders of the CIA, was a Uyghur. But because the Hui dominate the scriptural modernist movement and because the Uyghurs are mostly Sufi (or at least Sufi-influenced)[3], CIA publications, including the standardized textbooks for the Islamic Scripture Academies, can privilege the historical narrative of the Hui. The new curriculum tells all Chinese Muslims that they have inherited a long tradition of patriotism, *aiguo aijiao* (爱国爱教, 'loving country, loving religion') in which political loyalty to China was understood and articulated in Islamic terms. In fact, this account, already quite problematic and anachronistic, is questionably valid only for the Huis and far removed from the histories of the other Chinese Muslim ethnic groups. The CIA justifies its scriptural modernist agenda as the continuation of a uniquely Hui tradition that it then projects back onto all nine other ethnicities. Non-Hui Muslims who aspire to the pulpit must thus adopt a foreign tradition and in a sense become Hui in order to fulfill their religious calling.

The remainder of this chapter is divided into four sections. Part I considers the history and structure of the China Islamic Association and demonstrates how it is possible that one ethnic group in China could come to dominate an ostensibly unitary and non-denominational institution. Part II examines the CIA's targeting and objectification of Xinjiang. By framing its activities (including *Jiejing*) as responses to growing unrest in Xinjiang, the CIA establishes itself as a loyal supporter of the regime and increases the likelihood that the government will identify the promotion of the CIA's Hui-modernist understanding of Islam with its own interests and policies. Part III looks at the CIA's justification for *Jiejing* as an indication of the project's inherent partiality for the mostly Hui modernist movement. Finally, Part IV concludes with a discussion of the implications of this contradiction between ethnic harmony and Hui privilege for the stability of Xinjiang.

Structural Ethnic Bias in the CIA

Before examining the *Jiejing* literature and the surrounding discourse, it is worth considering the structural features and history of the CIA that might enable one group within the diversity of Chinese Islam to control it. Three factors have engendered an environment where the mostly Hui scriptural modernist movement is able to use the CIA to advance its own interests, sometimes at the expense of other groups.

First, the geographic basis for representation in the CIA disadvantages groups concentrated in a single region. There are hundreds of local district-, city-, and province-level Islamic Associations, but the central China Islamic Association in Beijing directs *Jiejing*. The Hui are scattered across China, with communities in virtually every major city in every province. In contrast, the vast majority of the Uyghurs live in Xinjiang. Because representation in the national-level CIA is allocated geographically rather than demographically (based on ethnicity, for example), the Hui are overrepresented and the Uyghurs are underrepresented when we compare CIA membership to population. Although the Hui and Uyghur nationalities constitute .79% and .76% of the total population of the PRC (Undata 2010), respectively, in the current CIA Committee the Hui hold 78% (211) and the Uyghurs hold 17% (45) of the seats (China Islamic Association 2011a). The disparity is even greater in the more powerful CIA Standing Committee, where the Hui hold 82% (64) of the seats and the Uyghurs have 10% (8) (China Islamic Association 2011a). This skewed representation would not enable the Hui majority to pursue an overtly pro-Hui, anti-Uyghur agenda — nor can we assume that the Hui majority would want to. Moreover, government demands for ethnic harmony and the ostensible ethnic inclusiveness of the CIA, expressed in its charter (China Islamic Association 2011b), would prohibit such an agenda. But the skew does suggest that the Uyghur minority is at a considerable disadvantage in ensuring that CIA activities do not harm its interests.

Second, Hui involvement in regional and national organizations for the advancement of Chinese Muslim interests dates back to the first half of the 20th century. During the Republican period (1912-1949), organizations supporting Hui educational and scholarly interests proliferated throughout the major Muslim urban communities in eastern China. In 1912, Hui intellectuals in Beijing founded the Society for the Advancement of the Hui Religion of China (*Zhongguo Huijiao Jujinhui* 中国回教俱进会), which, with its network of provincial branches, was the first nation-wide organization for China's Muslims. The Learned Society of the Hui Religion of China (*Zhongguo Huijiao Xuehui* 中国回教学会) and the Guild of the Hui Religion of China (中国回教工会) were established in Shanghai in 1925 and 1929, respectively. Several more similarly titled organizations sprouted in the 1930s, including the Society for the Promotion of Education of the Hui People (*Huimin Jiaoyu Cujinhui* 回民教育促进会) (Aubin 2006: 244-246). These organizations brought urban Hui intellectuals, educators, and businessmen together to promote Arabic and Islamic learning alongside modern education. They established schools that followed a dual Arabic-Chinese curriculum and financed Islamic libraries. The first half of the twentieth century was a period of major educational reform throughout China, and these Muslims saw themselves as one among many battalions united under the banner of 'saving the country through education' (*Jiaoyu Qiuguo* 教育救国). Chinese Muslim support for the resistance movement after the Japanese invasion of the 1937 (manifested in the creation of the Association of the Hui People of China for the Resistance to Japan and the Salvation of the Country, *Zhongguo Huimin Kangri Qiuguo Xiehui* 中国回民抗日救国协会) affirmed their patriotic credentials (Ibid, 246-248). Thus, since even before the founding of 'New China', many Hui and scriptural modernists have been engaged in the very pedagogical and political endeavors that are today requirements for all religious institutions in China.

Third, the compatibility of the national association structure with scriptural modernism further favors that mostly Hui movement. As stated above, not all Hui are scriptural modernists, and not all scriptural modernists are Hui. But the fact that most scriptural modernists are Hui has resulted in the overrepresentation of Hui in the CIA leadership, even if their support for the CIA — and the CIA's support for them — is sectarian and not ethnic. Islamic traditions that assert mystical sources of religious knowledge or attribute special status to certain individuals are inherently less compatible than scriptural modernism with the national organization model of religious education and authority. 'Mutual adaptation' demands that the CIA articulate patriotism on Islamic grounds, which in turn entails a contest to demarcate 'true' Islam. The mostly Hui scriptural modernists, who lead the CIA and whose reformist agenda suits the CIA's powerful publishing and educational apparatus, naturally have the upper hand in this contest.

The Objectification of Xinjiang

How does the CIA continue to earn government support for activities that privilege one ethnic group over others? In the CIA and the Chinese government, the official discourse and literature surrounding *Jiejing* identify unrest and separatism in Xinjiang as major impetuses for the project. This narrative frames *Jiejing* as an indispensible tool from within the Islamic tradition in the patriotic battle against the 'three forces'—terrorism, separatism, and religious extremism— that plague Xinjiang. Through this discursive strategy, the Hui-modernist leadership accomplishes two goals. By taking unrest in Xinjiang as the target of *Jiejing*, the CIA signals its political loyalty to the government, which in turn earns it greater support and resources to advance its interests. At the same time, by identifying the solution to the 'Xinjiang problem' (*Xinjiang Wenti* 新疆问题) as a project external to Xinjiang itself, the CIA incriminates those forms of Islam not associated with its particular tradition as complicit in Xinjiang separatism.

Jiejing began with the Religious Affairs Guidance Committee's composition and publication of sermons (*wa'z*) to be read at mosques on Fridays and holidays. Upon the Guidance Committee's completion of the first *New Wa'z Speech Compilation* (*Xin Bian Wo'erzi Yanjiangji* 新编卧尔兹演讲集), the CIA held the formal ceremony marking the book's publication in Urumqi, the capital of Xinjiang Province. The volume (China Islamic Religious Affairs Guidance Committee 2001), which comprised 12 speeches on topics ranging from patriotism's place in Islam to the religious obligation to respect one's parents, was heralded as a tool to help all of China's imams "actively devote themselves to the struggle against the 'three forces', to the refutation of ethnic separatists and the fallacies and heresies of religious extremism, and to the protection of the purity of Islam." (Ma 2001) This assessment of *Jiejing*'s debut publication tellingly conflates the government's political and security objectives vis-à-vis Xinjiang with the reformists' ambitions to purify Chinese Islam. Later writings similarly cast *Jiejing* as a weapon in the twin battles against 'false' Islam and Xinjiang separatism: *Jiejing* was a requirement both in the development of Chinese Islam, which suffered from lack of properly trained and knowledgeable imams, and in the struggle against Xinjiang separatism. Chinese Islam needed the CIA just as much as the government did (CIA 2006: Curriculum of Muslim Patriotism 408-409).

The association of 'false' Islam with the Sufi beliefs and traditions of many Muslims in Xinjiang (and elsewhere) mirrors this equation of 'true' Islam with Islam as represented by the CIA. The CCP has long opposed elaborate and expensive funerary customs, which in its view waste money and, even worse, empower the local religious leaders who carry out the attendant rituals. Reformist movements in China and other parts of the Muslim world have also targeted such practices as backward and, in attributing ritual powers to certain human beings, fundamentally contrary to 'true' Islam. Through *Jiejing*, the CIA can align its reformist opposition to such practices with the ideological opposition of the CCP. For example, the third *New Wa'z Speech Compilation* includes one sermon 'Islam Advocates Generous Care [for the Old] and a Thrifty Funeral' (*Yisilanjiao tichang houyangbozang* 伊斯兰教提倡厚养薄葬) with the subsection 'A Thrifty Funeral Is a Rule in Islamic Law' (*Bozang shi yisilajiao de guiding* 薄葬 是伊斯兰教教法的规定). The compilers have attempted to craft the volume as indisputable evidence that the CIA's version of Islam fully accords with state policy. However, the content of the sermon itself reveals a parallel religious argument against Sufism. Interestingly, the sermon begins not by admonishing frugality but by forbidding *shirk*, (CIA 2005: 148) or the association of things other than God with God — precisely the accusation many reformists level against Sufism. Later on, the sermon repudiates the custom, popular among many Uyghurs in Xinjiang (Bellér-Hann 2001: 15-20), of spending heavily on a funeral to honor the diseased and receive spiritual recompense for the meritorious act: such practice "not only causes waste and brings economic burdens to the host of the funeral, but is also contrary to the spirit and rules of Islam." (CIA 2005: 158)

By positioning itself alongside the government in opposing such funerary customs, the CIA can make a divisive religious argument that could offend many Muslims in Xinjiang, who would not want to be accused of heresy or acting against Islam by an organization that ostensibly represents them. Again, some Hui are Sufi, so they too would be the targets of this repudiation. However, given the government's anxiety over religious and ethnic hostilities in Xinjiang and how the CIA has portrayed *Jiejing* as a solution to those very problems, the state-supported rejection of Uyghur-Sufi practices is surprising and counterproductive. Indeed, despite the government's requirement that Chinese Muslims of all ethnicities unite in a 'harmonious society', the CIA is sharpening divisions between Chinese Muslims, not bridging them.

Hui Bias in the *Curriculum of Muslim Patriotism*

In the preceding sections I have described two aspects of the China Islamic Association and its connection to the issues of ethnicity, territorial integrity, and patriotism in China. First, the overrepresentation of the Hui and underrepresentation of the Uyghurs in the CIA make it possible for that organization to take actions that prioritize the interests of the former while neglecting or even harming those of the latter. Second, the CIA's demonstration of political loyalty and pursuit of official support rely on a discursive strategy of objectifying 'Xinjiang' and casting itself as taking actions against or in the interest of it. This objectification in turn both reinforces the binary of Islam in Xinjiang and Islam in the rest of China and superimposes it onto the binary of normal and abnormal, or legal and illegal, religion. These biases arise largely out of the intense political and ideological pressures the state exerts on the CIA. Because all social associations in China must constantly profess loyalty to the government and Party and promote their agenda (of which territorial integrity is a core component), the CIA has no choice but to articulate its agenda according to those terms. These pressures can privilege those groups who favor such self-organization and view religion, citizenship, and modern education as interdependent. But they can also aggravate groups that are not so well adapted, raising tensions between them and other groups as well as the state. In what follows, I will examine such tensions as they surface in the CIA's justification of the *Jiejing* project. Focusing on the *Curriculum of Muslim Patriotism*, I will argue that the CIA increasingly identifies its dominant constituents — the modernist Hui — as the progenitors and exemplars of legitimate, patriotic Chinese Islam.

Published in August 2006 by the State Administration for Religious Affairs' Religious Culture Publishing House, the 450-page *Curriculum of Muslim Patriotism* (*Yisilan Aiguozhuyi Jiaocheng* 穆斯林爱国主义教程) represents the CIA's response to government calls for enhanced patriotic education throughout China. The textbook opens with a general discussion of patriotism and the official history of a unified, multiethnic China. Still, the textbook, the product of five years of work by a nearly entirely Hui editorial team (there was one Uyghur), defines and enjoins patriotism in uniquely Chinese Islamic terms. I specify 'Chinese' here because the majority of the text elaborates the history and current circumstances of Muslims in China; only one section (1.2) focuses on the role of patriotism in Islam in general and its basis in the *Qur'an* and *Hadith*. However, other literature published by the CIA and the Religious Culture Publishing House are replete with arguments deriving patriotism as an Islamic value, especially since the 2001 initiation of *Jiejing*, which aims to justify Chinese Muslim patriotism via Islamic exegesis.

In contrast, the *Curriculum* principally recounts the history of Chinese Muslim political loyalty and harmonious relations with other Chinese peoples, from the peaceful coexistence and commercial interactions as early as the Tang Dynasty (618-907) to contributions to the war effort against Japan in the 1930s and 1940s and the commitment to preserving the territorial integrity of the PRC today. The authors, keen to offer members of each of China's ten officially recognized Muslim ethnic groups a justification for patriotism, trace the 'formation and development' (*xingcheng he fazhan* 形成和发展) of each group in Chapter 2, 'The Contributions of Muslims of Every Ethnicity to a Unified Multiethnic State' (*Zhongguo ge minzu musilin dui tongyi de minzu guojia de gongxian* 中国各民族穆斯林对统一的民族国家的贡献). The authors also devote a separate section (1.3) to 'Famous Historical Chinese Muslims' Patriotic Thought' (*Zhongguo lidai musilinren de aiguozhuyi sixiang* 中国历代穆斯林名人的爱国主义思想). Notably, the authors divide that section into 'Hui' and 'Uyghur and other Muslims in Xinjiang'. In 2011, the CIA reaffirmed this distinction in its massive *Overview of Islam in China*, which organizes its discussion of Chinese Islam into two main sections, 'Xinjiang' and 'Interior' (*neidi* 内地) (CIA 2011c:1). The priority here is proving that all Chinese Muslims, even those in Xinjiang, inherit a long tradition of patriotism. Yet at the same time, the division also implies that Hui, some of whom actually live in Xinjiang, are categorically removed from the peoples and problems of China's far northwest. In this way the *Curriculum* reflects the conflation of ethnicity, religion, and separatism prevalent in the reigning discourse on Islam and Xinjiang.

Several speeches and *China Muslim* (*Zhongguo Musilin* 中国穆斯林, the CIA's semimonthly magazine) articles by CIA leaders refer vaguely to difficulties the curriculum unification project encountered in its early phases. These references suggest the possibility of internal disagreement over the content of the new textbooks. The *Curriculum of Muslim Patriotism* alone took five years to complete. Despite the multiethnic audience—or targets—of the *Curriculum*, CIA accounts attribute the ultimate completion of the work to an institutional consensus rather than an ethnic one. As one author writing in *China Muslim* explains:

> The reason that this textbook, which is brand new and has faced many difficulties, was completed was that it benefited from the care and help of each of the local Islamic Associations and Religious Affairs Bureaus, the Islamic Scripture Academies, Islamic specialists and scholars, and many great mullahs and imams. (Jun 2008: 45)

The typical reference to interethnic harmony is conspicuously absent here. The Afterword of the *Curriculum*, which describes the book's composition and publication, similarly makes no reference to the representation of different ethnicities in the process. The CIA presents the *Curriculum* as a reflection of the 'fine patriotic tradition' (*Aiguozhuyi de youliang chuantong* 爱国主义的优良传统) of all of Chinese Muslim ethnic groups, but not necessarily as a product of it. To be sure, *Jiejing* and the curriculum-unification project still draw legitimacy from the CIA's ostensible representation of all ten ethnic groups. But given how frequently and prominently the CIA invokes its multiethnic composition, it is striking that a textbook intended to cultivate patriotism among each of China's Muslim ethnicities *as* ethnicities makes no such claim. In fact, all but one of the editors listed in the book's front matter, as well as the additional consultants listed in the Afterword, are Hui. As I stated previously, these editors' ethnicity does not determine their outlook or intent, but the absence of members of other groups facilitates a Hui bias in the textbook's content.

This Hui bias manifests itself principally in the patriotic narrative that the *Curriculum* ascribes to all ten of China's Muslim ethnic groups. Any historical account of Islam in China inevitably begins with the Hui, who are the descendants of China's earliest (mostly Arab and Persian) Muslim merchants, soldiers, and immigrants, many of whom eventually intermarried with the local Han population. The *Curriculum* similarly describes the 'formation and development' of the other nine groups, all of which have historically constituted important parts of the 'multiethnic Chinese nation.' The textbook loses the ability to give equivalent accounts for each ethnicity once it moves beyond the discussion of ethnicity alone and attempts to demonstrate the longstanding patriotism of China's Muslims in religious as well as ethnic terms. Even if we accept the text's anachronistic characterization of ancient China as a multiethnic state with patriotic minorities throughout, the authors run into trouble when they make the additional claim that China's Muslims have long viewed loyalty to China as an aspect of their religion. For the CIA and the government, *aiguo aijiao* ('loving country, loving religion') captures the rightful synthesis of patriotism and religious affiliation in a single concept. Although *aiguo aijiao* today inscribes the banners, books, and policies of the State Administration for Religious Affairs and the associations for each of China's five recognized religions (Islam, Protestantism, Catholicism, Daoism, and Buddhism), the phrase originated in Hui intellectual and religious circles (referred to in Part II) affiliated with the Chinese Islamic revival in the late Qing and Republican periods (Matsumoto 2006: 118). Besides the *Curriculum of Muslim Patriotism*, which virtually synonymizes the 'fine tradition of patriotism' with the 'fine tradition of *aiguo aijiao*', a wealth of articles, speeches, and policies, featuring such titles as '*Aiguo Aijiao* Is the Basic Spirit of Islam,' identify *aiguo aijiao* a central component of Chinese Islam. The CIA claims generally that all ten Muslim ethnic groups have inherited a long tradition of patriotism to China, but by construing patriotism through religion, or *aiguo aijiao*, as the essence of that tradition, it alienates those groups for whom *aiguo aijiao* is little more than a recent slogan of the state.

The CIA's attempt to establish the strong history of *aiguo aijiao* as a central feature of Chinese Islam sharpens the Hui-centric character of the *Jiejing* project. The *Curriculum* and related literature cast *Jiejing* and curriculum reform as the latest phase in a centuries-long process of Islam and China's 'mutual adaptation'. This process began with the spread of the 'Scripture Hall Education' (*Jingtang jiaoyu* 经堂教育) method of Islamic pedagogy in the 16th century, whereby Hui students — most of whom knew no Arabic or Persian — studied both the Chinese Classics and Islamic texts in a transliterated form (using Chinese characters to phonetically represent Arabic and Persian words). Mutual adaptation accelerated and deepened in the 17th and 18th centuries with the writing of several works — known collectively as the 'Han Kitab' — that used traditional Chinese (especially Confucian and to a lesser extent Buddhist and Daoist) terms and ideas to explain Islam and demonstrate its harmony with the local intellectual environment. The process continued in the late Imperial and Republican periods via the Hui-led nationalist movements and educational reforms discussed above. Although it was only in this later period that *aiguo aijiao* emerged as an expression of

Hui-Islamic patriotism, the authors of the *Curriculum* transplant the concept back into Hui history. Thus, they describe the Han Kitab and its authors as 'a concrete and active manifestation of *aiguo aijiao*' (*Aiguo aijiao de juti xingdong tixian* 爱国爱教的具体行动体现) (CIA 2006: 44).

By this logic, *Jiejing* is the culmination of *aiguo aijiao* in the present day. Although the Han Kitab authors were Hui Muslims, the CIA leadership apparently sees no contradiction in tying the ostensibly (ethnically) inclusive *Jieijng* project to the uniquely Hui history of 'using Confucianism to explain [Islamic] scripture' (*yi ru shi jing* 以儒释经). As Chen Guangyuan (陈广元), the president of the CIA and a principal architect of *Jiejing*, wrote in *China Religion* (*Zhongguo Zongjiao* 中国宗教, the flagship publication of the influential China Academy of Social Science's Institute for World Religions):

> Ever since Islam spread to China, arising from the requirements of their own development, Chinese Islam and Muslims have always exerted great effort to realize mutual adaptation with Chinese society. In history, the use of Confucianism to explain [Islamic] scripture is a typical example [of this effort]. (Chen 2011: 15).

Chen ascribes this history of 'mutual adaption' to all of 'Chinese Islam and Muslims', but the deployment of Chinese philosophical concepts in Islamic writings, along with the other alleged incarnations of *aiguo aijiao* noted above, is unique to the Hui. The *Curriculum* and other CIA writings elaborate the uniquely Hui tradition of *aiguo aijiao* through *Jiejing* and project it back onto all ten Chinese Muslim ethnicities. If imams in training must accept this tradition and support *Jieijng*, it is unclear how non-Hui students at the Scripture Academies can satisfy the political requirement of affirming *aiguo aijiao* without engaging in an ethnic tradition quite different from their own. Such a rigid distinction between 'ethnic' and 'religious' identity may be artificial, but it is precisely that distinction that informs, and is in turn perpetuated by, Chinese state policy.

Conclusion

In light of the Chinese state's overarching aim of constructing a 'harmonious society' and its proscriptions of ethnic and religious denigration, the endorsement of the CIA and its particularly Hui-modernist project is quite problematic. This is all the more true in Xinjiang, where the mostly Hui modernist movement clashes with the strong Sufi traditions of the Uyghurs. The CIA touts *Jiejing* as the solution to ethnic and religious problems in Xinjiang, but as we have seen, it may in fact be aggravating them.

The penetration of *Jiejing* into the curriculum of the Islamic Scripture Academies may be even more problematic and dangerous than the publication of sermons that espouse anti-Sufi views. Communities may disagree over which customs and beliefs are truly Islam, but as long as they enjoy a limited space to practice their religion as they see fit, conflict might be avoided. If, on the other hand, the government authorizes one group to administer religious education and license religious professionals for the rest of the country, local tradition and state authority may collide, quickly and powerfully. There is a general agreement among scholars that the perception of government constraints on the expression of ethnic identity contributes to tensions in Xinjiang. For its part, the government seems to acknowledge the danger of insulting minority ethnic groups, even if it continues to tightly constrain the free expression of their identities. But in endorsing the CIA and the *Jiejing* project, the Chinese government may unwittingly be exacerbating the ethnic and religious conflicts it is so desperate to resolve.

Notes

1   Although the CIA established a separate committee to carry out the second endeavor, government and CIA officials envisioned it as part of the *Jiejing* project. See, for example, Gao Zhanfu and Ma Jianlong (2009: 22-23).

2   These are, in descending order of population size, the Hui, Uyghur, Kazakh, Dongxiang, Kyrgyz, Salar, Tajik, Uzbek, Bonan, and Tatar nationalities.

3   For an account of Sufism and Sufi-influenced traditions among the Uyghurs, see Bellér-Hann, Ildikó (2001), and Schrode, Paula (2008).

References

Aubin, Françoise (2006). 'Islam on the Wings of Nationalism: The Case of Muslim Intellectuals in Republican China,' in Stéphane A. Dudoignon, Komatsu Hisao and Kosugi Yasushi, eds, *Intellectuals in the Modern Islamic World: Transmission, Transformation, Communication*. New York: Routledge, pp. 244-246.

Bellér-Hann, Ildikó (2001), 'Making the Oil Fragrant: Dealings with the Supernatural among the Uyghurs in Xinjiang', *Asian Ethnicity* 2 (1), pp. 9-23.

Chen, Guangyuan (2011), 'Advance Jiejing Work, Expound the True Spirit of Islam', *China Religion* (5), 15. (伊斯兰教自传入中国以来, 出于自身发展的需要, 中国伊斯兰教与穆斯林一直在努力现实与中国社会的相适应, 历史上的以儒释经就是一个典型的例子.)

China Islamic Association (2005), 'Islam Advocates Generous Care and a Thrifty Funeral,' in *New Wa'z Speech Compilation*, (3). Beijing: Religious Culture Publishing House. (...那样不仅造成浪费, 给丧主带来经济负担, 也是与伊斯兰教的精神和规定相悖的.)

Chinca Islamic Association (2006). *Curriculum of Muslim Patriotism*. Beijing: Religious Culture Publishing House, pp. 408-409.

China Islamic Association (2011a). '9th Session of the Committee,' available at http://www.chinaislam.net.cn/about/wygw/about188.html [Accessed March 17, 2014]

China Islamic Association (2011b). 'General Regulations', available at http://www.chinaislam.net.cn/about/xhgk/zhangcheng/201206/01-1015.html [Accessed March 17, 2014]

China Islamic Association (2011c). *Overview of Islam in China*. Beijing: Religious Culture Publishing House.

China Islamic Religious Affairs Guidance Committee (2001). *New Wa'z Speech Compilation* (1). Beijing: China Islamic Religious Affairs Guidance Committee.

Gao, Zhanfu and Ma, Jianlong (2009). 'Third National Islamic Scripture Academy Specialized Religious Classes' Uniform Educational Materials Work Conference Convenes in Lanzhou', *China Muslim*, 3, pp. 22-23.

Jiang, Zemin (1995). 'Attach High Importance Ethnic Work and Religious Work,' in *Selected Documents of the New Period of Religious Work*. Beijing: Religious Culture Publishing House, p. 253. (一 是全面、正确地贯彻执行党的宗教政策, 二 是依法加强对宗教事务的管理, 三 是积极引导宗教与社会主义社会相适应.)

Jun, Jing (2008). 'Adapt to the Times, Cultivate Human Talent', *China Muslim*, 3. (这部全新而又曾面临诸多困难的教材之所以完成, 得益于各地伊协组织和宗教局、有关伊斯兰教经学院、伊斯兰教专家学者以及许多大毛拉、大阿訇的关心与帮助.)

Ma, Liqiang (2001). 'China Islamic Religious Affairs Guidance Committee's *Compliation of New Wa'z* Book Donation Ceremony Held in Xinjiang', China Muslim, 5, pp. 6. (积 极投入与'三 股势力'的斗争, 批驳民族分裂主义分子和宗教极端主义的歪理邪,维护我们伊斯兰教的纯洁性.)

Matsumoto, Masumi (2006). 'Rationalizing Patriotism among Muslim Chinese: The Impact of the Middle East on the *Yuehua* Journal', in Stéphane A. Dudoignon, Komatsu

Hisao and Kosugi Yasushi, eds, *Intellectuals in the Modern Islamic World: Transmission, Transformation and Communication.* London: Routledge, pp. 117-141.

Schrode, Paula (2008). 'The Dynamics of Orthodoxy and Heterodoxy in Uyghur Religious Practice', *Die Welt des Islams*, 48, pp. 294-433.

Spiegel, Mickey (2000). 'China: Religion in the Service of the State', Statement to the U.S. Commission on International Religious Freedom. Available at http://www.hrw.org/news/2000/03/15/china-religion-service-state [Accessed April 17, 2014]

UNdata (2010), 'China, 2010', 'Population by national and/or ethnic group, sex and urban/rural residence'. Available at http://data.un.org/Data.aspx?q=ethnic&d=POP&f=tableCode%3a26 [Accessed March 17, 2014]

CHAPTER 4

Collective Feature, Identity Construction and Cultural Adaptation: Interaction between Hui Muslim Society and the State

Gui Rong

Yunnan University

The relation between Hui Muslim society and the state could to some extent be described as an interaction between communities as a small place and the state as a big society. The interaction between local Hui Muslim society and the state mainly depends on the 'jamaat' community and is always represented by collective features. Muslim society can constantly construct nation-state identity and seek for development throughout the history through continuous development practice and cultural adaptation of Hui Muslim society and real-time policy adjustment and institutional construction of state power. The national identity of Hui is essential to understanding the key issue of how the Hui Muslims survive in a non-Islamic country as a minority group and how they interact with the state power. Overall, the national identity of Hui Muslims is characterized by stable internal structure and dynamic subjective construction. The author attempts to reveal the essence and characteristics of the interaction between local Hui Muslim society and the state by analyzing the interaction history, interpreting the cultural expression of national identity of Hui Muslims and illustrating cultural adaptation and development practices of the Hui minority. The interaction history, national identity and practice of cultural adaptation of Hui Muslims are very important aspects that help to understand the relation between Hui Muslim society and the state.

Jamaat: Community Pattern and Collective Feature of Hui Muslim Society

The Hui minority in China is widely scattered in small settlements. As Durkheim noted, religion binds people into a single moral community through beliefs and ceremonies (Durkheim, 1912). The Muslim people usually term the Muslim community that shares Islam as their common belief, that lives around a mosque, and that is separated by a clear geographical border and identity boundary as *jamaat. Jamaat* is a transliteration from Arabic, meaning 'aggregating, gathering'. *Jamaat* shares a similar meaning with 'community' and 'society' in English and *shequ* (社区), *shehui* (社会), *shequn* (社群), *jiti* (集体) in Chinese. As a basic population unit in Hui Muslim society, the geographical border of *jamaat* roughly corresponds to that of a village or block under the state system. The size of a *jamaat* is usually directly related to the historical tradition, economic status and population size of the place where it is located. All Muslims in a *jamaat* believe in Islam and exert autonomous democratic management of religious affairs in the community. From this perspective, the *jamaat* is a traditional social organization for Chinese Muslims, a fundamental entity for the Hui Muslim society to interact with the state, and thus it determines that Hui Muslim society is represented by all kinds of collective features of local *jamaats*. It is the Islamic belief and values that hold all members of *jamaat* together (Ma 2006: 8-15).

To facilitate the understanding of cultural characteristics of local Hui Muslim society, I will analyze and summarize the stable cultural structure of the community of the Hui Muslim and put forward the notion of a cultural pattern of *jamaat* (Gui 2013: 42-47). American anthropologist Kroeber regarded the stable relationship and structure as a cultural pattern (Kroeber 1952). I use the concept for providing a perspective and theoretical framework for understanding the Hui Muslim community. Religious identity, public space, behavior pattern, economic system, and institutional guarantee constitute the basic structure and content of the cultural pattern of a *jamaat*. These five aspects are closely related to each other as a whole and tend to be marks and rules distinct from other ethnic groups (communities).

Religious identity is the most important identity of Hui Muslims in a *jamaat*, and Islam is the fundamental principle that every Muslim in a *jamaat* observes in their religious belief and living practice and often becomes an identity boundary between a jamaat and other ethnic groups. Local inhabitation provides a living pattern and focus of identity for every Chinese Muslim (Israeli 2002: 306). The local difference between jamaats is often related to Islamic sects and schools, in addition to the differences in local histories and traditions of different *jamaats*. For example, different Islamic sects and schools usually form into different *jamaats* and all the Muslims in a *jamaat* often belong to the same Islamic sect and school. For all *jamaats*, the mosque is an iconic symbol and public space where the Muslims worship Allah, hold community rituals and collective activities. The common and main social interaction as a behavior pattern in *jamaats* can be summarized into two types: substantive and virtual. The behavior patterns of substantive social interaction can be further divided into an aggregated pattern and a divergent patter. The former refers to inward institutional interaction within and between *jamaats*, including Islamic cultural education, festivals and celebrations, holding collective prayer ceremonies for the deceased (*janaza* in Arabic), family memorial religious activities, etc.; the latter refers to outward social interaction between the *jamaat* and other ethnic groups, such as participating in social activities arranged by the government, migration due to work in other places, and doing business. Virtual social interaction mainly refers to the use of modern media. Such interaction existing among *jamaats* is usually beyond the geographical boundary and has the quality of what Anderson calls 'imagined community' (Anderson 1983). The charity economy and public welfare system of Islam provide financial security for the normal operation of the *jamaat*. The most important regular collective events in a jamaat mainly include developing mosque education, celebrating festivals and ceremonies, organizing renovation of mosques, etc. The Democratic Management Committee of a mosque is the management organization of a *jamaat* and is managed by local Islamic associations.

Through the effective interaction between folk organizations, like Islamic management committees and Islamic associations, and government departments, religious and political harmony is achieved and provides the government institutional guarantee for the healthy development of the *jamaat*.

Amartya Sen argues that the construction of Muslim citizen society should emphasize the political and social position and democratic practices (Sen 2009: 72). Being a fundamental entity for Hui Muslim society, which carries out democratic practices and interacts with the state, to some extent, the cultural pattern of a *jamaat* reflects the basic development status of Muslim citizen society. Furthermore, the cultural pattern of a *jamaat* can help us understanding the universality of local Hui communities and the difference between Hui Muslim society and non-Muslim society.

History of Interaction between Hui Muslim Society and the State

Throughout the history of Hui Muslims in China, the state power is the fundamental institutional guarantee and social root for the establishment of the national identity of Hui Muslims. In fact, since the Yuan Dynasty, especially, by strengthening the national bureaucratic systems and implementing the various ethnic-religious policies, the state played an important role in the national integration and shaped the national identity of Hui Muslims and during some stages it was even decisive. In the process of formation and development of the Hui Muslim minority in China, their national identity is reflected in a stable cultural-psychological identity and flexible political-legal identity (Gui 2011a: 192-198).

During the Tang and Song dynasties, Hui Muslim ancestors were regarded as foreign residents. In the Yuan Dynasty, Hui Muslim ancestors were called 'Huihui people' (*Huihuiren* 回回人). They were registered according to residence, which meant that these Muslim ancestors became new members of the family of the Chinese nation as was recorded in Volume 17 of the Ordinances of Yuan Dynasty (*Yuandianzhang juan shiqi* 《元典章》卷十七). Huihui people in Yuan Dynasty enjoyed a social status inferior only to the Mongolian ruling class. Annals of governmental officials of the History of Yuan Dynasty (*Yuanshi Baiguanzhi* 《元史·百官志》) manifested that the central government set up special official positions and organs in charge of affairs of the Huihui people. Preferential national policies helped preserve their religious and cultural characteristics. In order to survive in the Confucian cultural context of Chinese Han nationality, Huihui people, still having diverse ethnic identities as well as the Muslim identity, on the one hand constantly learned from the mainstream culture while on the other hand contributing to the indigenization of Islam in China which lead to the final formation of Hui minority in Ming Dynasty (Bai 1984: 15-28).

In the Ming Dynasty, the government implemented limitation and assimilation policies, such as installing garrison troops or peasants to open up wasteland and grow crops, incorporating all the people into household registration, forced migration, and prohibiting marriage with people of the same ethnic origin. Volume 6 of the Law of the Ming Dynasty (*Minglü juan 6* 《明律》卷6) stipulated banning "Hu (minority)[1] clothing, Hu language and family names of Hu". The government strengthened the management and control on mosques and the Imams' judicial power was cancelled (Yu 2012: 109-110). State restrictions and assimilation policies stimulated the Hui people to strengthen their cultural self-consciousness and accelerated the process of national identity formation as Chinese. In this context, in the mid and late Ming Dynasty, intellectual elites of the Hui minority as represented by Hu Dengzhou raised the first wave of cultural self-awareness by establishing the Islamic mosque education system. In the late Ming Dynasty and early Qing Dynasty, the activities of interpreting scriptures using the Chinese language were carried out by a series of representatives including Wang Daiyu, Liu Zhi, Zhang Zhong, and Ma Zhu, which lead to the second wave of cultural self-awareness. These two waves of cultural self-awareness activities greatly promoted the adaptation of Muslim Islamic culture to the mainstream culture and the national identity of Muslims was greatly strengthened (Yang 1999: 32-37). In the Qing Dynasty, the state government took a series of policies to 'oppress, relegate, and even eliminate the Hui people'. Since the 1640's, Hui people had suffered an unprecedented oppression (Bai, 2003: 130). In the mid and late Qing Dynasty, the conflict between the Qing government and the Hui society was increasingly sharp and the Hui people in Yunnan and the Nortwest turned to a revolt.

With the great changes occurring in the late Qing Dynasty and early Republic of China, the country was faced with domestic strife and foreign aggression—it was on the verge of destruction. The Muslim religious figures and intellectuals formed into a larger elite movement to launch the third wave of cultural self-awareness to improve their religion, develop education, and save the nation from subjugation. They combined the destiny of the state with that of the Hui minority and Islam, and put the survival of the country in the first place. Loving the country and desiring to protect it, they founded newspapers, vigorously developed education and industries, and promoted religious reform. The Hui intellectuals in China organized an 'Islamic Education Association of Muslim Students Studying in Japan' and later 'China Islamic Association'. After the Anti-Japanese War broke out, the China Islamic Association for National Salvation was created (Mi and You 2000: 178-218; Yang 2000a: 78-84). Obviously, the national crisis strengthened the national identity within Hui Muslim society.

After the founding of the PRC, the national ethnic-religious policies provided political protection for the Hui people as national citizens. A large-scale undertaking of ethnic identification that was started in the 1950s established the legal status of the Hui people. Marked by the Third Plenary Session of the 11th CPC Central Committee in 1978, the Chinese government, on one hand, restored and implemented the policy of freedom in religious belief, and a series of preferential institutional arrangements and policies were designed for minority groups. This played a positive role in boosting the overall social, economic, educational and cultural development of minority communities. Especially, the modernization course that had lasted for more than half a century substantially promoted the interaction and common development of minority groups and the state. The Hui nationality enhanced their national identity in daily life through these benefits. On the other hand, since China's reform and opening up, confronted with the impact of globalization, modernization, and marketization, minority groups have shown increasingly apparent self-consciousness and interest appeal. The core of their interest appeal is the requirement for preferences in institutions, laws and policies to their ethnic group in a country with a multi-ethnic population and thus the accessibility to a larger share in the allocation of scarce resources (Zhang & Liu 2005: 98-101).

Common Islamic faith and Muslim identity are native roots of the Hui identity built across the largely dispersed spatial separation. This makes Islam a sensitive factor in the interaction between Muslim society and the state and the most important internal factor among many that influence the national identity of Hui Muslims. For specific Muslim communities, the Muslim ethnic identity, as a symbol of collective identity and a national institutional resource, is the carrier for the interaction between Muslim communities and the state and a means to enjoy preferential systems. On one hand, in interaction with the state, the Islamic cultural mechanism in specific Muslim community reflects cultural adaptation that keeps abreast of the times and maintains its own ethnic cultural properties under the impact of the strong mainstream culture. On the other hand, the state governs minorities and religious affairs by implementing ethnic-religious policies in different historical stages. The ethnic-religious policies implemented by the authorities are decisive factors in the relations between minorities and the state and also the direct cause why Islam has dual effects on the national identity of Hui Muslims. If the ethnic-religious policies are beneficial to the survival and development of Hui Muslims, Islam will become a cultural adjustment mechanism that promotes the Hui national identity; otherwise, Islam tends to be a tool that mobilizes resistance against the government. Due to the complex bureaucratic system of the state, as state authorities, government organs at all levels are, in the general sense, considered by the masses as spokespersons of the Chinese people. Once a spokesperson at a certain level fails to scientifically understand and seriously execute the Chinese national will or makes wrong decisions for not being able to fully mastering the conditions of the grass-roots, the result will surely be contradiction between local aspirations and Chinese national will, which may further leads to conflict between local communities and the state as both of them try to maximize their own interests. Such unequal gaming is often manifested in social events of conflict nature between local communities and grass-roots governments. The Shadian Incident[2] is an example.

The Shadian Incident was a special historical event that occurred under special circumstances in a special area during a special historical period (the Cultural Revolution). At that time Shadian was plagued by a complex conflict between political factions in the surrounding areas (Gejiu, Mengzi, Jijie, etc.), and the incident, coupled with religious issues, became even more complex than any other similar case in other Muslim localities. The local authority in Yunnan Province implemented ethnic-religious policies that were more aggressive than in other Muslim communities, thus exacerbating the conflict. Historically, Shadian was a place with strong political traditions, rich Islamic cultural characteristics, and flourishing economy and culture. The local community there had always demonstrated a strong national identity in history. As a traditional Muslim community, it had established its identity through the traditional way of religion. The significance and value of religion was nothing but the search for the meaning of life in the course of survival (Bell 1989: 207-222). Once normal religious life was destroyed, the significance of survival was bound to be threatened. As those who were involved in the Shadian incident said, the reasons they treated national policies as weapons to defend their religious freedom and sent representatives to appeal for help of the central government lied in their understanding of the national ethnic-religious policies and the requirements of civil rights. This showed that the Hui Muslims in Shadian had a strong sense of Chinese national identity. The focus of the conflict in Shadian was an attempt to secure the significance of the survival of a minority group by appealing to the supreme state authority rather than to deny the state power. The struggle of people in Shadian was a gesture of disagreement on the specific power initiatives taken by officials represented by Zhou Xing in Yunnan Province; the appeal to the supreme state authority showed exactly the measure of Chinese national identity and sense of belonging among the people in Shadian. This incident to some extent implied that: the political system of the state provided security and equitable benefits for all ethnic groups and constituted the prerequisite and basis for the political-legal identity of the ethnic groups. When there was crisis in the political-legal identity, a strong cultural-psychological identity might resolve the Chinese national identity crisis to a considerable degree; cultural-psychological identity was a sense of recognition and belonging towards the Chinese nation and was more lasting and consolidated than political-legal identity (Gui 2012b: 153-159).

By recalling the history of interaction between the Hui society and the state, a conclusion can be drawn: the interaction between the Hui society and the state is a dynamic relationship of two-way adjustment. Corresponding to the state religious policies in different stages of history, the contextualized political-legal identity endowed national identity with a dynamic subjective structure and the stable cultural-psychological identity of being Chinese endowed national identity with stable internal structure. Cultural identity and common development are the mainstream of the interactive relations. Politics (the implementation effect of ethnic-religious policies) directly influence the relationship between Muslim society and the state. If the ethnic-religious policies of the ruling government had put Hui society in a crisis of survival and development, religious and cultural conflicts would have occurred; however, the ruling government treated the Hui people fairly and ethnic-religious policies enabled them to live and work in the peaceful social environment and, thus the Hui society has maintained a harmonious relationship with the state.

Cultural Interpretation of the National Identity of Hui Muslims

The national identity of Hui Muslims is the core notion for understanding the interaction between Hui Muslim society and the state. I based myself on investigations and research from 2007, to argue that it can be understood well by the cultural interpretation built on the following outside-in cultural logic: the visualized cultural representations predominantly reflected in symbols, the behavioral expressions of cultural reproduction, the expressions of cultural power and practical interests and the identity psychology as being Chinese (Gui 2011a: 15-21).

Symbols are the most visualized direct representation of the national identity of Hui Muslims. To the Hui Muslims, both worshiping Allah and being faithful to the emperor were core concepts of adapting to Confucian culture. This core concept was fully reflected in architectural design, content layout and monument type of the mosques in the Ming and Qing Dynasties. According to the records of inscription and historical literature of mosques, tablets inscribed by emperors were set in mosques and praying for the emperor had been the responsibility and obligation of most mosques since the Yuan and

Ming Dynasties (Yang 2006:89-97). At the present time, the formal expression of the correlation between modern mosques and Chinese national orthodoxy is manifested by hanging a qualification certificate issued by the state ethnic-religious department, setting up bulletin boards to propagandize state ethnic-religious policies, or even hanging the five-star red flag or carving the flag pattern at the gates of mosques. As public arenas in the Hui Muslim society, mosques are the window and medium for Muslims to interact with the state.

The national identity of Hui Muslims can be understood as a Chinese cultural reconstruction based on the relevant philosophy of Islam. Especially, to survive in a non-Islamic country, the Hui Muslims in China should adapt to the mainstream society and obtain growing space through active cultural adaptation. The essence of cultural reconstruction is the sinicized interpretation of Islamic culture. Chinese Muslim scholars and religious authorities take the *Qur'an* and the *Hadith* as the religious law basis to carry out cultural reconstruction and interpretation through reasoning, deduction, comparisons and making judgments. The cultural self-renewal mechanism of Islamic culture is an important characteristic and historical tradition of Chinese Islam. Through the activities of interpreting Islamic writings carried out by Daiyu, Liu Zhi, Ma Zhu and Ma Dexin in Ming and Qing Dynasties, the New Culture Movement of the Chinese Muslims in the 20th century, and the scripture translation and book writing by the modern Chinese Muslim scholars, the inheritance, development and innovation of Islamic culture always keep pace with the times. Overall, the reproduction of Islam culture is carried out by families, *jamaats* and Hui social networks. Bourdieu argued that cultural capital is mainly found in the production field of knowledge and culture and the educational function of cultural capital should first be emphasized; in addition to technical or skill education, quality, morality and humanity education are more important (Bourdieu 1997: 192-201). As a kind of cultural capital, the value of Islam lies in its ability to provide a moral model for the Hui people through religious enlightenment to obtain dual qualifications of internal members and citizens of modern society. By the main educational forms, including cultural interpretation, knowledge innovation and folk society operation, the Hui people in China achieve social adaptation in multiple levels of interaction between Muslim minorities and the mainstream nationality, religious circle and government, civil society and state power.

As the Hui people are mainly scattered in rural areas, the interpretation of the discourse power of Hui should be recognized and understood in the rural political and cultural network in which the religious power (authority) interacts with other powers (authorities). In rural areas, there is a modern political order centering on legal-rational authority, which is regulated by the national legal system, while the rural order is regulated and controlled by folk powers, like customs, pacts, religious teachings and canons, and public opinions. Nowadays, Hui Muslim society, in a macro-view, demonstrates the power structure, in which dual orders and multiple authorities coexist and the interactive relationship between the religious circle and the local government. In a micro-view, some religious believers have dual identities as religious authorities and local grass-root officials, or representatives of state power. For example, some important members of mosque management committees are delegates of local congress (*Difang Renda* 地方人大) or CPPCC (*Difang Zhengxie* 地方政协). They are the institutional elites of the Hui minority who participate in the administration and discussion of state affairs and act like a safety valve in politics for Hui society.

Hui Muslims used to have a bicultural identity of the Islamic belief and Confucianism. Until the Republican period, some people from those in power to ordinary people, or even Muslim elites, had regarded Muslims as Han people who believed in a special religion (Yang 2000b: 4-8). Since ancient times, the Chinese cultural education that the Hui people have received is actually a subtle process to continuously strengthen their awareness of being Chinese and to bolster their national identity. Numerous historical texts show that the Hui people have tried to participate in the mainstream Chinese culture through various means like being officials by passing the imperial examination, defending the homeland, actively participating in social activities, and vigorously developing public interests, and they demonstrated a strong sense of being the master of the country. When the state was trapped in deep crisis, the Hui people made active efforts to protect their family and country, which proved their shared identity with the state and loyalty to the state; in the ages of peace and development, the Hui people were positively devoted to economic development, which is the testimony of their shared national identity and commitment to common development. All of these reflect the long-lasting cultural-psychological identity of the Hui people as Chinese.

Practice of Adaptation and Development of Hui Muslim Society

Muslim scholar Ramadan emphasized that Islamic principles come from three sources of *Qur'an*, *Hadith* and social situation (Ramadan 2004: 37). The former two remain fixed as holy religious texts, while the latter one is the specific field for Muslim belief and practice that is under dynamic process. This requires Muslims to keep the position and attitude of cultural adaptation and development practice. In particular, as a minority group and non-mainstream culture in a non-Islamic country, they need to adapt more to the social development and earn their growth space through positive cultural reforms and adaptation. The development practice and cultural adaptation of Hui Muslims contain two meanings: first, adherence to rigid religious belief and the essence of Muslim culture; second, cultural innovation and development that will not jeopardize the established religious belief. They are influenced by various factors such as the Hui Muslims themselves and the national political environment, globalization, modern media, and the market economy. As a minority that established itself in China, Hui Muslims share deep historical and cultural roots with the Han people, and because of their distribution pattern of being largely scattered in small settlements, thus Hui Muslim society has strong cultural adaptability and diverse local knowledge. Historically, Hui Muslims had made constant cultural adjustments to adapt to the social development and political needs through two-way means: first, the state dominating means like national institutional arrangements, policy of assimilation and mainstream culture education; and second, the Hui society dominating means like activities of interpreting scriptures using the Chinese language carried out by Hui intellectual elites. In the contemporary era, the main and common cultural adaptation and development practice are primarily reflected in these domains such as ethnic festivals, Muslim folk education, and building a harmonious society.

I have investigated and studied some Hui cases in Yunnan since 2008. The following cases reflect some major aspects of practice of adaptation and development of Hui Muslim society.

Case 1: *Mawlid al-Nabi* of the Hui Muslims in Weishan

Mawlid al-Nabi is the anniversary of Prophet Mohammed, one of the three major festivals of the Hui minority in China. Located in Dali Autonomous Prefecture of the Bai Nationality in Yunnan Province, Weishan Autonomous County of Yi and Hui Nationalities is the most populated area of Muslims in western Yunnan. There is a historic site of the uprising of Du Wenxiu in the Qing Dynasty, a Chinese historical and cultural village and a national model mosque here. It is a Muslim community with the richest and most typical traditional culture of the Hui minority in western Yunnan. Mawlid al-Nabi is the common traditional festival of more than twenty thousand Muslims in the 22 *jamaats* throughout the whole Weishan County. The Mawlid al-Nabi of Muslims in Weishan inherit the world-wide Islamic traditions, such as reciting *Qur'an*, glorifying Prophet Mohammed, prayers, and preaching the doctrine. In addition, traditions and religious customs with Chinese characteristics, like the dressing ceremony of graduates of Islamic education in mosques and collective banquets, are also observed. In the dressing ceremony, the prestigious religious figures dress the graduates of Islamic education in green gowns. This is related to the legend in which Prophet Mohammed gave his green gown to a follower who would go preaching. The ceremony acknowledges the reputation and responsibility for the graduates to preach Islamic belief. The most obvious change is that the contemporary Mawlid al-Nabi adds more activities with characteristics of modern times. Overall, by inheriting the tradition, the contemporary Mawlid al-Nabi has always maintained the continuity and stability of the main cultural pattern of the festival; through reconstruction of the traditional culture, it always keeps abreast of the times. The reconstruction of tradition is reflected in the reconstruction of religious folk traditions and the construction of a new culture.

The reconstruction of religious folk traditions can be divided into reconstruction of religious rites and reconstruction of religious folk customs. Reconstruction of religious rites includes, for example, an up-to-date preaching doctrine, chanting competition, and constantly innovated dressing ceremonies. The early preaching doctrine in Mawlid al-Nabi focused on *Qur'an* and *Hadith*, with poor social relevance. Now, the preaching doctrine is in combination with practical needs. According to the observation of the author, the speakers included different representatives ranging from villagers, imams, and members of management committee of mosques. The speeches cover Islamic history and culture, community religious affairs, management of mosques, and anti-drug publicity. In addition to celebrating the achievements of the Prophet Mohammed and introduction to Islamic history and culture, which are traditional themes in the preaches at Mawlid al-Nabi, the others are highly realistic new themes. In contrast, the chanting competition and dressing ceremonies of religious students are closely related to the religious traditions in content and significance, although the forms are products of the times. The contemporary Mawlid al-Nabi, apart from continuing the traditional content and form of chanting, also embraces the new form of chanting competition to arouse the enthusiasm for participation and to improve the quality and frequency of Mawlid al-Nabi. The gowns, certificates, gifts and other extrinsic signs at the dressing ceremonies of religious students are products of the new times. These new cultural elements built on the religious traditions undoubtedly strengthen the religious attributes of contemporary Mawlid al-Nabi and enhance the harmony between religion and social development.

New cultural events have been constructed, such as the basketball game of Mawlid al-Nabi Cup, 'national presence' of government officials, 'ritual reproduction' of the five-star red flag and national anthem, and the issuance ceremony of village choreography. The basketball game of Mawlid al-Nabi Cup and the 'national presence' of government officials, after more than two decades, have become new traditions at Mawlid al-Nabi of Weishan Autonomous County of Hui Nationality. The basketball game Mawlid al-Nabi Cup is a highlight in the new culture of contemporary Mawlid al-Nabi. It marks the extension of Mawlid al-Nabi activities from the religious and living spheres of the Hui in Weishan Muslim to the broad areas of social life. According to one representative of the Islamic Association of Weishan County, the first basketball game of Mawlid al-Nabi Cup was in 1984, initially organized by the people voluntarily in response to the call of the station for anti-drug campaigns. To highlight its positive significance, the imam cited the classics to emphasize that holding the basketball game also inherited the spirit of the Prophet Muhammad. The game enriched the national culture and promoted friendship and progress. The praise from government officials and the organisation of the basketball game enriched the cultural life of the masses and demonstrated to the outside world the positive and good image of the Hui Muslims in Weishan. The issuance ceremony of village choreography of Xiaoweigeng Village turned out to be a new bright at the Mawlid al-Nabi in 2012. The choreography of a small village implies deep cultural politics: it is the protection and inheritance of folk culture at the grass-roots level of the Hui nationality in Weishan, using the national cultural and publishing mechanisms; it reflects the cultural consciousness of cultural elites from the Hui nationality in Weishan to cope with the impact of modernization and globalization; it represents the positive attempt made by the Hui people in Weishan, as disadvantaged and minority groups, for the right to social discourse. The 'ritual reproduction' of the five-star red flag and anthem at the opening ceremony of the basketball game of Mawlid al-Nabi Cup and the 'national presence' of government officials at the opening ceremony of Mawlid al-Nabi in every *jamaat* as well as their speeches, similar to the anti-drug speeches in the preaching activities, promote state policy, patriotic education and legal education.

The emergence of new cultures that bear political significance is a prominent feature in the reconstruction of the contemporary Mawlid al-Nabi and represents the social value and era characteristics of the contemporary Mawlid al-Nabi. The leader of the Islamic Association of Weishan County mentioned that anti-drug propaganda and strengthening national unity are the political missions in the recent celebrations of Mawlid al-Nabi. In order to strengthen exchanges and solidarity between the Hui nationality and the neighboring non-Muslim nationalities, future Mawlid al-Nabi may invite the surrounding Han and Yi nationalities to join in. Apparently, government departments represented by the National Bureau of Religious Affairs at county level and the Islamic Association in the county are the leading forces in constructing the new cultures. The mechanism of using Mawlid al-Nabi to carry out ethnic-religious work has existed for more than two decades in Weishan. As a traditional cultural symbol and grand public cultural space, Mawlid al-Nabi has become a medium and platform for the Hui people in Weishan to have two-way interaction and seek common development with the government (Gui 2012a: 44-54).

Case 2: Elementary school of Muslim Arabic language in Yunnan

Most *jamaats* have folk educational institutions inheriting the Islamic culture. They generally rely on civil society organizations or mosques to carry out Islamic cultural education. There have been some successful attempts to actively explore possibilities for harmonious development between fundamental education and ethnic traditional education among the Hui in Yunnan. Among them, Hui Guang Primary School of San Jia Cun in Weishan County and the Arabic Language School of Na Jia Ying in Tonghai County can be considered as successful examples. Hui Guang Primary School is an example of a successful experiment to harmonize fundamental compulsory education and ethnic traditional education for Hui villages and towns. Since 1995, supported by the county and town level education departments, the two systems (*i.e.* national compulsory education and Hui cultural education) have been carried out together through the mechanism of 'public management and sponsoring by private enterprises', in which teachers from the education department undertook the national compulsory education, while grants from the Hui Guang Education Foundation were invested in the building of teaching facilities, the editing of Arabic teaching materials and the management of Arabic teachers and teaching. It became a completely up-to-date primary school with classical Hui traits where national compulsory education and Hui cultural education have been developed together very well. In September 2006, in the name of the 'Arabic Primary School of Na Jia Ying', the Na Jia Ying Management Committee organized the implementation of Arabic teaching for children, in which a rather haphazard Arabic teaching for children was replaced by a systematic management by the school; in compliance with the didactic principle of personal development alongside compulsory education, *Children's Arabic* was taught during the spare time of the students. Moreover, parts of the textbooks used in the statutory education syllabi for *Chinese, Mathematics, Ideology and Morality*, and *Science of Nature* were chosen to be taught in Arabic, whereby students could not only learn and understand the contents of the national education syllabus but could also master the fundamental listening, speaking, reading and writing skills of Arabic. Its pupils include kindergarten students and primary school students from the 1st grade to the 6th grade. Generally, after *Hun Li* (evening prayers), students have six lessons at the Na Jia Ying mosque each week. Na Jia Ying also introduced some brave innovations during its reformation of mosque education, by taking some of the contents of their religious tradition and culture as local teaching materials and inserting them into the nationally stipulated courses. The teaching material that they adopted, called *Gu Xun Ji*, was compiled by the mosque, the school and other departments with eleven chapters and 119 items on topics such as patriotism, education, behavior, morality and so on; parts of these are extracted from the *Koran, Hadith, and Arabic Proverbs*. The pupils from the Han nationality living in Na Jia Ying also received local knowledge education in the school. Through interviews with the Han students and their parents, I learned that they were highly willing to accept Islamic culture and Arabic education. They generally believed that "it is good to learn more about Muslim culture and master another language, after all. This is something that the Han people elsewhere are not accessible to."

Case 3: Building of a harmonious society in Shadian

Shadian is the administrative district attached to Gejiu City in Yunnan Province. In the 1940s, Jiang Yingliang, a famous scholar, called it "the most typical village of Muslims" (Jiang 1985:1-19). The place received wide attention for suffering catastrophe during the Cultural Revolution. From the painful memory of the Cultural Revolution to the current prosperity of the new countryside in a harmonious society, Shadian witnessed the great changes occurring to the society and lives of Chinese Muslims. Islam has become a major force in the construction of harmonious society in Shadian. The moral core of Islam has points in common with the socialist spiritual civilization and the spirit of the construction of a harmonious society, and it plays a key role in soft maintenance mechanisms for the building of a local harmonious society. In Islam, morality and religion are integrated as a whole, and religious obligations and ethics, daily life and religious rituals are hardly separable. The ethical contents in tens of thousands of *Hadith* almost cover all areas of social life (Zhou 2005 : 101-108). According to my survey done in 2008, about 94% of the respondents believed that Islam had a positive impact on the harmonious society construction in Shadian (Gui 2009:122-132).

Customs and village rules guided by Islamic ethics are the internal basis for the stability and harmony of a community. Customs and village rules are social norms of interpersonal interaction established by usage or collectively developed by the people, according to Islamic ethics and local traditions. They are a typical form of local knowledge. For example, prohibiting the running of bars or cyber bars in the Shadian, prohibiting pornography, gambling and drugs, and the prohibition of funeral ceremonies for drug addicts have become village rules that everyone in Shadian observes.

The Islamic doctrine and ethics play an important role in cultivating interpersonal relationships of solidarity and mutual help. The Islamic property concept not only encourages the running of business to seek wealth, but also provides a guarantee for the relief of poverty and the development of public welfare undertakings in Hui communities. It helps narrow the gap between the rich and the poor, ease social conflicts, and foster interpersonal relationships of solidarity and mutual help. The help for those in distress is mainly provided by individuals and mosques, and it demonstrates the characteristic of charitable economics. It provides folk relief to the poor class, plays a role of social security and control of the rich-poor division and facilitates the development of social welfare. This is consistent with the goal of building a harmonious socialist society that upholds a human orientation, fairness and honesty, and common prosperity. Over the years, a favorable atmosphere in which every one is engaged in charity has been created in Shadian. Every year millions of Islamic taxes and charity donations are used for poverty relief, folk education, and social welfare services.

To build ethnic relationships with the Islamic spirit of inclusiveness and fraternity is an important guarantee for the Muslims in Shadian to get along with other ethnic groups. Although Shadian is a Hui community where Islam is the dominant religion, there is a township of the Yi nationality and many villages inhabited by dozens of other nationalities including Zhuang, Han and Hani. The mosques in Shadian attach importance to guiding and fostering harmonious relationships between different communities and groups. The daily preaches advocate equality among all ethnic groups and require religious believers to actively participate in the public welfare programs that help other nationalities. The mosques have successively carried out activities like donations for the aged of the Yi nationality in Chongposhao Village and helping the poor of the Yi nationality to build new houses. In addition, marriage with non-Muslims is also a reflection of the harmonious ethnic relations in Shadian. Due to the developed industrial economy and the substantial increase of migrant workers, interpersonal relationships fostered by occupation have become the main driving force for inter-ethnic marriages. Since the 1990s, the ratio of marriages between Han and Hui nationalities has increased significantly. Generally, people from the Han nationality convert to Islam, and become Han Muslims of Shadian. According to the questionnaire analysis and interviews in May and August of 2008, 100% of the respondents (native Hui Muslim) acknowledged marriages with members of other ethnic groups that can convert to Islam[3].

Conclusion

As a product of Chinese localization of Islam and as a member of the 'Chinese nation', the Hui minority shows a stable cultural-psychological identity. Historically, the Hui people have been largely scattered in small settlements bonded by Islam, which gave rise to the basic community form of the *jamaat* under the national administrative system. The Hui Muslims are always collectively represented through interaction between *jamaat* and state. Such collective feature maintains coordination with the local cultural diversity. This consistency is reflected in the fact that *jamaats* as local Muslim communities in different areas of China always adopted flexible, diverse strategies and social practices in response to the ruling policies of different dynasties in the Chinese nation-state. Cultural adaptation that acts as an important and major form of social strategy and practice and the reproduction of Hui Muslim culture is its essence. Generally, the religious obligations and rites determined by the doctrines and canons of Islam are fixed, while Muslim social culture with contemporary characteristics is usually flexible. Different *jamaats* of Muslims generally show cultural adaptation that is compatible to the local social development in festivals, civil education, and harmonious society construction in communities.

The interaction between local Hui Muslim society and the state is a dynamic relationship of two-way adjustment. The Hui Muslim society has been holding the practical rationality during the interaction process all along and always stays between national control and local autonomy. In the interaction process Hui Muslim society takes the political and economic interests as the goal while preserving its culture and and development. Thus, it is characterized by practical rationality. For the state, the interaction is a process for the 'Chinese nation' to integrate multiple ethnic groups for social construction, and its ethnic-religious policies have to be real-time adjustments according to the needs of ruling and social development. Corresponding to ethnic-religious policies of the state in different stages of history, Hui Muslims demonstrate contextualized political-legal identity. Now Hui Muslims are achieving shared identity and common development with the Chinese nation through constant practice of adaptation and development to negotiate and integrate community action strategies with government policies. We can conclude that identity and development are a resource and guarantee for successful interaction between Hui Muslim society and the state.

Notes

1   Hu was the collective name of the alien northern and western nations used by the ancient Han nationality in Central China. The scope of 'Hu' varied with different historical periods. 'Hu' used in *Ming Dynasty Law* is supposed to be a collective name for all non-Han nationalities, including Muslims.

2   The event began in the elimination of 'four olds' during the 'Cultural Revolution' in 1966, and the mosques in Hui Muslim villages including Shadian were forced to shut down. At the same time, Muslims across the province were forced to raise pigs and change their customs and habits. Eating pork was even used as the criterion to distinguish between 'progressive' and 'backward'. The majority of Muslims considered that as 'ethnic and religious genocide', and a large number of Hui Muslims petitioned, requiring implementation of the Party's ethnic-religious policies. However, the head of the Yunnan Provincial Party then stuck to wrong beliefs and took a series of wrong measures that intensified the conflict and

seriously hurt the religious affections of Hui Muslims. The Muslim masses were indignant, and a bloody incident occurred in Shadian. On February 15, 1979, with the approval by the CPC Central Committee, the CPC Yunnan Provincial Committee and the Party Committee of Kunming Military Region jointly issued the 'Notice of Redressing Shadian Event' (《关于沙甸事件平反的通知》) to announce rehabilitation of the event. (See Wang Lianfang: *Forty Years of Ethnic Work in Yunnan* (《云南民族工作 40 年》), The Nationalities Publishing House of Yunnan, 1994, pp. 427; Liu Shusheng: *Echo of Footsteps: knowledge and from 70 Years of Eventful Experience* (《脚步的回声——70年风雨历程见闻杂记》), Press of China Federation of Literature Art Circles, 2002, pp. 906.)

3   From traditional days to modern days, the marriages of Hui Muslims in China have been tied by the common Islamic faith. Endogamy marriages were prevalent in rural Hui Muslim villages in China and Islamic religion was often intertwined with Hui nationality. Based on the experience and consciousness of Hui Muslims, Hui Muslims were those who believed in Islam and those who believed in Islam were Hui Muslims. Since the reform and opening up in the 1980s, due to the increased level of religious belief and expansion of social interaction, in the cross-ethnic marriages of Hui Muslims and other ethnic groups, the Muslim (Islamic religion) identity rather than the national identity was more and more stressed, and identity built on exogamy marriages tied by a common belief has become universal. This phenomenon is particularly common in Hui communities in Yunnan.

References

Anderson, Benedict (1983). Wu Ruiren, trans. (2011) *Imagined Communities: Reflections on the Origin and Spread of Nationalism*. Shanghai: Shanghai People's Publishing House. 本尼迪克特·安德森: 《想象的共同体: 民族主义的起源与散布》, 吴睿人译, 上海: 上海人民出版社, 2011 年.

Bai, Shouyi (1984). 'Formation and primary development of Huihui nationality', in The History of Hui Nationality Team, eds, *Collected Essays on the History of Hui Nationality*. Yinchuan: Ningxia People's Publishing House, pp. 15-28. 白寿彝: 回回民族的形成与初步发展, 回族史组编《回族史论集》, 银川: 宁夏人民出版社, 1984 年, 第 15-28 页.

Bai, Shouyi (2003). *Nationality History of Huihui in China*. Beijing: China Book Company. 白寿彝: 《中国回回民族史》, 北京: 中华书局, 2003 年, 第 130 页.

Bell, Daniel (1989). *The Cultural Contradictions of Capitalism* (Zhao Yifan *et al.*, trans.) Beijing: SDX Joint Publishing Company, pp. 207-222. 丹尼尔·贝尔: 《资本主义文化矛盾》, 赵一凡等译, 北京: 生活·读书·新知三联书店, 1989 年, 第 207-222 页.

Bourdieu, Pierre (1997). *Cultural Capital and Social Alchemy: An Interview with Bourdieu.* (Bao Yaming, trans.). Shanghai: Shanghai People's Publishing House, pp. 192-201. 布尔迪厄：《文化资本与社会炼金术——布尔迪厄访谈录》，包亚明译，上海人民出版社，1997 年，第 192-201 页.

Durkheim, Emile (1912). Lin Zongjin and Peng Shouyi, trans. (1999). *Les formes élementaires de la vie religieuse.* Beijing: Central University for Nationalities Press. 涂尔干：《宗教生活的基本形式》，林宗锦，彭守义译，北京：中央民族大学出版社，1999 年.

Gui, Rong (2009). 'Religion, power, culture: Shadian new rural construction of Hui nationality in Yunnan', *The Southwest Frontier Ethnic Studies*, 6. 桂榕：宗教、权力、文化：云南沙甸回族农村和谐社会的人类学研究，《西南边疆民族研究》2009 年总第 6 辑，第 122-132 页.

Gui, Rong (2011a). 'National identity of Hui ethnic group: from the perspective of cultural anthropology of construction and interpretation', *Journal of Beifang University for Nationalities*, 1. 回族的国家认同：建构与阐释的文化人类学视角，《北方民族大学学报》(哲学社会科学版) 2011 年第 1 期，第 15-21 页.

Gui, Rong (2011b). 'Hui's National Identity and Historical Reflections: Case Study on Hui Ethnic Group in Yunnan', *The Southwest Frontier Ethnic Studies*, 9. 张力与调适：回族的国家认同及其历史反思：基于云南案例的研究，《西南边疆民族研究》2011 年总第 9 期，第 192-198 页.

Gui, Rong (2012a). 'Inheritance and reconstruction of tradition: The contemporary change of Weishan Hui minority' Mawlid al-Nabi', *Journal of Studies on Nationalities*, 2. 传统的继承与重构———云南巍山回族圣纪节的当代变迁，《民族研究》2012 年第 2 期，第 44-54 页.

Gui, Rong (2012b). *History, Culture and Reality: Case study on National Identity and Social Adaptation of the Hui Muslim in Yunnan.* Kunming: Yunnan People's Publishing House. 《历史·文化·现实：　国家认同与社会调适———云南回族社区个案研究》，昆明：云南人民出版社，2012 年.

Gui, Rong (2013). 'Cultural pattern of Jamaat: Theoretical construction of Hui Muslims community life', *Journal of Beifang University for Nationalities*, 1. '哲玛提'文化模式：理解回族社群文化的一种理论框架：以巍山回族'哲玛提'为例，《北方民族大学学报》(哲学社会科学版) 2013 年第 1 期，第 42-47 页.

Israeli, Raphael (2002). *Islam in China: Religion, Ethnicity, Culture, and Politics.* Lanham, MD: Lexington Books.

Jiang, Yingliang (1985). 'Investigation on Shadian village of Hui minority in southern Yunnan', in Yunnan editor team, *Social and Historical Investigation on Hui Muslim society in Yunnan (1)*, Kunming: Yunnan People's Publishing House, pp. 1-19. 江应梁：滇南沙甸回教农村

调查, 云南省编辑组编《云南回族社会历史调查》(一), 昆明: 云南人民出版社, 1985 年, 第 1-19 页.

Kroeber, Alfred L. (1952). *Nature of Culture*. Chicago, IL: The University of Chicago Press.

Ma, Qiang (2006). *Floating Sprit Community: Study on Muslim Jammat in Guangzhou From Anthropological View*. Beijing: China Social Science Press, pp. 8-15. 马强:《流动的精神社区——人类学视野下的广州穆斯林哲玛提研究》, 北京: 中国社会科学出版社, 第 8-15 页.

Mi, Shoujiang and You, Jia (2000). *Brief History of Islamic Religion in China*. Beijing: Religious Culture Press, pp. 178-218. 米寿江、尤佳:《中国伊斯兰教简史》, 北京: 宗教文化出版社, 2001 年, 第 178-218 页.

Ramadan, Tariq (2004). *Western Muslims and the Future of Islam*. New York: Oxford University Press.

Sen, Amadya (2009). *Phantom Fate: Identity and violence*. (Li Fenghua, Chen Changsheng and Yuan Deliang, trans.). Beijing: Chinese People University Press, pp. 72. 阿马蒂亚.森:《身份与暴力——命运的幻象》, 李风华, 陈昌升, 袁德良译, 北京: 中国人民大学出版社, 2009 年, 第 72 页.

Yang, Guiping (1999). 'The new culture movement of Chinese Muslims', *Journal of Hui Muslim Minority studies*, 4. 杨桂萍: 中国穆斯林新文化运动,《回族研究》1999 年第 4 期, 第 32-37 页.

Yang, Wenjiong (2006). 'Hui community under the situation of transformation of relation between the state and Hui society during the Ming and Qing dynasties', *Heilongjiang Nationalities Periodicals*, 5. 杨文炯: 明清时期国家与社会关系转型境遇下的回族社区——以历史上西安回族社区文化变迁为视点,《黑龙江民族丛刊》2006 年第 5 期, 第 89-97 页.

Yang, Zhijuan (2000a). 'Big turning point in the history of Hui nationality–The awakening movement in modern times', *Journal of NorthWest Nationalities Studies*, 2. 杨志娟: 回族历史上的大转折——近代回族的觉醒运动,《西北民族研究》2000 年第 2 期, 第 78-84 页.

Yang, Zhijuan (2000b). 'Demarcation on ethnic identity and nationality: Taking an example of Hui nationality', *Journal of Hui Muslim Minority studies*, 4. 杨志娟: 族群认同与民族的界定——以回族为例,《回族研究》2000 年第 4 期, 第 4-8 页.

Yu, Zhengui (2012). *The Central Regime and Islamic Religion in China*. Yinchuan: Ningxia People's Publishing House, pp. 109-110. 余振贵:《中国历代政权与伊斯兰教》, 银川: 宁夏人民出版社, 2012 年, 第 109-110 页.

Zhang, Yonghong and Liu, Deyi (2005). 'On ethnic identification and national identification', *Journal of Guangxi Nationalities University (Philosophy and Social Science)*, 27(1).

张永红、刘德一: 论族群认同和国族认同, 《广西民族学院学报》(哲学社会科学版) 2005 年第 1 期, 第 98-101 页.

Zhou, Xiefan (2005). 'Islamic ethic: Traditional form and its modern meaning', *Journal of Studies on World Religions*, 4, pp 101-108. 周燮藩: 伊斯兰教伦理: 传统形式及其现代意义, 《世界宗教研究》 2005 年第 4 期, 第 101-108 页.

Part II:
Relations between Hui and non-Muslims

CHAPTER 5

Changes of Intermarriage Circle of the Pashi Dai (Muslims in Dai Society): A Case Study in the Hui Village in Manluan

Chuang Ma
Yunnan Open University

The ethnic group of the Parshi Dai (Dai-Hui) consists of two Muslim groups who live in the Hui village in Manluan and the Hui village in Mansai of Menghai County of Xishuangbanna Autonomous Prefecture in Yunnan, China. They are very different from the 'Chinese-speaking Muslims' for they have adoped the language, dress and customs of their Dai neighbours, whom believe in Theravada Buddhism. To some degree, they are culturally indistinguishable from the Dai people, but they identify themselves as Hui and are recognized as Hui nationality by the state. The word 'Parshi' comes from Burmese or Thai. Some scholars have pointed out that a large number of caravan merchants of the Hui ethnic minority from Yunnan had settled in Burma and Thailand during history. The Burmese call these Hui people 'Panthay' and the Shan call them 'Pansee', whereas the Dai ethnic minority in Xishuangbanna Autonomous Prefecture call them 'Parshi', which means people who don't eat pork. The Parshi Dai are called 'Parshi Dai' or 'Parshi' in the Dai language and 'Hui Dai' or 'Dai Hui' in Chinese both by themselves and other ethnic groups. The ancestors of the Parshi Dai were the Hui ethnic minority in Dali, Yunnan, who came to the Dai-inhabited region and settled there, intermarrying Dai women at the end of Qing Dynasty. Their descendants formed a Muslim group with a unique culture, shaped by frequent intermarriage and cultural exchange with the Dai people.

Three changes of the Parshi Dai's intermarriage circle

The intermarriage circle refers to the scope of choosing a spouse. There are usually two kinds of intermarriage circle, one of which is based on social estate, limiting the scope of choosing a spouse to a certain class, race and religion. While the other kind is based on the geographical conditions, namely geographical territory. This article would discuss the topic mainly in terms of ethnological preferences of mate choice scope of the Parshi Dai in the Hui village in Manluan. In the history of Parshi Dai, they experienced three changes of the intermarriage circle. The first change happened when they got into the Dai-inhabited region and got married to Dai women in order to survive. The second change was that they got married within their own nationality while the population was increasing. The third change was that more and more villagers married to the Dai and other people after realizing the damage of incest with the development of social communication.

Arrival in the Dai-inhabited region and intermarriage to the Dai
The survey of the Parshi Dai in Xishuangbanna Autonomous Prefecture records the history of how the ancestors of the Parshi Dai settled in the Hui village in Manluan. Two hundred years ago, a caravan merchant surnamed Ma of the Hui from Weishan County of Dali got into Xishuangbanna to do business. It was a time of social unrest in the Jiaqing and Daoguang period of Qing Dynasty when Du Wenxiu was about to uprise. The merchant was stranded in Menghai County for he was robbed halfway and couldn't go back home. So he gave the hereditary headman of Menghai three bags of salt and asked for abidance by the Liushahe river where the Hui village of Manluan is now located.[1] The headman agreed on the condition of three requirements, the first of which was that the merchant should behave well and respect the customs and habits of the Dai, who would treat him in the same way in return. Secondly, the merchant was requested to obey the hereditary headman. Thirdly, he should marry a Dai woman. After the caravan merchant surnamed Ma accepted these requirements, the hereditary headman ordered his men to distribute a piece of land to him on a hill, where the caravan merchant built a bamboo house and settled down. Later, the merchant surnamed Ma got married to Yuwen who was the headman's daughter of the Manyangkan village nearby. They had four sons and two daughters, and the sons established four families, which counts numerous members today.

It can be seen from the genealogy sorted by the Parshi Dai in the Hui village in Manluan that the first three generations of the Parshi Dai married to the Dai people and mainly chose spouses from Dai villages which were near the Hui village in Manluan. The population size of the Hui had expanded by marriages to the Dai people. But when the Parshi Dai people married to the Dai people, they had to follow the principle that only marriage into the village is allowed. That is to say, when a Parshi Dai man got married to a Dai woman, the woman must move into the Hui village in Manluan, and when a Parshi Dai woman got married to a Dai man, the man must move into the village and live with his wife's family as well, complying with Muslim habits.

Ethnic endogamy and intermarriage with villagers of the Hui village in Manluan
The population expansion of the Hui had made endogamy possible. The endogamy within the village happened in the fourth generation in the Hui village in Manluan. Moreover some Parshi Dai people married to the Hui people from other places in Yunnan. By the time of the fifth generation, marriage to the Hui people had become consensus of the Parshi Dai. According to the genealogy of the Parshi Dai, the intermarriage status of middle-aged and elderly villagers, and marriages within the village were the most common although some Parshi Dai people got married to Muslims who came from Eshan, Tonghai, Xinping, Menghai counties of Yunnan and another village of the Parshi Dai because of the restrictions of culture, economy and communication. Incest appeared in an inevitable quantity and some villagers got married to their own cousins.

Expansion of intermarriage circle
Since the 1980s, the intermarriage circle of the Parshi Dai has been expanded gradually. It was common for them to marry the Hui people, the Dai people and other nationalities. Th geographical scope has been expanded gradually too. The mates of the Parshi Dai came from other places of Yunnan or other provinces of China, who got to know the Parshi Dai through doing business or studying the Koran. At present, the Parshi Dai in the Hui village in Manluan not only marry the Parshi Dai from their own village but also the Dai, Han, Hui groups and other nationalities from other places.There are only a few young men getting married to young women from their own village, both of whom are Parshi Dai following Islam. And most of the Parshi Dai marry the Dai people or people of other nationalities. There is a difference between young men and young women

in terms of mate choice. Young men would marry mainly Dai women or women of their own village and few Hui women from other places would marry into the village. While mates of the young Parshi Dai women are mainly young men of their own village, Han, Hui from other places, Dai and people from other nationalities. The Parshi Dai people who marry Hui people from other places are mainly young women who have studied the Koran outside. They returned to the Hui village in Manluan to get married and settle down.

Reasons of changes of the Parshi Dai's intermarriage circle

Migration into a Dai-inhabited region and marriage to Dai people largely to meet survival needs

How to improve economic conditions, to get married and multiply are the most basic problems for either an individual or an ethnic group when leaving the original residence for habitancy in a place with a totally different ecosystem. At that time, marriage to Dai women was one of the requirements which the hereditary headman put forward to allow the caravan merchants settle down there. Meanwhile, it was the only choice for the Hui to get married to the Dai people in order to procreate considering that they were far away from any other Hui group and were confronted with the populous group of the Dai.

At the same time, marriage to Dai women embodied a friendly relationship with the Dai people. Mauss said that when two human groups meet, they would either trust or suspect each other completely, they would either execute mutual disarmement and magic-removal or give the other everything as presents including courtesy at first and daughters and properties at last. Mutual payments would take away reservations. Williams pointed out that different groups are banded together by ties of marriage identification and they keep up the ties by repaying each other.

It can be seen from the genealogy of the Parshi Dai that the first three generations of villagers in the Hui village in Manluan got married separately to the headmen's daughters of the three Dai villages adjacent to the Hui village in Manluan. As the guest settlers in the Dai-inhabited region, the hereditary headmen of the Dai not only distributed a piece of land to the Hui people who came from other places, to build houses, but also married their daughters to the Hui people in order to imply friendship after the ancestors of the Parshi Dai gave them salt as a gift. There is no doubt that the intermarriage was the supreme gift which had banded the two groups together closely.

Engaged in ethnic endogamy when the Hui people multiplied
The rule of forbidding exogamy of Islam has made the Hui generally inclined to endogamy. The Koran says: "You shouldn't get married to polytheistic women unless they believe in Islam... You shouldn't let your daughters get married to polytheistic men unless they believe in Islam." The Koran suggests that Muslims can marry people who convert to Islam. Since the fourth generation of the Parshi Dai, they not only married people of the same nationality in their own village but also intermarried to Hui people of other places in Yunnan Province. Endogamy began to prevail during that period mainly because the population of the Hui had increased and the scope of mate choice was not limited to the Dai people any more.

During the late Qing Dynasty and the beginning of the Republic of China, a large number of Hui caravan merchants from Yuxi City in Yunnan got into Xishuangbanna with the development of commercial trade there. In 1938, Hui industrialists from Shadian District led some Hui people to establish spinning factories in Menghai County and some of them settled down there later. Afterwards, some Hui people who came from Tonghai County and Eshan County came to Menghai to do business and settled down there too. The Parshi Dai got acquainted with a great quantity of the Hui people during this period. The Hui people generally have deep national feelings considering Hui people all over the world as family members; a Hui people therefore would be extraordinarily cordial if he meets other Hui people wherever he goes. The two Parshi Dai muslim groups in far away Xishuangbanna naturally attracted particular attention of the Hui. These Hui people helped the Parshi Dai to acquire Islamic knowledge and persuaded them to marry Muslims. A few of them had married Parshi Dai people.

Meanwhile, the population of the Parshi Dai had gradually increased with continuous intermarriages to Dai people. Owing to the limitation of culture, communication, etc, the scope of the Parshi Dai's endogamy was mainly within the village, namely marriage between the Parshi Dai people except that a few of them married Hui people of other places in Yunnan.

Prenatal and postnatal care improved and social technology developed: expansion of the intermarriage circle
The Parshi Dai people have practiced endogamy commonly since the fourth generation and the scope of endogamy was mostly limited to their own village, inevitable bringing about incest.

The relevant governmental department tested physique and health of the Parshi Dai in 1980. At that time, there were 92 married couples and 29 couples of them were incestuous. The survey concluded that incest was common in the Parshi Dai groups, resulting in a significant degradation of health levels, and stature and weight were below normal levels. Besides, there were obvious genetic diseases such as dementia, thalassemia, muscular atrophy, congenital cyanotic, Turner's syndrome, etc. The rare metabolic genetic disease of high uric acid metabolic syndrome was also found there. After this physical investigation and with some educated villagers' appeal, the villagers had gradually come to realize the disadvantages of incest and since then there has been a decrease of incestuous relationships among young villagers and a decrease of endogamy within the same village. In order to bear high quality offspring, the Parshi Dai began to prefer marrying Dai people and other ethnic groups.

Meanwhile, the Parshi Dai has more opportunities to interact with other ethnic groups along with the improvement of the technology, traffic and communication with the outside world. Some young couples of the Parshi Dai get acquainted with each other when they are either studying the Koran or outdoors recreation. The young Parshi Dai also make friends with netizens all over the country via the internet and a few of them have fallen in love and got married to their internet friends. At present, the marriage partners of the Parsi Dai not only include Hui people, but also Dai, Han and other people. During this period, the geographical scope of their intermarriage circle is enlarged day by day.

Influence of the intermarriage circle of the Pasi Dai on formation of culture and customs

The results of getting married to the Dai people: blending of Hui and Dai culture

Islamic culture and the culture of Theravada Buddhism blend with each other in the process of intermarriage between the Parshi Dai and the Dai, which has made both sides adjust constantly to adapt to each other's culture.

The Dai people would bring their original culture such as Dai language, costumes, food and behaviour, all influenced by Theravada Buddhism, into Parshi Dai families. For example, practices like divination and wearing amulets for peace and health flourish in Parshi Dai villages. Besides, some Dai people will go to temples and pray to Buddha when their family members are sick. As a result, The Parshi Dai people have learned some cultural practices of the Dai people and adopted similar customs of the Dai's. The Parshi Dai people, however, also stick to their Islamic faith and they tell or teach the Dai people customs and taboos of the Hui nationality. Before getting married to a Parshi Dai, a Dai has already known more or less that his own beliefs and customs are different from the Parshi Dai's. After they get married, family members and the villagers of the Parshi Dai would instruct the new couple continually in family life, religious activities, weddings, funerals, festivals and other activities. Therefore the Dai can get further knowledge of religious cultures and customs of the Hui, including not eating pork, not going to Buddhist temples and no longer practicing any kind of religious activity of Theravada Buddhism.

The Parshi Dai people have formed a kinship with the Dai people through intermarriage. The in-laws not only visit each other frequently but also often cooperate in economic activities. Families of both sides will invite each other on significant days when they either begin to build a new house, hold a wedding or host a celebration for a one-month baby. On these occasions, the Dai people who are Parshi Dai's in-laws would prepare new pots and bowls for their in-laws and children. The increasingly frequent interaction between the Parshi Dai and the Dai has made the relationship between the two groups closer.

The ethnic consciousness of the Parshi Dai was maintained and strengthened by endogamy

The customs of the Hui nationality were taught to the offspring of the Parshi Dai by their first ancestor, the caravan merchant surnamed Ma. Many aspects of Hui culture were ignored slowly under the strong cultural influence of the Dai nationality except the food exlusion since they were isolated from mainstream Hui society. Hui caravans and merchants who did trade contacts from Xishuangbanna to other places became the key figures to help the Parshi Dai preserve the Hui customs in the Parshi Dai history. Xishuangbanna was the historical spot and the only access where caravans who came from Yunnan transfered to Burma and Thailand. The children and grandchildren of the caravan merchant surnamed Ma, who was the ancestor of the Parshi Dai, were not only engaging in agriculture and handicraft but also ran the inns for the travelling merchants including the Hui people from the inland of Yunnan. The travelling merchants followed great interests and paid more attention to this special Muslim group that was far away from the other Hui people. The consciousness and sense of identity of the Parshi Dai as Muslims was strengthened through the frequent contacts with these

Hui people. Some of these merchants stayed at the Parshi Dai village to serve as imams, and they played an important role in preserving the Islamic cultural customs of the Parshi Dai.

Some scholars believe that endogamy is inextricably linked with strengthening ethnic consciousness and ethnic identity which is always developed through the interaction among ethnic groups in the specific historical environment. From the fourth generation on, the Parshi Dai have advocated endogamy, which became a main factor to avoid assimilation and enhance ethnic cohesion.

3.3 Expansion of the intermarriage circle strengthened the ethnic identity of the Parshi Dai

With the introduction of various media in modern society and the expansion of social intercourse, the intermarriage circle of the Parshi Dai also transformed from the Parshi Dai and the Dai people, the Parshi Dai and the Hui people (or the Parshi Dai) to broader groups. The boundary of 'our group' and 'their group' (which mainly consists of tDai people) was broken up gradually. The Parshi Dai were noticed and influenced by more and more ethnic groups or individuals.

Due to the expansion of the intermarriage circle and the improvement of transportation and communication, many Hui groups in other places knew there was a special Muslim group: the Parshi Dai, living in remote Xishuangbanna. However, they thought the religious beliefs of the Parshi Dai were not 'pure'. Therefore, they tried their best to guide them onto the 'orthodox' Islamic way. Some devout disciples went to the village to missionize. They led the villagers to worship and taught them the Koran. They also give financial assistance to some young people to receive formal religious education outside. Under these circumstances, the religious life of the Parshi Dai experienced a renaissance. The people of the Hui village in Manluan rebuilt a mosque and reintroduced the celebration of three Islamic religious festivals, which are Lesser Bairam, Corban Festival and Maulid al-Nabi. Since then, they invite Hui people from all over Yunnan to celebrate the Maulid al-Nabi every year.

With the recovery of religious consciousness, the ethnic consciousness of the Parshi Dai has become stronger day by day. The Parshi Dai initiatively began to trace their roots and energetically sort out their developing history. Two people in the Hui village in Manluan have reorganized the genealogy of the village. In 2005, in order to seek the sources of their ancestors, eight representatives of the Hui village in Manluan were sent to the counties of Binchuan and Weishan in

Dali Prefecture where the Hui people live and which could also be the land of their ancestors to visit their ancestral homes.

At the same time, along with mixed marriages among the Hui, Han, Dai and other ethnic groups all over the country, the Parshi Dai recognized the charm of their unique culture. Their ethnic pride was greatly enhanced. They started to display their own ethnic identity using a variety of symbols. For example, the new houses in the village are totally different with the architectural style of the Dai people. They garnish their houses with Arab style dome ceilings on the roof and inscribe the saying "There is no God but Allah" in Arabic above the door. The architectural style of the new mosque combines Arab influences with a traditional Chinese style, which formed a strong contrast with the Burmese herringbone temples nearby. Both ends of the bridge of the Hui village in Manluan were decorated with Arab style domes and pavilions of the Dai style. They say these embody the history that their fathers were Hui people and their mothers were Dai people.

Conclusion

Since the ancestors of the Parshi Dai settled in Xishuangbanna region, it has been nearly two hundred years until now. In this process, the Parshi Dai experienced three changes of the intermarriage circle. The first change was that their ancestor moved into the Dai-inhabited region and got married to Dai people. The second change was that endogamy appeared in order to keep the purity of their race and for increasing the population size. The third change was that endogamy brought great trouble to the Parshi Dai's health, and the scope of the Parshi Dai's intermarriage circle expanded from nation to geography as social communication diversified and widened. The changes of the intermarriage circle made the Parshi Dai develop a unique culture which blends the customs of the Dai with the religion of the Hui. In daily life, they speak Dai, wear Dai costumes, eat Dai food, use Dai names, etc. But they also adhere to the Islamic customs such as not eating pork, Islamic worship, fasting and so on. At the same time, they also recognized the unique charm of their own culture, and began to use all kinds of symbols and ways to display and promote their own culture.

References

Gregory Chris A. (2001). *Gifts and Commodities* (Du Shanshan *et al.*, trans.). Kunming: Yunnan University Press.

Luo, Yi (1989). 'The Investigation Report of the Branch of the Parshi Dai', in *The Physical survey about Jinuo and the Parshi Dai of Yunnan*. Kunming: Yunnan National Publishing House.

Ma, Weiliang & Li, Jia (1986). 'The survey of the Parshi Dai in Xishuangbanna' in The Yunnan Editorial Board, *The Survey of the Social History of Yunnan Hui Nationality*. Kunming: Yunnan People's Publishing House, pp. 51-52.

Mauss, Marcel (2002). *The Gift*. (Ji zhe trans.). Shanghai: Shanghai People's Publishing House.

Qur'an (1996). (Ma Jian, trans.). Beijing: China Social Sciences Publishing House.

Yang, Deliang (2005). 'Marriage System, Ethnic Consciousness, Cultural Identity: the Historical Origins and Cultural Connotation of the Marriage System of the Hui Nationality', *The Journal of the North University For Ethnics*, 1.

CHAPTER 6

Being Chinese and Being Muslim –
Portrayals of the Hui Minority by Muslims,
Non-Muslims, and the Media[1]

Frauke Drewes

Munster University

Where do Hui people belong in the complex Chinese society? For finding answers to this question, it is important to regard various relevant stakeholders. Not only Hui people themselves have to be heard, but also members of the Han majority, of other ethnic minorities, as well as official representatives. In this chapter I will present impressions from all of these stakeholders, knowing, however, that these also cannot reflect the complete situation but only provide glimpses into the perceptions of individuals. Anyway, it is hardly possible to present daily life realities of any group this size and the more so of a group that is internally differentiated to such an extend as the Hui are. Discussions on the invention of this heterogeneous group are well known and will not be repeated here (Gladney 1996:17),[2] nevertheless we need to be aware of them whenever discussing Hui people, so as to always consider that environments are very different for Hui living in different areas and under different conditions.

While having studied the situation of all Muslim nationalities[3] in China, in this chapter I will summarize some of my findings regarding the Hui people.[4] These include five in-depth interviews with Hui from various regions in China, eleven interviews with non-Muslims from China (while the majority of all interviews was conducted abroad for reasons of openness) and some results from analyzing online newspaper articles.

Hui Muslims' Perceptions

First, I will explore self-perceptions of the Hui Muslims I interviewed regarding their positions in Chinese society and in state policies, so as to examine their sense of belonging to society as a whole. In the course of my dissertation I conducted in-depth interviews with five Muslims belonging to the Hui nationality (among others). Four of the five interviews took place in Europe and Egypt, so that these respondents were freer from a restrictive political environment than the one in China. In addition, I assured all respondents that the interviews will be dealt with anonymously, so that I have reason to hope for quite open answers. The interviews lasted for 20 to 90 minutes and dealt with various topics, focusing mainly on their self-perceptions as Muslims as well as their self-perceptions as Hui. I present here those excerpts that deal with their relations with non-Hui people on the one hand and with the Chinese state on the other hand.

Relations to Han Chinese

All Hui people I spoke to described their relations with the majority Han Chinese to be very close (contrary to their Uyghur co-religionists). One respondent from Northeast-China even described the Hui to be almost completely assimilated:

"There are differences, I think there are differences. But there are people who think that there are already no differences anymore."

When I asked him about the kind of differences existing between Hui and Han he explained that many of the young generation Hui in his home area now 'ate with Han' which means in this case that they gave up Islamic dietary distinctions and chose to consume even pork and alcohol in order not to be separate from their Han friends, even though their parents would not like this if they knew. The interviewee added that these young Hui were "already Hanified".[5] It is remarkable at this point that in the course of the whole interview he stressed various times that many Hui were 'already' very similar to the Han, which means that he sees their 'sinicization' as a progressive development, probably leading to all Hui being *the same* as Han in the end. To paraphrase him, the Han have *already* reached a very high stage of civilization, while the Hui are following up. This understanding is closely connected to the official Chinese Communist view still powerful today that sees religion as "a historical phenomenon pertaining to a definite period in the development of human society" that will disappear in the end (as stated in the still valid 'Document No. 19', see Central Committee of the CCP, 1982).

Another respondent from Qinghai supports the view of Hui and Han not having any conflicts due to their similar cultures – with the main exception being dietary discrepancies:

"Regarding us in China, there are basically no problems. For example, because we are living in a wide Han environment, in this whole wide environment there is no religion, there is no faith, so in such a wide environment this means that our learning and our lives take place in close contact with non-Muslims. For example, when we are in school, in one class there may be only five or six, seven or eight Hui pupils, the other over 30 of 40 pupils all are Han. So, as long as we do not pass through systematical religious studies, [we] only know 'I am Hui, I do not eat pork.' Many Muslims are like this."

It can be concluded that on the side of the Hui I spoke to, no problems with the Han Chinese majority were mentioned. Rather similarities and even the trend to complete assimilation were highlighted. The main if not only difference between Han and Hui for many seems to be pork (and to a lesser degree alcohol) abstention. In the interviews I conducted, Hui Muslims do not express any feeling of being discriminated against or segregated by the Han Chinese majority.

Relations to other majoritarian Muslim minorities
In order to approach the Hui sense of belonging in the overall Chinese society, it is also relevant to examine their views on other ethnic minorities, particularly those that are also Muslim by majority. In this way, their position between the linguistically related Han and the religiously related 'Muslim' minorities can be determined more clearly.

Clear preferences were shown by two Hui respondents from Northeast-China who stated that for them the unity or connection between the Hui people were more important than that between Muslims. This means that they value their ethnic identity over the religious one. In addition, for all the Muslims I spoke to, their sense of religion was connected tightly with their sense of nationality. When asked about Muslims in China, respondents from all nationalities referred mainly to their own nationality. Only after I pointed out that there were also other 'Muslim nationalities', some of them considered them in their following answers. But the initial connection with 'Muslim' was that of the own nationality group for all respondents. It seems that especially the two main groups of Hui and Uyghurs in many cases are not aware of each other – apparently in many areas of China they live in completely different worlds. So, in China, the concept of 'nationality' in most parts obviously has more power than that of 'religion'.

Uyghurs I spoke to clearly locate the Hui closer to the Han than to themselves, while Han people are seen in quite a hostile way. There is even some sense of hostility emerging between some Hui and Uyghurs, in the way that some Uyghurs see Hui as betrayers (to their co-religionists, leaving them alone in their protest against the government) and some Hui adopt the common stereotype of Uyghurs tending to be 'criminal', 'separatist' or at least somehow 'backward'. As one Northeastern Hui respondent told me regarding Uyghurs:

"Hui and Han basically already have reached integration, they are very harmonious, but other nationalities do not accept the term of China's unity."

Here, the interviewee refers to the common Chinese political slogan of 'Unity of nationalities',[6] meaning that all nationalities should stand together in a united China. One Hui interviewee who had lived in Xinjiang for some years, described relations between the various peoples living there also to be defined strictly along the borders of nationality. As he put it: "The ethnic factor plays a bigger role than the religious one." He described that each ethnic group in Xinjiang basically formed an entity on its own, even the smaller ones such as Kazakhs or Kirghiz.

In some areas in the West of China (here: Yunnan and Qinghai) with considerable Hui communities but far less political tensions than in Xinjiang, things are different. Respondents from these areas described the various nationalities to be 'very united' with inter-ethnic marriages and friendships (in contrast to Xinjiang) being quite common. For the interviewees from these regions, it was more important if someone was a Muslim and if so, which 'school' of Islam he belonged to.[7] The following statement of a Hui from Yunnan stands in sharp contrast to the description on relationships in Xinjiang:

"You can say that the Hui basically do not have any problems with any nationality. But when the Hui find distinctions in the field of religion, there may occur problems, no matter which nationality it is."

Altogether, results from the interviews suggest that in many areas, nationality is more relevant in forming the Hui identity than religion. This is the case both in the East of China with few Muslims as well as in Xinjiang with various Muslim nationalities distinguishing from each other. Only in those areas in Western China with major Hui communities the nationality marker is second to the various religious schools that only under these conditions find room to develop and compete against each other.

Relations to the state

The third relationship that has to be considered for evaluating the Hui people's position within Chinese society is that to the state. I summarize here those answers referring to the respondents' views on state policies towards them. All in all, the Hui I spoke to consider state policies towards them as Muslims and as Hui people to be quite good (contrary to Uyghur respondents). One *'ālim* (Islamic scholar) from Western China concluded on the overall situation of Muslims in China:

"Although there may still be some limitations for them in the religious field,[8] [...] Chinese Muslims may go abroad for studying by various ways, they may be able to gain religious knowledge and then after returning to their home country, they may spread the Islamic knowledge by various communication channels. I consider this to be quite a good situation for Muslims in China."

Following this statement, he draws an analogy to the Jewish people in the USA:

"Thus I think that the Chinese Muslims are now in a very good position. This position might lead to something, if the Chinese Muslims this time used the opportunity well - similarly to the Jews in the USA who hold a certain distinct position within the American society."

Here, the respondent does not wish the Hui to become assimilated (which would mean giving up their religion, as shown in the examples above), but to gain a certain privileged position within the Chinese society by re-emphasizing Islam (via studies abroad) and thus highlighting 'ethnic' characteristics. Hui people enjoy the reputation of being excellent businesspeople, similarly to Jewish Americans being considered to be very successful in various fields, so comparisons between the two groups are common (Gladney 2004: 283-84; Lynn and Kanazawa 2008; Gladney 1996: 282).

Another Hui respondent from Northeastern China did not see any advantages or disadvantages given by the state due to being a Muslim or Hui. When asked about the privileges for ethnic minorities[9] he answered that these were only relevant to those minority members who wish to have children. He added that some Muslim members of minorities found disadvantages due to their non-Chinese mother tongues, for example in job-seeking. However, according to his opinion these were only for linguistic reasons. Regarding the overall situation of Islam in China he concluded:

"Indeed, the state supervises, but does not interfere in all affairs. For example, regarding theological details, the state usually does not interfere."

Although it is known that indeed the Chinese Islamic Association since the beginning of the 21st century has increasingly been interfering in 'theological details',[10] the respondent seems not to be aware of this development. Another Hui respondent from Northeast-China criticized some difficulties in gaining religious knowledge. When asked if Muslims in China were disadvantaged compared to Non-Muslims, he stated: "A bit, a little bit. For example, when you cannot find any Islamic books in a library." He explained that finding 'Islamic things' was increasingly rare and that he was not able to find a *Quran* in a book shop. He continues:

"But when I want [to buy] a party statute, such things with Communist and Marxist thoughts, you can buy them."

He did not know anything about minority privileges. So both respondents see state policies towards them as Hui people to be almost neutral and as Muslims to have little disadvantages.

One interviewee from Yunnan disagreed with this view. He stressed that Hui and Han lived together without any problems in his home area, whereas problems sometimes were initiated by the local authorities:

"Let us suppose the local authorities for nationality affairs do not execute the central government's nationality policies very well, then this would lead to some nationality problems. (...) This is a conflict between rulers and non-rulers, because the Hui can be as any other nationality, [we] are all the same common people,[11] [we] are all the same nation, even the nationalities can be on good terms with each other. But the true conflicts emerge as soon as a regime restricts the Hui or other nationalities, this can arouse conflicts."

It is striking here that the interviewee emphasized that the general policies were not the problem, only if local authorities executed them in the wrong way this could lead to problems. However, this restriction may be due to considerations of political correctness and of carefulness not to express too open criticism towards the Central government. He emphasized the general harmony among the people which was only destroyed sometimes by the rulers. In using this Confucian-based concept, he claims that the current government (or local authorities) did not fulfill their duties as just rulers (Rainey 2010: 96-97).

Altogether, Hui Muslims I spoke to regarded state policies towards them to be sufficient, with little restrictions but no tendencies of suppression or open discrimination. However, none of them emphasized the preferential policies valid for them as members of a minority nationality. Instead, restrictions of religious freedom are highlighted and in one case state authorities were seen as initiators of inter-ethnic conflicts (with no details given on the reasons).

Non-Muslim Perceptions

For locating the Hui within the overall Chinese society, it is not only important to consider their own views, but also outside views from the majority population. Here I summarize the findings from interviews with 11 non-Muslim persons[12] from China (most of them during their stay in Europe), asking them on their opinions on and experiences with Muslims in China.[13] Not all of the answers are relevant here, as many refer to other nationalities, I therefore focus on summarizing contents and explicating a number of statements clearly referring to Hui.

Altogether, most non-Muslims in China are not well-informed about the religion of Islam. When I asked the respondents on their spontaneous associations with Muslims in China, one interviewee (who did not know any Muslims personally) did not have any idea at all. Among the others, the most frequently mentioned issues were conflicts and criminal activities (which mainly referred to Uyghurs), certain clothes and certain food and restaurants. Although I asked explicitly about Muslims, only one respondent referred to their religion, while the others mentioned cultural or ethnic traits (which are in large parts influenced by religious elements though). One respondent even stated that Muslims believed in some religion that he was not able to name. In another question I directly asked about knowledge on the religion of Islam, and obtained only limited responses. Among three people who did not know any Muslims personally, only one knew one characteristic of Islam, the pork taboo. Four respondents who knew Muslims superficially (e.g. as classmates or colleagues), were able to name between 1 and 3 characteristics of Islam, and only those having close Muslim friends knew more details about the religion (mentioning between 2 and 7 characteristics). Additionally, the background knowledge on these characteristics for most respondents is poor, too, as can be seen in one not untypical answer by one of the interviewees:

"I know that pigs are holy and respected by all people in Islam. Because of this they do not eat pork."[14]

When asked about the kind of personal relations with Muslims, comments on Hui people were mostly positive. One respondent thought they were 'likeable', according to experiences in a Hui restaurant. Another one said they were 'the same as Han' and not distinguishable at all. Others, who knew Hui people personally, also said that they were as any other friend apart from the fact that they would not ask them to eat pork but had to choose a Muslim restaurant when eating together. Another interviewee compared Chinese Muslims (meaning Hui) with Taiwanese:

"I actually think they are even like Taiwanese. It is difficult to separate this or so. But they actually still belong to us. Taiwan does, too. But as I said, after a while – they always have this own kind of culture and thoughts and mentality, too."

Two respondents from Xi'an emphasized that in their home town many Hui lived in a somehow separate community in the 'Hui quarter' with their own infrastructure. However, they confirmed that many Han people frequently go to this quarter for eating in one of the many Hui restaurants, as I also experienced during my own stay in Xi'an. Friendships between Han and Hui in Xi'an were also common. However, when invited to a Han's home, the Hui in Xi'an did not use any of their dishes as they regarded it to be unclean (on the particular habits in Xi'an see also Gillette 2000). One respondent describes that drinking alcohol by most Hui was not regarded as a problem, though. So in this city, clear differences between Hui and Han are noticed and upheld, while common friendships show that ethnic frontiers are by far not as clearly drawn as with Uyghurs in Xinjiang.

Only one respondent from Shandong had some negative views on Hui in his home town. He explained:

"When dealing with Muslims, I have to be very careful and may not show any disrespect to their belief. And we avoid talking about cultures. In addition, I have to avoid conflicts with them, as I know that the government will be on their side, even if I was wronged."

He described that in his home town sometimes there were conflicts between Hui and Mongol or Han groups. Hui people there formed a strongly united group that sometimes attacked members of other nationalities, particularly Mongols, and destroyed possessions such as houses or cars. He admitted however that he had never seen this kind of incident personally, but had read many articles on these issues online. Similar experiences on protected Hui were made by one respondent from Xi'an. When asked about advantages or disadvantages given by authorities to Muslims, he answered:

"Yes, they have many advantages. Study. They can study with much less achievements than others. And they can have more children. And also the school. In our home town there is a special one for other [i.e. minority] nationalities. (...) And if the children beat each other it is always our fault. They cannot say this is his fault. Always our fault. Yes, when they always say this is your fault I sometimes think we are being discriminated against."

So two out of eleven respondents see the Hui to be especially protected by the government, even to the degree that criminal deeds were not punished and members of the Han majority felt discriminated against. There is one other respondent who considers the Hui (as members of the ethnic minorities) to be wrongfully treated preferentially by admitting to find the positive discrimination in school entrance exams 'a little bit unfair'.

Four respondents thought that Muslims in China generally had more advantages than disadvantages (mainly through their nationality status), but did not judge these advantages. Two interviewees emphasized particularly the facilitated university access. Another one concluded on that point:

"But I do not see myself impaired by that. Just because my colleague has had more points at the entrance examination – I don't see any disadvantages."

One interviewee emphasized the little constraints for Muslim minorities:

"The Chinese government respects their religion, they can do everything in the way they like it, as long as their actions are legal. They can go everywhere and eat everything they want."

Only two respondents mentioned any possible disadvantages for Muslims in China, however, both referred to Uyghurs.

On the perceptions of non-Muslim interviewees it can be concluded that they also connect to the nationality concept more than to religion. When asked about 'Muslims', most respondents referred to cultural traits and ethnic stereotypes and most of them had only very limited knowledge on the religion of Islam. The majority of interviewees described Hui people in positive terms, perceiving them to be very close to Han Chinese with only certain distinct characteristics – which were seen more in the way of particular cultural habits than totally differing worldviews. Only one respondent thought of Hui as aggressive and criminal people, while he and two other interviewees thought that the Hui were unrightfully treated preferentially. Yet the majority consider state policies towards Hui people to be good as they are.

Media Portrayals

In this third and final part I summarize some of my findings based on analyzing articles published in the years 2003-2011 on the Chinese website of the major

Chinese newspaper and party organ 'Renmin ribao'[15] (its English language version is known as 'People's Daily'). By searching articles via the website's search engine, I firstly found out that articles mentioning the key words 'Muslim' (穆斯林 *musilin*) and 'Islam' (伊斯兰 *yisilan*) were very rare – only about 0.2/ 0.4% of all articles mentioned these terms – compared to 1.7/ 3.8% in a comparable major German newspaper, which means that Islam and Muslims are referred to about eight times more frequently in the German than in the Chinese newspaper.[16] A rough analysis of contents showed that still by far the biggest number of hits referred to issues outside of China. For both key terms, 44% of articles were classified into the category 'International' (国际 *guoji*), and many articles from the other 51 categories of the website also completely referred to international cases, not being relevant for analysis here. These numbers demonstrate that articles mentioning Islam or Muslims inside China are very rare.

In the following, I analyzed contents from articles classified into the most relevant categories, such as 'current policies' or 'society'.[17] The majority of the articles dealing with Muslims or Islam in China describe certain 'cultural' or religious activities, usually called 'traditions' (传统 *chuantong*). Most relevant other topics include economy, emergency aid, extremist groups, Muslim institutions and projects, or international exchange. Below I summarize some of the contents referring to Hui people.

The articles on the occasion of certain Muslim holidays, such as Eid al-Adha or Eid al-Fitr, all refer to these feasts as 'traditional feasts' almost every time they are mentioned, supporting the impression that religions are seen as something traditional, different from the 'modern' atheist culture of many Han. Apart from this, they are often described as 'happy' feasts, with everyone celebrating cheerfully. Activities on these days are in some cases described meticulously. The Muslims' actions and emotions and the whole atmosphere during these days and even during Ramadan are described consistently in a very positive way. In some cases, very detailed information on the religious backgrounds are given.

Not surprisingly, most of the articles praise the government's support and efforts for the Muslims and that high officials not only celebrate with them during their feasts (mainly in regions with a high Muslim share of the population), but even get up very early in the morning to convey their congratulations. Political slogans are not missing either, with the most frequent ones being those of "unity of the nationalities" (民族团结 *minzu tuanjie*), "Love the country, love the religion" (爱国爱教 *aiguo aijiao*), and the praise of the great "socio-economic development" (经济社会发展 *jingji shehui fazhan*) due to the government's support.

There are other articles that describe the everyday lives of Chinese Muslims, which also portray the Muslims consistently in a positive way. For example, one article portrays a model-Hui-woman who even won a price for her and her family's exemplary way of life – farming land, raising cows, sending the children to school and attaining above-average earnings (Voice of the Heart, 2006). Another article similarly highlights the exemplary conduct of inhabitants of a Hui village, who were not only excellent businessmen but even shared their knowledge generously and in a friendly way with Han newcomers so that these were also able to increase their incomes (Yang et al. 2004). So, in both articles Hui are portrayed as being even superior to Han people, both in economic success and in moral conducts.

Other articles describe for example the situation after a major earthquake in a region where there are many Hui living. Here, mainly the great cooperation and mutual help between members of various nationalities are highlighted (Wu 2010). The generosity of the Muslims is also emphasized in an article on their contributions to aid for Tsunami-hit areas in 2005 (Zhou 2005).

Thus it can be concluded that the Renmin ribao firstly reports very little about Chinese Muslims and secondly makes sure that those articles that are published on the Hui are consistently positive. Hui are represented as friendly and hard-working people with fine morals who stick to their traditional but very likeable religion.

Compared to some media reports in European countries, it is striking that there are no discussions about violence, terrorism or criminality referring to Hui Muslims, nor are there any reports about perceived threats or even nuisance by 'Islamic-style' buildings or cloths or the suppression of women. On the contrary, Renmin ribao offers a category named 'Women' which does not contain a single hit of altogether 47,570 articles containing the word 'Muslim' or 'Islam'! Even though it really seems that by reporting in this positive way, possible inter-ethnic tensions shall be avoided, the pure existence of various nationalities is always emphasized - firstly by naming them and secondly by highlighting differences between them (even if the Hui are portrayed to be superior) and thirdly by consistently calling the culture and religion of Hui people 'traditional', meaning not as modern as Han culture.

Other state policies support these views. There are huge Million-Dollar projects with the label of 'Muslim' or 'Islamic' at present raised mainly in the Hui Autonomous Region Ningxia (such as the Global Muslim City, Hui Culture

Park or Muslim Trade City, all located in Yinchuan), which on the one hand were initiated to foster economy and international contacts in the rather poor area, but on the other hand always portray the 'traditional culture' of the Hui, which in many cases is not Hui but Middle Eastern style, as Hui actually do not really set apart from Han people. These accord with the overall trends of Chinese 'ethnic' tourism (Gladney 2004: 28-50) on the one hand and of the common equation of Islam with 'Arabic culture' on the other hand.

Conclusions

The main conclusion that can be drawn from findings presented in this article is the dominance of the category of ethnicity, supporting Gladney's assumption of a fourth tide called 'ethnic nationalism' in China's Islam (Gladney 1996: 62-63). Hui are not seen by members of the majority population, and also do not see themselves, primarily as Muslims, but as Hui. This is remarkable, as particularly in their case the main characteristic that makes them 'Hui' and not 'Han' is their religion (Gladney 1996: 17-21). Particularly in their case it has been shown that their 'ethnicity' has been quite arbitrarily 'invented', as groups from various regions speaking various languages are subsumed as 'Hui' solely for their religious orientation. It is thus notable how state policies can and do influence people's perceptions of the own group and belonging. It seems to me that the only areas where Hui people have the possibility to differentiate in their self-perceptions are those Western areas where there are large Hui communities not rivaled by big groups of other Muslim nationalities (as in Xinjiang).

This overwhelming ethnic factor of identity does not lead to exclusion, however, but to a predominantly friendly relationship to Han people, so that most Hui people surely see themselves as being different but not really inferior to Han – just a little bit more 'traditional' than the 'modern' Han. The wish for reaching modernity surely contributes to the development of growing assimilation in some areas in Eastern China, along with the pressure of adaptation due to small numbers of Hui in these areas. All in all, Hui can be considered to be very close to the Han majority – closer than to co-religionists of other nationalities. Nevertheless, realities for Hui in different areas are still very different and so certainly are their senses of belonging to the society as a whole.

Notes

1 This paper summarizes some findings from the author's dissertation, published in German language (see Drewes, 2016).

2 Dru Gladney states that as Chinese nationalities were identified and categorized by the state mainly in the 1950s according to various criteria that not always correspond to previously existing groups and identities, some of these nationalities can be regarded as having been 'invented'. This view applies particularly to the Hui people who speak various languages and hold a remarkable cultural variety and thus prior to their categorization rarely identified themselves as one ethnic group.

3 The term 'nationality' here and in the following refers to the Chinese term '民族 minzu', which denotes the 56 officially registered 'ethnic' groups in the PRC. It shall be noted at this point that there are also some Chinese Muslims not belonging to any of the minority nationalities, as they are Han people who chose to convert to Islam. Similarly, not all members of the 'Muslim' nationalities are indeed Muslims. Both categories are just overlapping in large parts and so are seen to be identical by many Chinese. In this article I will also refer only to the mainly Muslim nationalities for reasons of clarity, bearing the inaccuracy in mind.

4 In particular I made comparisons to the other main Islam-influenced nationality, the Uyghur, so as to highlight the differences between the concepts of 'religion' and 'nationality'. For background information it shall be noted that Uyghurs live almost exclusively in the Northwestern Autonomous Region of Xinjiang. They have significantly more problems with state authorities, and even accuse them of systematical suppression.

5 Chinese original wording: "已经汉化了 yijing Hanhua le".

6 In Chinese 民族团结 minzu tuanjie.

7 In China, the three main Islamic schools (or 'tides') are the Gedimu (Chinese-influenced, 'traditional' Islam), various Sufi orders, and the 'new' scriptural teachings (in China summarized as 'Wahhabi') (see Gladney 1996: 36-62).

8 The respondent does not explicate these limitations, restrictions (outside of Xinjiang) are known for example in the fields of hajj admission and performance, religious activities of officials and students and control of religious personnel.

9 The 'preferential policies' for members of ethnic minorities include most prominently facilitated university access and the permission to have more children than Han.

10 In particular, the China Islamic Guidance Committee (中国伊斯兰教教务指导委员会) has been established in 2001 in order to re-interpret Islamic sources and accordingly set up Islamic textbooks as well as the so called 'new sermons' (新卧尔兹) (see Erie 2014).

11 Chinese original wording: '老百姓 laobaixing'.

12 Nine of these are Han, one is registered as Manchu (whereas she considers her culture to be identical with that of the Han people surrounding her), and one was born in Taiwan but is currently living in mainland China.

13 It might be argued that the results may be distorted due to the respondents' stay abroad and influences from media and society here. This actually may be true in some very limited cases, but for the majority of the respondents this is not very probable as most interviews as a whole show. Most of the respondents stayed in Europe for the purpose of studies, dealing mainly with other Chinese and rarely consuming European media. The alternative of conducting interviews in China is not considered to be advantageous, since the issue is regarded as being politically sensitive and answers would probably lose quality and frankness. Even during the preparation of the interviews in Europe, some respondents showed serious concerns about possible negative consequences for them and some even disagreed for these reasons to the idea of conducting an interview – although anonymity was guaranteed. Thus, the lesser evil is accepting minor possible influences by European experiences, which, however, are not very relevant in the statements cited here.

14 Various authors note that in China the assumption of pigs being holy to Muslims as a reason for the Islamic pork taboo seems to be quite common, although it is contrary to the taboo's true reason of the assumed 'impurity' of pigs (Chen 2007:13).

15 In Chinese: 人民日报. The website can be found at: http://www.people.com.cn (accessed on June 30, 2015).

16 In both cases I compared the number of matches with the number of matches to a neutral character calculating the overall number of articles, which was 'to be' (是 shi) in the case of the Renmin ribao and '*' in the case of the German newspaper, 'Süddeutsche Zeitung'. Though this method may not lead to 100% exact results, it shows a clear tendency in this case.

17 I analyzed only those articles showing the key terms in the title. The chosen categories were 'Current Policies', 'Opinion', 'Society', 'News from the National People's Congress', and 'Media'. Altogether, this method showed 109 articles for more in-depth analysis.

References

Central Committee of the CCP (1982). *Document No. 19: The basic viewpoint and policy on the religious question during our country's socialist period* (Original title: 19 号文件; 关于我国社会主义时期宗教问题的基本观点和基本政策, Donald MacInnis trans.). English translation available at http://www.purdue.edu/crcs/itemResources/PRCDoc/pdf/Document_no._19_1982.pdf [Accessed February, 27, 2014].

Chen, Jessica (2007). 'Pigs, Purity, and Protection: Food Taboo in Hui Chinese and African American Muslim Minority Communities'. Available at http://apps.carleton.edu/curricular/religion/assets/Comps2.doc [Accessed February 28, 2014].

Drewes, Frauke (2016). *Orientalisiert, kriminalisiert, propagiert? Die Position von Muslimen in Gesellschaft und Politik der Volksrepublik China heute.* Würzburg: Ergon.

Erie, Matthew S. (2014). 'Defining shari'a in China: State, *ahong*, and the postsecular turn', *Cross-Currents: East Asian History and Culture Review*, E-Journal No. 12 (September). Available at https://cross-currents.berkeley.edu/sites/default/files/e-journal/articles/erie.pdf [Accessed June 30, 2015].

Gillette, Maris Boyd (2000). *Between Mecca and Beijing: Modernization and Consumption Among Urban Chinese Muslims.* Stanford, CA: Stanford University Press.

Gladney, Dru C. (1996). *Muslim Chinese: Ethnic Nationalism in the People's Republic.* Cambridge, MA and London: Harvard University Press.

Gladney, Dru C. (2004). *Dislocating China: Muslims, Minorities, and Other Subaltern Subjects.* London: Hurst and Co.

Lynn, Richard and Kanazawa, Satoshi (2008). 'How to explain high Jewish achievement: The role of intelligence and values', *Personality and Individual Differences*, 44, pp. 801–808.

Rainey, Lee Dian (2010). *Confucius and Confucianism: The Essentials.* Chichester: Wiley-Blackwell.

Wu, Bin (2010). Qiang Wei qinqie kanwang dizhenzaiqu musilin jiaozhong (Qiang Wei pays an amicable visit to Muslim earthquake disaster zones). 强卫亲切看望地震灾区穆斯林教众, 人民日報 *Renmin Ribao (People's Daily)*, April 21st, Available at http://politics.people.com.cn/GB/14562/11437437.html [Accessed February 28, 2014].

Voice of the heart of an ordinary woman in the new Mumin-village (2006). Mumin xincun li de yi ge putong musilin funü de xinsheng (2006), 穆民新村里的一个普通穆斯林妇女的心声, 人民日報, *Renmin Ribao (People's Daily)*, March 2nd. Availabe at http://politics.people.com.cn/GB/14562/4159398.html [Accessed February 28, 2014].

Yang, Jing, Zhang, Yan and Cui, Qingxin (2004), Hanzu: shenghuo zai 'musilin zhi xiang' de 'shaoshu minzu' (Han nationality: Life of the minority nationality in a Muslim community). 杨静, 张彦, 崔清新. 汉族: 生活在"穆斯林之乡"的"少数民族" 人民日報 *Renmin Ribao (People's Daily)*, July 7th. Available at http://www.people.com.cn/GB/shizheng/1026/2633708.html [Accessed February 28, 2014].

Zhou, Zhizhong (2005), 'Yinchuan Yisilan Xiehui zuzhi zongjiaojie xiang haixiao zaiqu juankuan (Yinchuan Islamic Association organizes donations of religious circles for Tsunami disaster zones)'. 周志忠, 银川伊斯兰协会组织宗教界向海啸灾区捐款, 人民日報 *Renmin Ribao (People's Daily)*, January 7th. Availabe at http://politics.people.com.cn/GB/14562/3105259.html [Accessed February 28, 2014].

CHAPTER 7

The Diversity of Chinese Muslim Identities: A Special Hui in Yunnan[1]

Feng Yu

Yunnan University

Suchart Setthamalinee

Payap University

Chinese Muslim Identity

The present theoretical assumptions in the studies of Muslims in China seem to divide the possible accounts into two paradigms: secessionist and assimilationist.

Secessionist Paradigm

Israeli (2002: 7) fiercely argues that the Muslim presence in China, which dates back to the Tang dynasty, has always posed a challenge, and at times even a threat, to the Chinese establishment. This was due to their understanding of the nature of Islam, which made its members far from willing to acculturate into Chinese society, and on the contrary nurtured a set of distinctive traits and stressed its own superiority, something almost unheard of in other minority cultures in China.

According to Israeli (2002: 45), the energetic Chinese policy of sinicization that began in the 1720s under the Qing Dynasty did not succeed with the Muslim population for two main reasons: first, there was no single territory shared by the Muslims in China, which meant that the Muslims as a group were relatively free from the control of the Chinese government; and second, the Muslim Hui chose to remain outside mainstream Chinese society, and therefore had their own sense of superiority, their own festivals and religious symbolism, and their own learning and culture.

Israeli (2002: 16-24) asserts that the Muslims in China felt they were an alien people, more akin to other members of the world community--the Umma--than to their Chinese neighbors. Because their main concern was their religion, and because their identity was focused on the universal Umma, the deeply ingrained Chinese tradition of identification with the locus of domicile did not pertain to them. The Muslims had become better members of their community through strong communal organization, inculcation of Islamic values, communal worship and activities, a total and unqualified identification with their fellow Muslims in the congregation, and moral submission to the authority of the Imam. They did not become Chinese.

The Chinese scholar Wang Jianping, in an historical study of the Yunnan Hui, adopts a similar line of reasoning. He argues that the coherence of the Hui in their encounters with non-Muslim neighbors was obvious. If an argument occurred with the Han, if it was a trifling matter, the community would disregard the facts and stand up together to defend their interests or even take revenge against the other side. According to Wang Jianping (1996: 242), such group unity had been cultivated during the long formation of the Hui community.

Taken to its extreme, this paradigm defined the Muslims solely in terms of their religion. In this case the Muslims in China were totally distinct from the Han majority, and likely to either rebel against the non-Muslim state or, failing in that endeavor, to totally assimilate. Assimilation or secession were the only options available to Muslims in China, according to this view (Gladney 1996: 21).

For Michael Dillon (1996; 1999), even though he argues that it is not possible to consider Muslims in China solely as a religious minority, he also portrays the Muslims as a group separated from the Han Chinese majority, divided by familial, ethnic and linguistic ties in addition to their religious difference. Differences in lifestyle in the past have contributed to distinct identities and a sense of national identity, which in turn have supported the demand for political autonomy.

An Assimilationist Paradigm

At the other extreme are those writers who regard the Muslims as virtually indistinguishable from the larger population, referring to them as 'Chinese Muslims' or 'Sino-Muslims.' The scholars in this camp include Isaac Mason and Jonathan Lipman.

In this view, the Muslims are portrayed as completely assimilated to the Han, the dominant ethnic group in China, and as differing from them only in certain minor religious beliefs and customs. This position seems to be appealing because Muslims often appear physically and linguistically similar to the Han amongst whom they live. Isaac Mason (1929), quoted by Gladney (1991: 25), notes that he "found little in the facial or physical appearance of Moslems [he had] known to distinguish them from their neighbors of other faiths."

Some writers continue to suggest that the Hui Muslims are distinct from Han only in their religion. A reporter noted that we could find little different between Han and Hui: "Frequently indistinguishable in features and dress from Han Chinese.... It is then only their rejection of pork, the common surname Ma (Mohammad), and Arabic inscriptions in mosques built like Buddhist temples, that serve to distinguish them from Han neighbors" (Gladney 1991: 25).

The other primary scholar working within this paradigm, Jonathan Lipman, voices another common supposition in his study of the history of the Hui in northwest China. He coined the term 'Sino-Muslim' to describe the Hui prior to the emergence of the People's Republic of China (PRC). Lipman (1997: xxiii) suggests that, prior to the founding of the PRC, the word 'Hui' meant Muslim and that "they were Chinese-speaking Muslims - but they would not have used that name themselves." Lipman (1996: 98-99) likewise argues that in order to understand Chinese society accurately, "we must hyphenate the Chinese, writing about Manchu-Chinese, Subei-Chinese, etc., and Chinese-speaking Muslim." He quotes Jo-Ann Gross (1992) to demonstrate that the Hui identity has been constructed and reconstructed over time throughout Chinese history, and, ultimately, the Sino-Muslim identity was formed.

Thus Muslims, according to Lipman, can be Chinese and Muslim at the same time, in part because religion is seen as only one of many different ways that identity is constructed. Along the same lines, Lipman (1997: 102) also asserts that the vaunted unity of the Muslim Umma, the universal congregation of Islam, did not always save Muslims from conflict with one another anywhere in the Muslim world, and China has been no exception. Lipman states:

"In short, according to this view, the identity negotiations occurring here remain trapped by the dichotomy between Muslim and Chinese. Even as people negotiated between the two identities, the two identities themselves remained fixed and problematic. The key question for each person was which group they belonged to, and the extent to which the diasporic group acquires the identity of the host culture. Taken as a model, then, this account of the relation allows us to consider whether Chinese Muslims in Yunnan completely adapted and assimilated to the host society."

Five Special Hui Ethnic Groups in Yunnan

There are five special Hui ethnic groups in Xishuangbanna Dai Autonomous Prefecture, Dali Bai Autonomous Prefecture, Diqing Tibetan Autonomous Prefecture, Wenshan Zhuang Autonomous Prefecture, Yuxi Xinping Dai and Yi Autonomous County, and Ninglang Xiao Liangshan Yi Autonomous Prefecture of Yunnan province. It is difficult to distinguish these five special groups among the surrounding ethnic groups by the appearance, since they speak the same language, live in the same local ethnic style houses, and their customs are similar to other local ethnic minorities. However, they believe in Islam, and do not believe in any other religion.

The five special groups are not the people who were converted to Islam. Their formation has two approaches. One is the localization process through a long interaction with other ethnic groups. The other is that many Hui people escaped and hid in the ethnic group areas after the failure of the Du Wenxiu uprising in the Qing Dynasty. They had to change some living habits in order to adapt to the new environment. Since the 1990s, along with the religious revival in China, many faithful Hui people in the inland have paid much more attention to these 'special Hui people'. They came to promote a pure Islam and tried to change some non-Muslim habits of the local people. By doing the so-called "returning to Islam", it brings with it many new ideas and some changes in local society. This action has inspired many local people to consider the issues of religion, culture, identity, ethnic relations, and some other interests.

Diverse Identities of Parshi Dai

Parshi Dai live in the two villages of Manluanhui and Mansaihui in Xishuangbanna, Yunnan province. They speak Dai, wear Dai clothes, reside in houses of *ganlan* style, but have retained their belief in Islam while not adopting their neighbors' Buddhism. In the Dai language, the Hui nationality is called 'Parshi.' Tracing their roots to mainstream Yunnan Hui Muslims, the 'Parshi Dai' in the Qing Dynasty (1644-1911) until the present, have gone through a process of adapting to the cultural and social mores of the Dai, and established a highly unique and different set of customs and beliefs. Today, the village of Manluanhui has 63 families and a population of 360 people. The village's primary source of income is derived from tea, sugarcane, and transportation. The other village, Mansaihui, has 76 families and a population of 360. The village economy is dominated by raising cattle. Between them are 4 villages Manjiang, Manduan, Manpai and Mansailong.

The appearance of the distinctive 'Parshi Dai' appellation has its particular history. Historically, Yunnanese Hui often served as the caravaneers who transported goods and did business throughout Yunnan and its foreign neighbors. In order to travel to Southeast Asia, many caravans passed through Xishuangbanna.

Hui—Muslim Identity

Religious Buildings

The Parshi-Dai's mosque, with a green dome and star-and-crescent sign, represents that Parshi-Dai have a different religion from the Dai nationality. Manluanhui village has recently built a mosque in which the main hall is about 10 meters high. The first floor is used as the classroom for Islamic study, and the second one as the prayer hall for *salat*. Between the two floors, the name of the mosque with the versions of Chinese, Arabic, and Dai characters is written on the building. It reads 'Manluanhui Mosque' and 'Parshi Dai Hui Mosque'. Four eaves are warped in each direction, which is typical in Chinese mosques. A 20-meter-high Minaret is built on the left of the main hall with an Arabic dome and the green star-and-crescent sign on its top. There is a wooden carving with the Islamic creed Shahada, both in Chinese and Arabic, hanging in the middle of the hall gate. In the 120-square-meter prayer hall, there are a built-in closets on the left side for the scriptures, a place in the front of the hall for the imam to lead prayers, and a platform in the middle for delivering *Khutbahs* (Muslim sermon delivered on Fridays). The prayer hall is divided into two parts by a curtain. Two-thirds of the hall on the left is for the men to pray, and the other one-third for the women. The mosque is exquisitely designed with a special style. The newly-built mosque in Mansaihui village is a reinforced concrete structure, with a style combining Arab and modern elements. The main hall is separated from the teaching building and the inner decoration is similar to the one in the mosque of Manluanhui.

Residential Buildings

The new storied houses of Parshi Dai are built with Arab domes. The head of the gate is carved with Arabic characters, which are mainly the content of Shahada ("there is no god apart from Allah, and Muhammad is the Messenger of Allah").

In the living room of most families, usually there are tapestries displaying the Kaaba and quotations of the *Qur'an*. Some families take the first floor as the living room, and the second one for religious use, in which the imams recite scriptures.

Dress and Grooming

Some of the boys like wearing the Islamic white cap, and girls wear the hijab in different colors, such as white, pink and blue.

Eating Habits

Parshi Dai do not eat pork, according to the Islamic eating habits. They usually fry the traditional dessert *you xiang*[2] for celebration. Like many Hui in other places, Parshi Dai like drinking tea. For example, the aged people make their own tea, which the villagers call 'the old tea'. The tea leaves are large and yellow. It tastes good and has a mildly fragrant scent.

Intermarriage

Parshi Dai are willing marry Hui. If they want to get married to Dai nationals, they will ask the person to convert to Islam before marriage, in line with the *Qur'an*. The most common ritual is the same among different Hui groups. The process often includes proposal, saying *salaam*, and doing the *nikah* (marriage prayer).

Funerals and Burials

Parshi Dai practice inhumation. The deceased will be brought to the mosque and be washed in the prescribed manner. The body will be shrouded in pieces of white cloth named *kafan*, and be placed into a wooden coffin of the mosque. After the male relatives practice prayer for the deceased, the body will be transported to the mountains to be buried. The body will be taken out from the coffin and be put into the grave. The head will be put towards the north, the feet towards the south, the face towards the west[3], and the back towards the east. People will put a piece of wooden board to cover the grave and cover it with earth. After the burial, people will hold memorial ceremonies at intervals. During the ceremony, the imam and caliph are invited to the house of the deceased to recite verses. The host will offer *jing qian* (money), fruit and snacks to the guests. It is polite to serve the imam and caliph first and then the guests. The family members usually have dinner last.

Language

Parshi Dai speak in Dai, but the language is mixed with some Chinese Muslims dialects, and use words like iman, (faith and trust in Allah), Muslim, prayer, faith, imam, jumat (Friday prayer), and khutbah (speech). Some children will greet strangers with *salaam alaykum* in Arabic, which means 'peace be upon you'. Along with the practice of religion policy in China and religion revival around the world, Parshi Dai revive the enthusiasm to communicate with Hui in the inland of China. In recent years, many young Parshi Dai have been sent to Shadian, Gejiu city or Najiaying in Tonghai County, Yunnan. Both regions have famous Hui communities, where youngsters can acquire religious knowledge. At the same time, many Hui from Lincang, Zhaotong, Jujing and Menghai will visit the two villages to communicate. Nowadays, most villagers can recite eighteen Surahs of the *Qur'an*, which contain the basic knowledge of the scriptures.

Life Etiquette

Parshi Dai will ask the imam to name their newly-born infant in Arabic, which is normally a name of a prophet or sage. In this sense, people believe that children can live up to their hope to become a useful person, with the excellent merits and behavior of these prophets.

Festivals and Ceremonies

Parshi Dai celebrate three important festivals: Eid-ul-Fitr (celebrating the end of the fasting month of Ramadan), Eid al-Adha (Muslim holiday commemorating the willingness of Ibrahim to sacrifice his son Ismael as an act of obedience to Allah) and Mawlid (Muhammad's Birthday). They will invite Hui communities in the county or other nearby places to participate. During Ramadan, people practice fasting. In the past, fasting was practiced by elderly people, but at present, many young people have joined them. During Ramadan, the imam will be invited to three to five houses every day to recite verses of the *Qur'an*.

Dai Identity

Residential Buildings

Like Dai people, Parshi Dai also reside in houses of the *ganlan* style. Dai people usually take the first floor to keep livestock and the second floor for habitation. However, Parshi Dai use a second smaller house to keep the livestock separate from their living places. The houses normally have one gate and three walls, but some houses now are newly built with a reinforced concrete structure, and the bamboo houses have gradually disappeared.

Dress and Grooming

Parshi Dai girls are dressed like the Dai Nationality. They usually wear a tight short sleeve shirt with wide shoulders and a straight skirt. Nevertheless, some girls who have studied Islamic scriptures and the *Qur'an* wear a long sleeve blouse and wear the hijab.

Eating Habit

According to Islamic etiquette, Parshi Dai do not eat pork products. In the past, they usually ate duosheng, a special dish prepared by chopping and mixing raw beef, chilli, olive skin and fresh svegetables with seasonings. Now Parshi Dai rarely eat this food. Like other Dai people, they also love to eat glutinous rice, and they generally like spicy, sour, and crispy food,. When holding a memorial ceremony, glutinous rice is the main food. Some of the men smoke, and drink alcohol.

Intermarriage

Before the marriage ceremony, there is an engagement banquet called *jin qiannan* in Dai dialect. The family of the bridegroom will invite the relatives and the family members of the bride to have a meal together, in order to announce the marriage. An auspicious day is chosen by the imam to plan the wedding date. The family of the bridegroom needs to prepare a brand-new dress for the bride, and two suits of garment or a bolt of cloth for the parents-in-law as presents. The bridegroom family also prepares rice and meat for the bride family to cater for the guests. Like the marriage customs of Dai people, Parshi Dai also have the convention of 'marriage service', which means that the bridegroom lives in the house of the parents-in-law to serve them for a period of time that is agreed to by both sides before marriage. The wedding ceremony is firstly held in the bride's family, and the bridegroom will be sent there by his family before dark. The new couple will present cigarettes and serve food to the guests. On the third day of the marriage ceremony, the bridegroom will take his bride to visit his own family. This marriage ceremony is a long and complex process.

Funerals and Burials

In the past years, Parshi Dai used a temporary wooden box instead of a coffin to carry the deceased. They would split the box after the burial and throw it away in the wild, because they were afraid that the box might bring the ghost home. At present, Parshi Dai have abandonned the old custom and have adopted funeral conventions of inland Hui people. Nevertheless, some particular details of the local features are still kept. During our field research, we took part in a memorial ceremony in Mansaihui. The process was found to be similar to the ceremony of the inland Hui, but the meal is special. The host makes glutinous rice balls as large as a fist. The rice is put into plastic bags for each guest to eat. People take the rice roll with the left hand, and the chopsticks with the right. The food includes duck, fried fish, cold rice noodles dressed with sauce, pumpkin and pickles.

Language

Parshi Dai can speak Dai dialect, and they communicate with other Dai people conveniently.

Life Etiquette

When a baby is born, the family will go to the nearby temple to ask the *kanglang* (the first-class Buddhist monk, or the second-class Buddhist monk in Dai language) to give a Dai name. The *kanglang*, as the secular religious scholar, is respected by Dai people. The Dai name is important for the kids, because a good name will protect the kids against disease. The Dai only use given names, they have no surname. 'Ai' and 'Yu' are the first given names to distinguish the gender. 'Ai', meaning 'rock', introduces a male name, and 'Yu' meaning 'jade', introduces female names[4]. The first-class Buddhist monk will engrave the name and the birth date of the baby in Tai Tham script onto a tube made of so-called 'golden bamboo', or *phyllostachys aurea*. The carved bamboo tube, which is 10 centimeters long, is called *miebi*. This tube will be kept until death, after which it will be split and burned. Parshi Dai believe that the soul will rest in peace after doing that. Since a piece of cotton cloth is more convenient than a bamboo tube, many young people nowadays use cloth to replace the *miebi*. The *kanglang* will write the name on the white cloth using a brush. When the baby is one-month old, the Parshi Dai will ask the imam in the mosque to name the baby in Arabic. After the child is old enough to go to school, the family will give the children a Chinese name. Therefore, Parshi Dai have at least three names during their lifetime, for instance, Aijian is a Dai name, Ali an Arabic name, and Ma Rongjin the Chinese name. There are many examples in the 'genealogical history', and two versions of names are recorded together. The Arabic name or Chinese name in brackets is put together with the Dai name. For example, Ailuan in Dai (Ma Jin'an in Chinese), Aiwen in Dai (Ma Baoren in Chinese), Ai Kanjian in Dai (Ma Zhanyuan in Chinese), and Ma Changshun in Chinese (Isa in Arabic)

Festivals and Ceremonies
Parshi Dai do not celebrate the traditional festivals of Dai people, like the Guanmen Festival (it means 'to send Buddha into the temple', or 'to close the door for abstinence', which lasts for three months), Kaimen Festival (it means 'to send Buddha out of the temple', or 'to open the door for entertainment', the end of Guanmen Festival, lasting for three days) and Dai's New Year Festival. However, if the Dai invite them to celebrate, they will bring their own pan and bowls to cook by themselves.

Discussion

Muslim Identity
Parshi Dai have always regarded Islam as their only religion, and Hui-Muslim culture as the culture passed down by their ancestors. During the past 200 years, they have bee making efforts to preserve their faith and conventions. They have formed a small community in which their philosophy of life and society has been taught and exchanged, which has a great influence on their daily life. Hui-Muslim culture makes it possible for Parshi Dai to build an affinity with other inland Hui people.

When some Parshi Dai narrate the historical stories of their village, I discovered that two versions of the story are repeated and cherished. One is about how Parshi Dai adhere to their own religion, for example, when the ancestor married Dai woman, they would insist that the wife should convert to Islam; during the first stage of the construction of the village, the ancestors would plant two wooden pickets with a curtain as the prayer place; and during the cultural revolution, they resisted against the pressure and did not raise pigs. The other story is about how they showed their braveness and wisdom as Hui people. For instance, the clever ancestors had been appreciated and accepted by the local chieftain and the chief's daughter married him. The ancestors got their own land and were allowed to preserve their own religion. The ancestor Ma Wulong once helped the local chief of the Dai to defeat the enemy's invasion, and he was rewarded by the chief and all the Parshi Dai were exempted from taxation. In the time of Ma Jin'an, Parshi Dai relied on their diligence and wisdom to build a bridge, which is helpful for the local transportation and especially the caravan transport.

Even for the young generation, being Muslim is one of the most basic standards to identify themselves and others. They will consider whether the person has faith in Islam, how faithful the person is, and whether the person is a Muslim. These become one of the most important criteria for them in selecting a spouse.

Double Identities: Both as Muslim and Parshi Dai

Concerning their group identity, Parshi Dai believe that they are not Dai, because they belong to the Hui people in a large sense. In the larger group of the Hui, Parshi Dai think they are special and different from other Hui, which makes them Parshi Dai.

Belonging to Hui, although the Parshi-Dai's region is quite remote, the Parshi Dai feel a link to this larger community. Their relationship is like a network, which connects the whole people, though separated from each other, as a big family sharing common ideology, behavior and customs. As a member of the big family, Parshi Dai and other members share weal and woe. For instance, at the end of the Qing Dynasty, in the eleventh year of Tongzhi (1872 AD), the Yunnan Hui anti-Qing uprising failed, and many Hui people escaped in the border areas. Because they shared the same religion, many Parshi Dai sheltered and hid the fugitives. After the war, these escapees had settled in Parshi Dai villages, and became important members. For a long time, the Muslims in other places continued to support Parshi Dai in material and spiritual development. For instance, in the 1930s, under the leadership of Bai Liangcheng, inland Hui people helped Parshi Dai. In recent years, some Hui in the inland paid more attention to Parshi Dai and provided donations. They helped to find imams for Parshi Dai, and accepted children of Parshi Dai to study, and they employed teachers working in the Parshi-Dai area, and set up kindergartens. Parshi Dai love to say that they are Hui people when they go out or on business, and they like to find a local mosque to lodge, and find local Hui for help.

The sense of belonging to Parshi Dai, from another perspective, gives Parshi Dai a greater living space, since Parshi Dai subconsciously admit the influence of Buddhist practices of Dai people in their daily life. It is also accepted as a potential link between Dai and Parshi Dai people. Relationship between Parshi Dai and the nearby Dai people are more intimate than their relation to Hui people within a scope of 8 kilometers. This is because they live together, sharing habits in the same living environment, dress, language and diet. This relationship is well proved by the intermarriage between Parshi Dai and Dai people. The economic life of Parshi and Dai is closely linked as well.

Theoretical Discussion on the Study of Chinese Muslims

The studies on Muslim identity in China over the past three decades have clearly made a worthwhile contribution to theoretical debates on ethnicity and ethnic identity. Scholars tend to split into two camps, affirming either an assimilationist or a secessionist model. The history of Yunnan in particular offers evidence that both secession and assimilation paradigms have some limitations in their ability to clarify the complexity of the Muslim identity.

On the one hand, the secessionist paradigm, which discusses the compatibility of being Muslim with the 'Chinese Order,' ignores the tremendous contributions that Muslims and their minorities have made to Chinese society. Yunnan was governed by famous Muslim officials, like Sayyid Ajall, while state expeditions were led by Muslim Yunnanese explorers, like Zheng He. On the other hand, the assimilation or sinicization paradigm mistakenly suggests that the Muslim identity was purely religious, and ignores evidence that the Hui were resistant to the Han hegemonic power, even as they changed aspects of their identity in relation to other local groups.

The history of Yunnan is filled with shifting power alliances where Hui united with Hui, and sometimes with the Han Chinese, against a Muslim who was often a rival Hui warlord. For instance, the struggle between the two Hui leaders, Du Wenixie and Ma Rulong during the Panthay Rebellion (see Atwill 1997; 1999; 2003). Likewise, arguments over who are the 'real' or 'better' Muslims have persisted until the present (Caffrey 2004: 257). In Yunnan, the Hui minority and the Han have lived together for many centuries and have durable traditions of their own creation despite the presence of the central authority. Here, locally negotiated identities represent an example of local people having a rich and long term reservoir of relational forms which are found in local history and convention and which can actually serve as alternatives to the excesses of the nation-state.

However, the two main schools of thought on the study of Chinese Muslims have neglected to adequately describe and failed to explain the construction of the Muslim identities as a continuing process and the internal diversity. Moreover, the transnational Muslim movements and new information technology as a channel for the transformation and contestation of Muslim identities in the age of globalization have been ignored by those paradigms. Thus this study attempts to bridge the gaps by emphasizing the transformation of Chinese Muslim identities through various stages, the contestations and negotiations of their multiple identities across time and space as they have experienced in their everyday lives.

Notes

1 This paper is an initial result of research project Research on Religion and Culture about Yunnan Muslims in Northern Thailand (13XZJ012) sponsored by National Social Science Fund of China; 'GaoDi' research project from Migrants to Merchants: Study on Oral History of Yunnan Muslim Caravan in Northern Thailand sponsored by Yunnan University of China.
2 A precious fried food made by flour and brown sugar, which is a special dessert in Chinese Muslims.
3 Since the holy land of Islam is in Mecca, which is located west of China, Chinese Muslims will put the face of the deceased towards the west in order to face the direction of Kaaba.
4 *Menghai County Annals*, Ed, Cai Shunpeng, compiled by Yunnan Menghai Chorography Committee, Yunnan People's Publishing House, 12(1997):102.

References

Cai Shunpeng, ed. (1997) *Menghai County Annals*. Compiled by Yunnan Menghai Chorography Committee, Yunnan People's Publishing House, 12. (云南省勐海县地方志编纂委员会编纂, 蔡鹏顺主编《勐海县志》, 云南人民出版社, 1997 年 12 月版.)

Chen Longwen (1998). 'A Survey about Social and Historical Development of Manluanhui and Mansaihui. Menghai', in *Cultural and Historical Information of Menghai* (Part four). (陈龙文《勐海县曼峦回社会历史发展调查》, 见中国人民政治协商会议勐海县委员会文史资料委员会编, 《勐海文史资料(四)》, 1998 年 1 月版.

Dillon, Michael (1996). 'Muslims in Post-Mao China', *Journal of Muslim Minority Affairs* 16 (1), pp. 41-48.

Dillon, Michael (1999). *China's Muslim Hui Community: Migration, Settlement and Sects*. Richmond, Surrey: Curzon.

Gladney, Dru C. (1991). *Muslim Chinese: Ethnic Nationalism in the People's Republic*. Cambridge, MA: Harvard University Press.

Gladney, Dru C. (1993). 'The Muslim Face of China', *Current History*, 92 (575), pp. 275-280.

Gladney, Dru C. (1998). *Ethnic Identity in China: The Making of a Muslim Minority Nationality*. Orlando, FL: Harcourt Brace College Publishers.

Gladney, Dru C. (2004). *Dislocating China: Muslims, Minorities, and Other Subaltern Subjects*. Chicago: The University of Chicago Press.

Gladney, Dru C. (2008). 'Islam and modernity in China: Secularization or Separatism?', in Mayfair Mei-hui Yang, ed., *Chinese Religiosities: Afflictions of Modernity and State Formation*. Oakland, CA: University of California Press, pp. 179-205.

Israeli, Raphael (2002). *Islam in China: Religion, Ethnicity, Culture, and Politics*. Oxford: Lexington Books.

Lipman, Jonathan N. (1996). 'Hyphenated Chinese: Sino-Muslim Identity in Modern China', in Gail Hershatter, Emily Honing, Jonathan N. Lipman and Randall Stross, eds, *Remapping China: Fissures in Historical Terrain*. Stanford, CA: Stanford University Press, pp. 97-112.

Lipman, Jonathan (1997). *Familiar Strangers: A History of Muslims in Northern China*. Seattle and London: University of Washington Press.

Luo, Yi (1989). *A Physical Survey about Jinuo and Parshi Dai of Yunnan*. Kunming: Yunnan Nation Press.

Ma, Jianxiong (1996). 'A Survey about Parshi Dai of Menghai', *Survey and Research of Ethnology*, 1. (马健雄，《勐海帕西傣调查》，载于云南省民族研究所编《民族学调查研究》, 1996 年第一期.)

Ma, Jianxiong (2001). 'Forming of Community Identity: Taking Parshi Dai as an Example', *Journal of Yunnan University of The Nationalities*, 6. (马健雄《社区认同的塑造: 以勐海' 帕西傣' 社区为例》，载于《云南民族学院学报》 2001 年第 6 期.)

Ma, Weiliang and Li, Jia (1986). 'A Survey of the Parshi Dai of Xishuangbanna', in *A Survey of Society and history of Hui of Yunnan* (Part 3). Kunming, Yunnan People Press. (马维良、李佳《西双版纳傣族自治州' 帕西傣' 调查》，见《云南回族社会历史调查》(三), 云南人民出版社, 1986 年 12 月版.)

Mason, Isaac. (1929). 'The Mohammedans of China: When and how they First Came', *Journal of the North China Branch of the Royal Asiatic Society*, 60, pp. 1-54.

Wang, Jianping (1996). *Concord and Conflict: The Hui Communities of Yunnan Society in a Historical Perspective*. Lund: Studentlitteratur.

Yao, Jide (2002). *Horse Caravan of Hui and Southwest Silk Road: a Case Study of Muslim in the North of Thailand*, PhD Dissertation.(姚继德 博士学位论文《回族马帮与西南丝路网络—泰国北部云南穆斯林的个案研究》 (2002 年 10 月).

Part III:
Hui Identity and Islam

Localizing Transnationalism in Post-Reform China: Sino-Islamic Identities among Hui-Muslim Women in Yunnan[1]

Lesley Turnbull
New York University

"We *Huizu* have a genetic link to the Qur'an, so we are Muslims whether or not we practice the teachings of Islam."
-Mr. Ding, 61, retired Kunming city employee, September 2010[2]

"Ethnicity is irrelevant. What matters is that one believes in Allah and faithfully practices the teachings of Islam."
-Mr. Ma, 58, administrator of the Shadian Great Mosque, May 2011

As the two quotes above illustrate, what constituted Islamic 'authenticity' in Yunnan Province differed ontologically in different localities. During my two years of fieldwork among Hui-Muslims there, my interlocutors in both the provincial capital of Kunming and the rural Muslim enclave of Shadian positioned themselves as uniquely authentic Muslims, but they did so in distinctly different ways. While local Hui-Muslims in both places recognized the shifting, malleable, and processual nature of Hui-Muslim identity, they nevertheless envisioned and utilized essentialist categories to illustrate what constituted authentic and legitimate Hui practices. No matter their residence, my interlocutors relied on hierarchies of authenticity in which certain practices were viewed as inauthentic; however, what constituted authenticity was locally-defined and negotiated. Furthermore, locally-constituted constellations of discourses and practices of authenticity collaboratively reflected and shaped Hui-Muslim notions of trans/national belonging and modernity.

During my fieldwork among Hui in Kunming, I noticed that for most of the educated Hui elite with whom I worked, the state of being a Muslim was divorced from Islamic practice. Most of my interlocutors fervently declared their authenticity as Muslims, though few prayed five times a day and many regularly imbibed alcohol. From my perspective, these Hui seemed quite secularized, despite their protests to the contrary.[3] As the first quote above suggests, these urbanized, educated Hui elite positioned themselves as Muslims who were uniquely absolved from the duty to practice the teachings of Islam. Many of these Hui appropriated biological rhetoric as a means to create their own 'authentic' Muslim ethnic identity, one that simultaneously linked them to both an imagined Arab past and an imagined modernity.[4] In these imaginings, the scientific glory and advancement of their Arab past merged with China's current ascendancy in global capitalism to shape the ways in which they imagined their present identity as modern Muslim subjects of the Chinese nation-state. This identity as Muslims was predicated less on Islamic practice than on a mythologized genealogy that situates urban Hui at the center of the Muslim world.[5] In Kunming, urbanized Hui elite relied on localized practices of interpreting lineages, genealogies, and oral stories of descent transmitted through generations, along with scientistic notions of *minzu* 民族 (nationality), and cosmopolitan consumerist practices to construct a Hui-Muslim identity that prioritized ethnicity.

In contrast, my Hui interlocutors in the rural Muslim enclave of Shadian repeatedly emphasized Islamic practice as key to authenticity, asserting that ethnicity is irrelevant. Whenever I asked a question about *Huizu* 回族 (Hui nationality) in Shadian, I was promptly, and gently, chided: one's *minzu* (nationality) is of no importance; all that matters is whether or not one is a Muslim. In Shadian, even the language that Hui-Muslims used to describe themselves differed from Kunming Hui usage: whereas Kunming Hui largely appropriated the state-designated nationality category, *Huizu*, Hui-Muslims in Shadian preferred to describe themselves not as *Huizu* (Hui nationality) but as *Musilin* 穆斯林 (Muslim) or *Zhongguo Musilin* 中国穆斯林 (Chinese Muslim). Furthermore, Hui-Muslims in Shadian argued that true Islamic faith erodes in the secular city and that in order to preserve authentic forms of Islam, 'real' Muslims fled the city and its secularizing, Hanifying influences for religious enclaves such as Shadian.

Throughout this article, I refer to an urban—rural dichotomy as a means to unpack how place influenced different localized notions of belonging.[6] Although my interlocutors often reified this dichotomy, in actuality, the imagined urban—

rural dichotomy is neither static nor clearly-defined. What is perceived as 'urban' or 'rural' may shift depending on the residence of the viewer: for instance, a Miao peasant from the village outside of Shadian may view Gejiu as a city (indeed officially it is one), whereas a longterm urbanite in Kunming would view Gejiu as a *nongcun* 农村 (a rural area). However, for most Chinese people today, this urban—rural dichotomy is one of the most salient ways of organizing their world: it may not be absolutely fixed, and the values allocated to 'urban' or 'rural' certainly shift depending upon context, but this dichotomy shapes both how they imagine the world and how they live in it.

For the purposes of this article, it is crucial to recognize that even though the rural—urban dichotomy is not static, Muslim lives in urban Kunming were quite different from lives in rural Muslim enclaves like Shadian.[7] The urbanized elite Hui-Muslims with whom I worked in Kunming had to negotiate the dominant capitalist modes of living there, which included work hours that did not accommodate prayer times, along with the lack of a spatially connected Muslim district, inconvenient distance from mosques, CCP religious restrictions, and other impediments to living a devout Muslim life. Some urban elite Hui negotiated this liminality by 'passing' as Han in certain settings, even as their Hui-Muslim identity was deeply felt. Despite their ambivalence, urban Hui accommodated, negotiated, and contested locally-dominant modes of living in ways that enabled them to assert their own claims to Islamic authenticity. In comparison, state agents and capitalist modes of production exerted less authority in Shadian, where Muslims were able to remake their religious authenticity after the turbulence of the Cultural Revolution.

Ethno-Religious Identity and Trans/National Belonging

Huizu 回族 is arguably the most ambiguous category of the ten Muslim *shaoshu minzu* 少数民族 (minority-nationalities) in China: although the Hui officially comprise a *minzu* 民族 (nationality), the Huizu category noticeably lacks the defined, unifying traits by which minzu were differentiated in accordance with the Stalinist model of nationality, that is, "common language, common territory, common economy, and common psychological nature manifested in a common culture" (Fei 1978; Lin 1986; Harrell 1995; Gladney 1996; Lipman 1997; Litzinger 2000; Allès 2000). While many of China's 56 official shaoshu minzu groups lack such a unified definition (see Harrell 1995, 2001; Pan 1997, 2010; Litzinger 2000;

Schein 2000; Tapp 2003), and certainly, as many scholars have argued, the *minzu shibie* 民族识别 (ethnic identification campaign) of the 1950s drew on imperial and Republican Chinese ethnic classification schemes in addition to the Stalinist model (Fei 1989; Mullaney 2004, 2011; Fiskesjö 2006; Yang 2008), the Hui category is especially problematic (Gladney 1996, 1998; Harrell 1995:33; Lipman 1997). Hui are scattered throughout China, claim descent from multiple ethnic groups, and while most speak some variant of Chinese, others speak Tibetan or other minority languages (Gladney 1996:32-34; Hillman 2004; Bai 2008) and some speak Chinese dialects that incorporate transliterated Persian and Arabic words (Wang 1996, 2001).[8] Some scholars assert that belief in Islam ultimately defines the Hui (Bai 1994; Israeli 2002), yet as Dru Gladney (1996, 1998) attests, there are those who identify as Hui but who neither believe in nor practice any form of Islam, such as the Ding lineage of Fujian, who petitioned the Chinese state for classification as Hui based on their Arab and Persian ancestry. Gladney (1996, 1998) posits a spectrum of Hui identities ranging from those, mostly located in Northwest China, who identify as Hui primarily on religious grounds, to those like the Ding lineage, whose identity is based on other characteristics, including descent from foreign Muslims, cultural practices (including abstaining from pork and endogamy) and a sense of a shared history.

While the state-propagated minzu classification scheme strives for scientific objectivity, it paradoxically enables multiple, conflicting practices and discourses to exist within a single minzu category. Hence, we see the spectrum of locally-produced Hui ethnic identities that Gladney (1996, 1998) describes and the processual, context-specific minzu that Louisa Schein (2000), Nicholas Tapp (2002), Kevin Caffrey (2004), and others articulate. With this in mind, I aim to emphasize that although the minzu shibie campaign and its subsequent nationality-focused state policies profoundly shaped the ethnic consciousness of China's peoples, Han and minority alike (see esp. Gladney 1996), the process of engendering minzu identities was far more complex than simply imposing state-designated categories onto on-the-ground social realities (Hansen 1999; Schein 2000; Litzinger 2000; Tapp 2002; Caffrey 2004; Fan 2012). As Tapp (2002) argues, we must unravel the variety and diversity of authenticity by investigating locally-produced constructions, particularly at the 'sub-ethnic level,' even when they are essentialist. In the case of Hui-Muslims in Yunnan, 'sub-ethnic' notions of transnational belonging — to the Umma and to an imagined cosmopolitianism more generally — added yet another layer to the localized production of their identities. Local production of Hui-Muslim identities was thus collaboratively influenced by national identification projects and notions of national belonging, notions of belonging to a specific minzu, and differentially formed notions of transnational belonging.

Below, I will provide a glimpse of these divergent configurations of Hui-Muslim practices and discourses by imagining a day in the lives of two ideal-typical Hui-Muslim women, one living in Kunming, one in Shadian. For the purposes of this article, I will focus primarily on how life is temporally and spatially structured, both in everyday practice and in imaginings of one's place in history, modernity, the Muslim world, and the Chinese state. By setting out details of the daily lives of these two women, I aim to elucidate how temporal and spatial structures of life, which are tied to urban or rural location, reflect and shape local identity formation. The two composites below are directly based on my field notes, although I have merged multiple days, conversations and interlocutors. During the 'day in a life' sections, I use the ethnographic present in order to make the fictive aspects more visible, and to mark shifts from analytical passages.

Muslims in China are perceived as (at least) dually peripheral: as a group, they are peripheral both to the imagined center of the Islamic world and to mainstream Chinese cultural and political spheres. Yunnan's distance from China's urban and state centers — imagined and real, cultural, historical, economic, geographical, political — produces yet another layer of peripherality for Hui-Muslims there. Scholarly papers, local gazetteers, and popular Chinese discourses have long characterized Yunnan as remote (*pianpi* 偏僻) and peripheral (Skinner 1977; Giersch 2006; Tapp 2010); this was reinforced during the Qing, when Yunnan allegedly was plagued by a contagious miasma (*zhangqi* 瘴气) that afflicted Han government officials with malaria (Bello 2005; Zhang 2005). Even today, Yunnan is oriented not only toward Beijing but also toward Southeast Asia (Evans 2000; Michaud 2007; Scott 2009),[9] and Yunnan's reputation as a pleasant hub for tourists stems largely from being imagined as an exotic paradise far from China's metropolitan centers (Xu 2001; Hyde 2001; Davis 2005; Ateljevic and Swain 2006; Zhang 2010).

Kunming City: 'Catching Up' with 'Cosmopolitan Modernity'

Although Kunming may not be considered a major metropolitan center on par with Beijing, Shanghai, or Hong Kong, in the past decade the city has transformed from a far-flung provincial backwater into a shiny modern metropolis, complete with steel-and-glass skyscrapers, high-rise condominiums, luxurious gated communities, an IMAX cinema, three Starbucks coffee houses, and even a Marc Jacobs retailer. In 2012, city officials unveiled a new subway system and launched a new international airport, reportedly the fourth largest in China. In the wake of China's economic reforms, the real estate market is 'booming', private enterprise is flourishing, and officials and some residents, responding to a sense that the city is 'lagging behind', have encouraged massive development projects in an effort to 'modernize' the city (Zhang 2010, 2006).

While many Kunming residents expressed optimism about the 'progress' symbolized by these projects, even residents who welcomed these recent changes mourned the loss of a cherished cityscape. For Yunnanese Hui, especially those who lived in Kunming's Shuncheng Jie Muslim District, this loss is particularly poignant: in 2004, after prolonged protests and negotiations with the local Wuhua District government and the Sailun Real Estate Corporation, the historic Hui neighborhood was demolished, displacing thousands of Hui residents (Zhang 2010:153-156; Zhu 2005). While some residents and remnants of Shuncheng Jie's Muslim past remain, the site has been supplanted by a sprawling, shimmering temple to capitalist consumerism: an upscale shopping mall.

A Day in the Life of Mrs. Na of Kunming

Mrs. Na, 58, is a retired schoolteacher and homemaker who has long resided in Kunming. She wakes around 8 a.m. and prepares a breakfast of spicy *mixian* 米线 (rice noodles) for herself and her husband before he leaves for work. Everyday lives in Kunming are structured by the work patterns of capitalist production, and as such they generally do not accommodate scheduled prayer times, but rather conform to dominant Chinese temporalities with regards to sleeping, eating, and other aspects of daily life. After breakfast, Mrs. Na dons a pair of brown trousers and a long-sleeved aubergine blouse. She walks ten minutes through her luxuriously landscaped *xiaoqu* 小区 (residential community) to the bus stop where she takes a bus fifteen minutes to the nearest well-stocked *qingzhen* 清真 (halal) market. She can buy a few items closer to home, but ever since she and her husband moved out of the city center she has had to commute at least fifteen minutes by bus to buy quality *qingzhen* meat. It's even farther to the nearest *qingzhen* bakery.

Back at home, Mrs. Na phones her youngest brother in Ohio to update him on their parents' health problems. Her brother settled in the U.S. after attending a university there, and, like many urban Hui in Kunming, Mrs. Na values

Western-style education, believing that Chinese-style education inhibits creative thinking. She had hoped that her daughter Lingling would go abroad to the U.S., U.K., or Australia for university, but, even though Lingling's TOEFL and IELTS scores were high, she stayed in Kunming and attended Yunnan University. After Mrs. Na and her brother hang up, she begins preparing lunch and then watches a Qing dynasty soap opera. Kunming Hui consumption patterns are a bricolage of Chinese soap operas, Western-style university educations and Hui *qingzhen* foodstuffs; through these practices, they imagined themselves as an exceptionally modern minzu, a people with the illustrious heritage of an Arab past, and the cosmopolitan discernment to appropriate what is useful from the West and from present-day China.

When her husband comes home shortly after noon, Mrs. Na quickly prepares a lunch of *chaocai* 炒菜 (stir-fried dishes) and sits down to share it with him. They discuss the upcoming Mid-Autumn Festival holiday. "It's not really our holiday, we should be celebrating Hui holidays. Why don't you ever get those off?" she complains. "You know why. We Huizu technically have those days off, but if I miss work then, all my Han colleagues will notice and create problems for me. It's much easier this way. We can still spend time together as a family on the Han holidays, even if they're not really ours."

After lunch, Mrs. Na phones some friends to arrange to play *majiang* 麻将 the day after tomorrow. Two of these friends are Hui women who were neighbors when she and her husband lived in the Muslim District in the city center. After the Muslim District was demolished in 2004, most of its residents were dispersed throughout the city. Among other things, this has made it more difficult to buy *qingzhen* products and to arrange social gatherings with other Hui.

Mrs. Na's bookcase is stocked with books on Hui history and culture, along with genealogies, lineages, and biographies of famous Hui personages. Her sister recently sent her a new compilation of biographies of notable Hui from their home county in rural Yunnan. The biographies go back as far as the Yuan Dynasty, and Mrs. Na eagerly reads them to glean further insight into her own lineage and heritage. In their close readings of genealogies, biographies, and histories, Kunming Hui imagined a linear ancestral past structured by generations; spatially, this links them at once with the Arab world of their imagined past and with the intimate geography of their home counties. And yet, these genealogical links are quite speculative: in some cases, elite urban Hui claimed Arab or Persian rather than Central Asian descent, even though official historical documents indicate Central Asian descent for most Yunnanese Muslims. In a majority of cases, urban

Hui relied on patrilineal descent to claim their authenticity as Muslims, despite the fact that nearly all Yunnanese Hui patrilines were obliterated during the 1873 massacres that followed the Qing suppression of the Panthay Rebellion.

After reading for a while, Mrs. Na begins to prepare dinner. Her daughter Lingling is coming over, so she will make her favorite dish: *hongshao niurou* 红烧牛肉 (red-braised beef). Once both her husband and daughter have arrived, they all sit down to dinner together, complete with thimbles of *qingkejiu* 青稞酒 (barley wine). After several years as a businesswoman at a well-regarded local company in Kunming, Lingling has recently transferred to an international startup where she hopes her years of studying English can be put to good use. The family discusses how her job is progressing, and her mother guarantees Lingling's success. "We Huizu have a long history as successful business people and traders. It's in our genes." After dinner, the family watches various game shows on TV until the parents go to bed, and Lingling returns to her apartment.

Localizing Identity Formation in Kunming

Although Hui-Muslims in Shadian often bemoaned the 'corruptive' process of 'Hanification' (*Hanhua* 汉化) that occurred in Kunming, the process of identity formation for Kunming Hui was much more complex than mere assimilation. Kunming Hui argued that although they remained Muslims, the turbulence of the past fifty years had contributed to the gradual erosion of their religious beliefs. Religious suppression during the Cultural Revolution, assignments to *danwei* 单位 (work units) in which Han were the majority, practical conformities to dominant temporal structures in order to ease work relations, the demolition of the Kunming Muslim District and subsequent dispersal of its residents — these events all recognizably contributed to shifts in Kunming Hui identity formation, but not only by diluting this identity. According to Kunming Hui, the erosion of their religious beliefs and their lack of opportunities to practice Islam engendered within them a sense of ambivalence about their identity as Hui-Muslims that eventually sparked in them a desire to cultivate a sense of 'Huiness' that distinguished them from the Han majority.

Although some Hui in Kunming consumed alcohol and even married Han people, shared practices such as normative endogamy, pork abstinence, readings of lineages, and storytelling provided them with the means to distinguish themselves from the Han. As Mrs. Su, a fifty-three-year-old middle school teacher recounted in Kunming in October 2010:

When I was a young girl, I used to pray at the mosque with my mother. But then, during *Wenge* 文革 (the Cultural Revolution), such things were no longer allowed. At home my mother told me stories of our ancestors and still tried to get me to *nianjing* 念经 (recite the Qur'an), but the words meant nothing to me. They were just empty syllables, meaningless, and besides, that stuff just didn't interest me. Later, I was accepted to Yunnan Normal University and went to study in Kunming. I became a Chinese language teacher at a middle school there... Back then, no one wore the hijab. It was the 80s, we just didn't wear it. I didn't pray either, and I began to think that the only thing that really separated me from my Han colleagues was that I didn't eat pork... My mother always told me stories about our ancestors so eventually I became interested in studying *Huizu* history, culture and genealogy.

Through their own local practices, influenced by specific temporal and spatial modes, Kunming Hui constructed their own version of an authentic Hui-Muslim identity predicated not on Islamic religious practice but rather on practices of reading a genealogy that, due to mythologized descent from Arab traders and/or the Prophet, situated them at the center of the Muslim world. These genealogies were read as marking particular patrilineal descendants as authentic Muslims, whether or not the descendants in question practiced Islam. In the words of one self-proclaimed *sayyid*, "Why should I pray five times a day, or abstain from alcohol? I am the [patrilineal] descendant of *Sai Dianchi* 赛典赤 (Sayyid 'Ajall Shams Al-Din).[10] I have a genetic relationship with the *Qur'an* (*wo gen gulanjing you jiyin de guanxi* 我跟古兰经有基因的关系); there is no need [to practice Islam]."

Most Hui in Kunming proffered more than their word as descendants of sayyids or other notable Muslims, a category that could include Arab traders, imams, or religious scholars:[11] when I further probed my interlocutors about the authenticity of their Islamic pasts, they 'proved' to me the truth of their patrilineal descent by showing me genealogies, lineages, and biographies, at times handwritten but more often printed and bound, that traced their lineages back to unquestionably authentic ancestors. In practice, my interlocutors often moved between different texts to demonstrate who their notable ancestor was: that is, they might use multiple lineages and local genealogies to trace their ancestry back to a specific person, and then investigate that person's life by way of local compendiums of biographies of notable personages. In this way, they used oral histories, lineages, and biographies to triangulate the validity of their claims.

Interestingly, my interlocutors figured their descent patrilineally, despite the well-known historical fact (at least among most educated Hui) that, after Du Wenxiu's defeat in 1873,[12] Qing Imperial forces massacred up to 90 percent of the Yunnanese Hui population, of which the remaining survivors were primarily young women (Armijo 2001; Yang 1994). Statistically, at least some of these cases of 'patrilineal' descent must be at least partially matrilineal. A Kunming Hui-Muslim woman of the Ding lineage acknowledged that "at least some" of the many Yunnanese Hui-Muslims who claim patrilineal descent from Sai Dianchi must be re-figuring that descent matrilineally, or through a combination of patrilineal and matrilineal descent. However, in her own case, she assured me that her patrilineal descent was indeed authentic: she traced her descent back to the Ding lineage in Fujian, and showed me documents that "proved" that her patrilineal male ancestor and his "younger brother" left Fujian for Nanjing during the Ming Dynasty. She told me that the elder brother "remained Huizu" while "the younger brother became Hanzu."[13] Her ancestors slowly migrated westward and only settled in Yunnan after the massacres of 1873.

Whether or not such reckonings of genealogical relationships and descent are true historically, they nevertheless shaped the ways in which my interlocutors articulated and practiced their ethnic identity in present-day Kunming. In discussing the Ding lineage of Fujian, Dru Gladney (1996) notes that, "The importance of [the Ding] genealogy is not its authenticity, but its acceptance by the current members of the Ding clan in validating their descent from foreign Muslim ancestors" (377 n. 22). Indeed, we should read genealogies of Hui-Muslims in Kunming similarly.

To an extent, authentic identity for Kunming Hui precluded religious practice: because a solid ethnic pedigree could absolve one of the religious obligation to practice Islam, a known Hui-Muslim who did not pray five times a day could be, among certain elite urban Hui, viewed as more ethnically authentic than one who had to prove his Huiness. While this was most commonly explained casually, as in, "Of course he doesn't pray regularly; he's a descendant of the Prophet", a conversation with a mixed group of Hui and Han men that I observed and participated in during my first forays into fieldwork especially illuminates how Hui-Muslims in Kunming employed this sense of primordial ethnicity in order to define their Muslim (and hence, religious) authenticity. After I outlined my intended research on Yunnanese Hui to a group of officials, a Han man piped up:

Hui in Yunnan aren't interesting; here the only thing that separates them from the Han is that they don't eat pork. They don't sing or dance like the other *shaoshu minzu* (minority nationalities), so what's the point in studying them? You should either choose a different *minzu* to study or go to Ningxia [Hui Autonomous Prefecture] to study real Hui who actually pray.

Clearly offended, a Hui man interjected:

No, she should study Hui here. We're as interesting as any other *shaoshu minzu* in Yunnan, even if we don't sing or dance... Ningxia Hui are just backwards (*luohou* 落后) and impoverished (*pinkun* 贫困) converts to Islam. Of course they have to pray: they're not real Hui; they are just the descendants of Han who converted, and they lack any Arab or Persian ancestry. If they were descendants of Arabs, do you think they would be so poor? No, they lack the gene for commerce, ha... Besides, those Ningxia Hui are uncivilized (*bu wenming* 不文明) and of low quality (*suzhi hen di* 素质很低)...They just ask Allah to help them, and they never help themselves... Here in Kunming, we Hui are advanced and modern, due to our Arab and Persian ancestry. We are the authentic Huizu.

In this re-positioning of Hui-Muslim authenticity, Kunming Hui disparaged prayer and the practice of 'religious converts,' instead articulating a uniquely Muslim modernity in which their own lack of prayer at once signified their authenticity as 'true' descendants of 'real' Muslims, and as vanguards of modernity, commerce, and science, further symbolized in their use of genetic 'science' to assert their claims of authenticity. Here, Kunming Hui's hierarchical situating of themselves vis-à-vis other, less authentic, religious Hui, and other non-Muslim Chinese, resonates with how Stacy Pigg (1996) untangles the ways in which the absence of traditional belief can become a marker of a modern identity: through voicing a lack of belief in shamanistic practices, 'cosmopolitan villagers' in Nepal hierarchically positioned themselves as 'modern,' 'scientific,' and 'advanced' in relationship to other, shaman-believing villagers.

Moreover, whereas encounters between Shadian's Muslims and other Muslims heightened their consciousness of being members of the Umma, Kunming Hui rarely encountered foreign Muslims. Instead, encounters with other Hui or with Han often, though not always, enhanced the ethnic consciousness of Kunming Hui rather than their sense of religious community. In this sense, the cosmopolitanism of urban elite Hui-Muslims was largely imagined.[14] Furthermore, in Kunming, Hui-Muslims relied on an imagined past of Islamic advancement and modernity to position themselves *within* China's modernization narrative. Thus imagined, Kunming Hui were dually modern, advancing ahead of the Han, who lacked claims to a glorious Islamic past, and ahead of non-Chinese Muslims, who lacked claims to China's ascendancy in global capitalism.

Shadian: Preserving the 'Tradition of Islamic Modernity'

Not far from the Vietnam border, Shadian *qu* 区 (administrative district) is a cluster of hamlets under the administration of Gejiu City, Honghe Hani and Yi Autonomous Prefecture, in a region populated mostly by ethnic minority groups. My interlocutors there reported that approximately 95 percent of Shadian's population were Hui; the rest were mostly Hani, Yi, Miao, or other minority groups, and a fraction were Han majority *nongmingong* 农民工 (peasant or migrant workers), most of whom resided in nearby Jijie township. As Gladney (1996) reports, Shadian was a "flourishing Muslim community...as early as the Ming dynasty...[and] became a center for Islamic learning throughout Southeast Asia and Southwest China, producing the first Chinese translation of the Qur'an" (137). My interlocutors relied on interpretations of Shadian's past glory to position it as a unique site in China, one that, in the words of a teacher at one of the local *madrasahs*, "preserved the tradition of Islamic modernity."

Before I visited Shadian, Hui interlocutors in Kunming insisted that spending time in Shadian was 'crucial' for my research, and yet, at the same time, that it was too 'dangerous' for me to go. Some claimed it sheltered 'religious zealots' and even 'wahhabi terrorists.' Rumors circulated that a 'fortress' or wall encircled the township, built by the villagers themselves after the notorious Shadian Incident, in which, after a series of 'uprisings' during the Cultural Revolution, the PLA allegedly launched heavy cannons, artillery and even used MIG jets to fire rockets in attempt to quell 'resistance', killing over 1,000 Hui villagers and razing the village.[15]

Hopping off the bus on the highway outside of Jijie, I caught a lift into Shadian with friendly newlyweds, and was astonished when we saw no walls nor met any resistance; rather, we glided into town via welcoming boulevards marked with signs in Chinese, Arabic, and English. From the bus, I had glimpsed the glinting domes of eleven mosques. Countless other buildings flaunted Arab-style architecture, including, I would later learn, the building that housed the local governmental administration. Palm trees dotted the landscape and gated mansions evoking oil baron owners flanked the town.[16] At the junction of the broad boulevards sat the Great Mosque, the largest mosque in China, funded mainly through private donations and constructed in a grand, Arabized style.

A Day in the Life of Mrs. Yang of Shadian

Mrs. Yang, 51, is a homemaker and native of Shadian. By the time the familiar sound of roosting hens filters through the pre-dawn calls to prayer, Mrs. Yang has already performed her morning ablutions. While her husband scurries down the street to the nearest mosque, she quietly slips into an alcove reserved for women's prayers in the home. In contrast to Kunming's dominant temporal mode of capitalist production, everyday lives in Shadian are structured by Islamic religious practices; prayer times, religious obligations, and opportunities such as *Qur'an* classes largely determine the timing of sleep, meals, and community events. After prayers, Mrs. Yang prepares a breakfast of spicy *mixian* 米线 (rice noodles) for herself and her husband before he leaves for work. She dons a navy *changpao* 长袍 (*abaya*) with black trousers underneath and covers her hair with a black, rhinestone-encrusted hijab. She walks down the street to one of Shadian's eleven mosques in order to attend a morning class on the meaning of the *Qur'an*.

After class, Mrs. Yang heads down the street to the market. In Shadian, practically all foodstuffs and restaurants are *qingzhen;* the few restaurants that aren't are clearly marked *Hanzu Fandian* 汉族饭店 (Han restaurant). Back at home, she begins preparing lunch and then flips through a range of television stations that she receives because of her satellite dish: Lebanon TV, Syria TV, Jordan TV and of course the CCTV Arabic channel. Although she only speaks Chinese, Mrs. Yang enjoys watching television series and news programs from the rest of the Muslim world, and feels that it connects her more to other Muslims' lives and experiences. When her husband comes home shortly after the noon prayers, she quickly prepares a lunch of chaocai and sits down to share it with him.

After lunch, she e-mails her son, who is in Syria studying to become an Islamic scholar.[17] In the afternoon, several of her friends stop by for tea and light snacks: dates, apricots and pastries imported from Turkey. Her friends are all Hui-Muslim women in their 40s and 50s who live in Shadian, but many of them were born in other parts of Yunnan or even parts of China as distant as Lanzhou and Jinan. They moved to Shadian for the 'strong Islamic atmosphere' (*nonghou de yisilan fengqi* 浓厚的伊斯兰风气). As one of their daughters exclaims, "If you walk around Shadian, you feel like you're not in China but instead in some advanced, modern city in the Middle East or maybe Pakistan or Malaysia. We even have palm trees!" The older women remark that Shadian is granted much more religious freedom than many other places in China, and that the "strong Islamic atmosphere" ensures, for example, that employers will provide Muslim workers with prayer halls and time off to pray during working hours.

The women chat about local affairs. Recently, a woman from Sichuan who studied for several years at one of Shadian's many *madrasahs* returned to live in Shadian with her four children. After leaving Shadian, she had become a Chinese-Arabic translator in Guangzhou and eventually married an Iraqi man. They moved to Jordan where they lived for over a decade, but when he died unexpectedly, she moved her family to Shadian, where she could count on community support. One woman from Lanzhou comments, "You know, more and more *Zhongguo Musilin* (Chinese Muslims) are marrying foreign Muslims. I heard that Lao Li's daughter met a Pakistani man on the internet and they plan to marry soon. And when Ma Laoshi returned from his studies abroad, he brought back a wife from Iran." "Well, and why not? Sharing the Islamic faith is the most important criterion for a marriage partner; one's country of origin or ethnic background should not matter. We are all Muslims." "Yes, but how can these foreign Muslims communicate with their Chinese in-laws? And the customs of these other places are quite different. We Chinese Muslim women have a much higher status than women in other parts of the Muslim world. How can we be sure that these foreign Muslims will respect that?" When the afternoon calls-to-prayer reverberate throughout the hamlet, Mrs. Yang accompanies her guests to pray at the nearest mosque.

Mrs. Yang's bookcase is stocked with books on Islam, Arabic language, and Middle Eastern culture and history. Many of them are Chinese translations of foreign books and some were printed abroad. Mrs. Yang selects a text on Islamic faith and settles into her armchair to read. Whereas Kunming Hui read Hui histories and genealogies that are primarily oriented toward a localized past, Hui-Muslims in Shadian read about Islam and the rest of the Muslim world. By consuming international Islamic literature and media, Shadian Muslims imagine a religious past, present, and future that temporally and spatially incorporates the Umma as an entirety and marks them as members of that Umma. After reading awhile, Mrs. Yang begins to prepare dinner, taking time to pray again around sunset. Once her husband is home, they have dinner together and decide to go watch the inter-mosque youth basketball tournament before evening prayers.

Afterwards, Mrs. Yang and her husband watch a subtitled Turkish TV series followed by a CCTV Arabic news program before they head to bed.

Localizing Identity Formation in Shadian

In contrast to Muslims in Kunming, Muslims in Shadian emphasized their attachment to the Umma through their consumption of, for example, Turkish soap operas, Malaysian Islamic educations, and Jordanian *halal* foodstuffs; through these practices, they, too, imagined themselves as uniquely modern. Although Shadian may appear more isolated than Kunming, Muslims in Shadian have experienced on average far more actual cosmopolitan encounters than have their counterparts in Kunming: through study abroad, *hajj*, meetings with foreign Muslims who visit Shadian, and even through marriages with Muslims from abroad, in addition to imagined encounters through books, TV and other media.

Unlike in Kunming, for most in Shadian, practices of authentic Islam constituted not an advance toward a modern, cosmopolitan, future stage of development but rather a *return* to authenticity and, at the same time, a return to a previously-dominant Islamic modernity.[18] Most evidently, this process of returning to authenticity was embodied in the Arabization of Shadian's architectural styles, foodstuffs, media consumption, and clothing. Additionally, Shadian Hui-Muslims often imagined Islamic modernity as the singular, global modernity that sparked other, lesser (secular) modernities (cf. Dirlik 2003), and, in doing so they positioned the Chinese state as hampering, not spurring, their modernity. Like their counterparts in Xi'an (Gillette 2000), Hui in Shadian resisted the CCP evolutionary scale of modernization while also producing their own model of modernization.

However, unlike those in Xi'an, Shadian Hui conceptualized the early PRC era (1949-1966) and especially the Cultural Revolution (1966-76) as inducing an objectionable, forced break with an authentic, localized Islamic past. Their opposition to CCP religious policies materialized in the Shadian Incident, which in addition to being a traumatic lived and memorialized experience for Shadian Hui-Muslims, also bestowed upon them a level of Islamic righteousness and authenticity that others in China, who did not resist the CCP, could not claim. Shadian Hui asserted that their own lived 'backwardness' in past decades was due to China's various modernization projects, and that when they have been able to pursue authentic lives of Islamic faith, they have been more modern than non-Muslims. In the words of one of my interlocutors there, "Capitalist and socialist systems alike deny the deep significance of faith; there is more to life than working, eating rice, drinking tea, buying things. That is actually a feudal (*fengjian* 封建) way of living. In order to live a modern (*xiandai* 现代) life, one must have faith in Allah, and practice the teachings of Islam."

In addition, whereas Gillette (2000) argues that increased contact with the Middle East since the 1980s partially accounts for Arabization in Xi'an, Hui-Muslims in Shadian repeatedly insisted that such increased contact — through the *hajj*, through media consumption, and through cosmopolitan encounters with foreign Muslim guests — had very little impact there. Instead, Shadian Hui-Muslims contended that Shadian's Arabization originated in improved local access to Chinese language copies of the *Qur'an*, beginning in 1981. Through exposure to the translated version of the *Qur'an*, Shadian Muslims gained insight into the 'true' meanings of Islam, and, accordingly, were able to practice Islam more authentically. In this narrative, Arabization arose naturally from authentic, orthodox Islamic practice, so that the Arabized architecture and consumption practices of Hui-Muslims in Shadian linked them to other authentic Muslims not hierarchically but horizontally. Thus the Arabization of Shadian simultaneously subverted the CCP monopoly on modernity while creating a space for a de-centered Islamic authenticity in which Shadian Muslims were no longer imagined as peripheral to Islam. Whether or not the stylistic details of Islamic practices emerged organically from reading translated copies of the *Qur'an*, the Arabization of Shadian's public spaces and architectural styles, along with consumption practices and cosmopolitan encounters, connected Shadian's Muslims in practice and in imagination both to other Muslims in China and to Muslims throughout the world while also influencing local identity formation, which above all emphasized authentic Islamic religious practice.

To be sure, Hui-Muslims in Shadian have appropriated Chinese cultural traditions and practices; however, they do so in a way that at once syncretizes and juxtaposes Chinese cultural practices with locally-defined notions of Islamic authenticity (Allès 2000). Linguistically, for instance, they incorporated transliterated Arabic and Persian terms into their Chinese dialect and gave their children both Arabic names and Islamo-centric Chinese ones. On Eid-ul-Fitr, they breakfasted upon *tangyuan* 汤圆, glutinous rice dumplings traditionally consumed during the Han Lantern Festival. For Hui-Muslims in Shadian, these diverse practices underscored not the appropriation of Chinese customs but rather the central importance of Islamic religious practice in all aspects of life. That is, Hui-Muslims in Shadian reinforced the significance of Islamic religious practices through the syncretization and juxtaposition of Chinese cultural traditions with Islamic ones.

From their perspective, authenticity in Islamic practice radiates out from an idealized Saudi Arabian center, with officially Islamic nations considered more authentic than secularist China, though Muslims in Shadian argued that their local authenticity in China is just as valid as that of officially Islamic nations. After all, Muslims there have endeavored to make Shadian as authentic as possible: the sale and consumption of alcohol, for instance, is banned within the Shadian administrative region.[19] And, as some of my interlocutors there told me, Shadian is in some ways a more authentic expression of Islam: according to many people there, women in Shadian have a much higher status than women in other parts of the Muslim world, and this is in accord with what the Prophet intended for all Muslims. Relying on *Hadith* that proclaim the importance of education for and the high status of women, on Islamic histories that document women's high status, and on CCP ideology and legislation that advocate equality of women, my Hui-Muslim interlocutors positioned themselves as unique practitioners of an enlightened Islamic authenticity.[20] Together these local discourses and practices combined to create a community of individuals who emphasized authentic Islamic practice, rather than ethnicity, as the central facet of their identities.

Conclusion

Although throughout this article, I have focused on the local practices among Hui-Muslims at two different sites in Yunnan Province, my intent was to deepen our understanding of the variety and diversity of 'authenticity', and the complex processes of identity formation: even within a single province, among a single official *minzu* that P.R.C. propaganda, media, and scholarship often construct as a unified, static group, localized practices and processes of identity formation are remarkably diverse. What constituted authentic Hui-Muslim identity depended to a great extent upon the residence of the interlocutor. This ambiguity in what constituted authenticity for Hui-Muslims in Yunnan destabilizes typical Han assumptions that all Hui possess a deep ethnic consciousness that unites them no matter what.[21] Even for those Hui who advocated a primordial ethnic Huiness, there is a sense not only of difference but also of hierarchical order in that, "Those Hui over there are different from us and they are less authentic or legitimate."

This ambiguity, flexibility, and diversity in processes of identity formation extends to other places within China and beyond. This article seeks to open a conversation onto such concerns, and one of my aims here is to begin to destabilize both 'Islam' and 'China' as totalizing, monolithic forces that, whether through orthodox religious authority or through governmental disciplinary techniques, impose identities and practices on the (perceived) cultural automatons who live in those worlds. Rather, I sought here to illustrate how, as actors involved in their own self production, Hui-Muslims in Kunming and Shadian negotiated, appropriated and contested both monolithic notions of Islam, and the official state-propagated *minzu* classificatory system.

Finally, another one my aims for this article was to begin to investigate how the processes of transnationalism and the yearnings and imaginaries that accompany it shaped locally-produced constructions of identity and authenticity. Even though Hui-Muslims in Yunnan often imagined 'genetic' or 'religious' authenticity as radiating from a Saudi Arabian center, in practice what constituted authenticity for these Hui-Muslims was constructed through locally lived experience and practice. In other words, although transnationalism was an important factor, ultimately these were locally-produced versions of 'authenticity', dictated neither by some distant imam nor by some Beijing bureaucrat, but rather constructed in tandem with local processes of self and community (re)production, and shaped by local spatio-temporal practices.

Notes

1   Acknowledgments: I presented a version of this paper at the workshop on 'Islam of the Everyday: Focus on Islam in China' held at Cornell University in April, 2012. I thank Matthew Erie for organizing the workshop, as well as all of the participants for their helpful comments, particularly Jeanette Jouili, whose thought-provoking questions have helped me re-shape this draft. I also thank Miishen Carpentier, Amanda Flaim, Inga Gruß, Edmund Oh, Yang Wang, and Yuanchong Wang for providing substantive feedback on drafts. Thank you to all of my pseudonymous interlocutors in Yunnan, and to Lu Yuan, without whose help I would never have secured research permissions in Yunnan, and certainly not in Shadian. Finally, I thank Zainab Khalid, who accompanied me to Shadian and spent time with me during my fieldwork in Kunming; her astute insights into non-Chinese Islamic practices have significantly informed my own interpretation of Islam in Yunnan.

2   All names and identifying information have been changed.

3 Interestingly, even those urban Hui who were atheists simultaneously claimed to be
   Muslims; for these individuals these positions were not contradictory. Ben Hillman
   (2004) mentions that when he asked a group of non-practicing Hui "youths studying in
   the county seat" if they were Muslims, they "answered [his] question as if it were absurd:
   'We are Hui — of course we're Muslims'" (63-64). Perhaps we should not be so surprised by
   this: during the Ming, Qing, and Republican eras, and indeed up until the 1950s, the term
   Hui meant *Muslim* (see Lipman 1997:xxiii; Gladney 1996, 1998, 2004; Harrell 1995:34).
   It is arguable that residual meanings of the term *Hui* continue to operate within self and
   community understandings of Hui identity (Williams 1977).

4 Regarding my use of the 'imagined', I intend to invoke both Arjun Appadurai's (1996)
   sense of 'imagination as social practice' and Benedict Anderson's (2006 [1983]) 'imagined
   communities', particularly in the sense that imaginings "are to be distinguished not by their
   falsity/genuineness, but by the style in which they are imagined" (Anderson 2006:6).

5 On biological 'myths of descent' in the P.R.C., see Barry Sautman (1997). On Qing
   Dynasty Era mythologizing of the origins of Islam in China, see Ma Haiyun (2006). On
   the mythologized descent of the Guo and Ding lineages in Fujian, see Fan Ke (2003). On
   the life and legend of an oft-claimed ancestor, Sayyid 'Ajall Shams Al-Din, see Jacqueline
   Armijo-Hussein (1997). On genealogy as the basis for identity among Omani Muslims, see
   Mandana Limbert (2002). Compare to Aomar Boum's (2011) analysis of the mythologized
   origins and imagined pasts of Saharan Jews.

6 When I speak of 'urban Hui' in this article, I do not mean simply 'Hui who reside in urban
   areas.' The urban Hui to whom I refer were almost exclusively well-educated and often
   wealthy, but their defining trait for the purposes of this analysis is that they identified
   strongly as *Kunmingren* 昆明人 (people from Kunming). They have all lived in Kunming
   long term, and some grew up there. In contrast, urban-dwelling Hui who hailed from
   the countryside and expressed strong attachments to their rural hometowns did not
   necessarily share the discourses or practices of Huiness of longterm city dwellers. Hui who
   resided in rural Muslim enclaves like Shadian, Najiaying, and Weishan exhibited the most
   deeply religious practices, though even Hui from other rural parts of Yunnan had deeper
   attachments to Islam than most of those who grew up in the city or had strong ties to the
   city. Finally, it should be noted that not all Hui who resided in Shadian were from rural
   areas; some had left cities as distant as Kashgar and Dalian to live a religious and harmonious
   (*hexie* 和谐) life surrounded by other Muslims. This accords with what Shadian Muslims
   argued: that 'real' Muslims 'fled the city' in search of an authentic Muslim life, away from
   the corruptive influence of the city. For most urban Hui in Kunming, however, this was
   unthinkable: they had internalized and valorized the urban–rural hierarchy that saturates
   contemporary China, and that, while allowing for pastoral fantasy holidays in quaint or

scenic rural destinations, discriminates against the rural in favor of the urban (see Jacka 2005; Siu 2007; Kipnis 2007).

7 In light of these differences in urban–rural patterns of Hui practice, I should mention that every Hui person I met during my fieldwork in Yunnan avoided pork, even if they drank excessively. That's not to say that they kept halal; some Hui in Kunming were willing to eat at non-halal restaurants so long as we didn't order any pork. In addition, almost every household, urban or rural, religious or secular, possessed a copy of the *Qur'an*, typically keeping it in an honored place. These two cultural practices appeared to be the only ones which were consistently shared among all Hui I encountered in Yunnan.

8 My own fieldwork in Shadian confirms this: Hui-Muslims there frequently peppered their conversations with transliterated Arabic and Persian words such as *hajji* 哈吉 as well as Arabic phrases like *Insha'Allah* إن شاء الله and *Alhamdulillah* الحمد لله.

9 Both historically and today, trade, migration, and religion link Yunnanese Hui-Muslims to Southeast Asia. In Thailand they are called the Haw, in Burma the Panthay (Hill 1982; 1998; Forbes 1986a, 1986b, 1988, 1997; Sen and Chen 2009).

10 Sayyid 'Ajall Shams Al-Din, a Central Asian governor of Yunnan during the Yuan Dynasty, is an oft-claimed ancestor of Hui in Yunnan. See Armijo-Hussein (1997).

11 Such notable persons were viewed as having an inextricable connection to the Holy *Qur'an*, whether through *jiyin* 基因 (genes) or *xuetong* 血统 ('blood' lineage), as in the case of Arabs, or through religious authenticity, as in the case of imams or religious scholars, whose own ancestry was almost always traced back to an Arab, Persian, or Central Asian.

12 On the Du Wenxiu or Panthay Rebellion, see Bai Shouyi (1953); Ju-k'ang T'ien (1981); Wang Jianping (1995); David Atwill (2005).

13 It is fascinating that she employs 20th century terminology here, both in her use of the minzu category and in her re-figuring of the elder—younger brother relationship, one so often used in post-1949 propaganda to show the Han elder brother guiding the shaoshu minzu younger brothers. Because she was certainly familiar with this typical hierarchical relationship, her appropriation potentially suggests a resistance to and re-working of it.

14 The vast majority of 'cosmopolitan encounters' for Hui, urban or rural, were imagined, typically through books and electronic media, and even those that were not imagined could be classified as what Hebdige (1990) terms 'mundane cosmopolitanism' (also see Szerszynski and Urry 2002). Some elite urban Hui in Kunming occasionally vacationed in the West, though usually as part of tour groups. A handful studied at Western institutions abroad (where they were usually classified as 'Chinese' by their non-Chinese friends) or, more often, at Western-style institutions in China where they encountered *waijiao* 外教 (lit. foreign teachers, most often English language teachers). However, few urban Hui developed close relationships through these encounters, and, particularly when compared

to the long-term relationships between some Shadian Hui and foreign Muslims, these urban Hui cosmopolitan encounters were only occasionally profound experiences for the actors involved.

15 For accounts of the Shadian Incident, see Ma Shaomei (1989); Wang Jianping (1996); Dru Gladney (1996:137-140); Raphael Israeli (2002:264-270); Ma Ping (2008).

16 Shadian Hui-Muslims explained the region's thriving economy in various ways, ranging from Allah's blessing to governmental reparations for the Shadian Incident. Whether or not it is blessed by Allah, the local economy benefits significantly from its mining industry, which is focused mainly on metals, including tin, copper, lead, zinc, silver, gold and tungsten.

17 Addendum: When I originally wrote this sentence, I was thinking of a particular interlocutor whose son was in Syria. Since then I have spoken with her, and she told me he had moved to Malaysia to continue his studies.

18 Compare this to Maris Boyd Gillette's (2000) description of a similar process of Arabization in Xi'an, where she posits that such styles excluded the Han majority (110) and were 'attractive because they embodied the prosperity, technological development, and modernization of the Middle East' (233). In Shadian, however, the 'meanings of change and the politics of pastness' (Appadurai 1996:3) were quite different from those in Xi'an, and significantly influenced Shadian's notion of a return to authenticity.

19 Wang Jianping (personal communication) raised the question: Why were Shadian Muslims able to ban alcohol successfully, whereas Muslims in Henan and Xi'an failed to do so? Shadian Muslims repeatedly stressed that because of specific historical and economic circumstances, particularly after the Shadian Incident, they were able to exert more legal and governmental authority locally than were Muslims in other parts of China. See also Gillette (2000:167-184) on the failed alcohol ban in Xi'an's Muslim District.

20 These *Hadith* and stories are too numerous to list here. In practice, Shadian Hui-Muslim women were indeed relatively well-educated, whether through state schools or Quranic ones, and many older local women continued to pursue Quranic education at one of Shadian's many *madrasahs*. A surprisingly high number of local women had pursued bachelor's or master's degrees, and many women pursued careers and other leadership positions outside the home, even after marriage and children. Local women interpreted Islamic prescriptions for modest dress and the wearing of *gaitou* 盖头/*toujin* 头巾 (*hijab*) as liberating: such styles of dress not only marked a woman's relationship with Allah, but also enabled her to focus on developing her intellect and other skills, safe in the knowledge that others would not judge her by her looks. Submitting to religious authority empowered some women (cf. Mahmood 2005). Mosques, too, provided 'spaces of their

own' for women: women's mosques and female imams, rare or absent in other parts of the world, are common in China (Jaschok and Shui 2000; 2012; Allès 2000; Tatlow 2012).

21 Hanzu in Yunnan often deplored what they viewed as preferential treatment of the Hui by the government, at national, provincial, and local levels. This 'preferential treatment' consisted of official preferential policies (*youhui zhengce* 优惠政策) as well as governmental actions allegedly based on a fear of Hui historical and genetic tendencies for 'violence' and 'rebellions'. According to many Han interlocutors, if any incident occurred between a Han and a Hui, the Hui people would rush to defend their 'brethren', so the government took careful steps to placate the Hui. Han explained that this was due to the deep ethnic consciousness of the Hui, even though some Han believed this unification had no basis in genetic truth. Many Han expressed a desire that, like the Hui, they, too, could unite together as an ethnic group against others in China, and lamented the fact that most Han lacked a primordial ethnic consciousness and seemed ambivalent about expressing ethnic pride. For more on Han views of Hui in Yunnan, see Blum (2001); Caffrey (2007); Zhang (2010:153-156). See Allès (2003) for relationships between Han and Hui villages in Henan. For more on Han ethnic consciousness (and lack thereof) see the Mullaney et al. (2012) volume *Critical Han Studies*.

References

Allès, Elisabeth (2000). *Musulmans de Chine : Une Anthropologie des Hui du Henan*. Paris: Éditions de l'École des hautes études en sciences sociales.

Allès, Elisabeth (2003). 'Some Joking Relationships Between Hui and Han Villages in Henan', *China Perspectives*, 49, pp. 49–60.

Anderson, Benedict (2006). *Imagined Communities : Reflections on the Origin and Spread of Nationalism*. London; New York: Verso.

Appadurai, Arjun (1996). *Modernity at Large : Cultural Dimensions of Globalization*. Minneapolis, MN: University of Minnesota Press.

Armijo, Jacqueline (2001). 'Narratives Engendering Survival: How the Muslims of Southwest China Remember the Massacres of 1873', *Traces – Multilingual Journal of Cultural Theory and Translation*, 2, pp. 293–332.

Armijo-Hussein, Jacqueline M. (1997). *Sayyid 'Ajall Shams Al-Din: A Muslim from Central Asia, Serving the Mongols in China, and Bringing 'Civilization' to Yunnan*. PhD Harvard University.

Atwill, David G. (2005). *The Chinese Sultanate : Islam, Ethnicity, and the Panthay Rebellion in Southwest China, 1856-1873*. Stanford, CA: Stanford University Press.

Bai, Chongren (1994). 'Yisilan Wenhua Shi Huizu Wenhua de Neike (Islam is the Internal Nucleus of the Hui's Culture)', *Huizu Yanjiu*, 16(4).

Bai, Shouyi (1953). *Huimin Qiyi*. Shanghai: Shenzhou guo guang she.

Bai, Zhihong (2008). 'The Ethnic Identification of the Zang-Hui or Tibetan-Hui in Tibet-Yi Corridor and Their Subjectivity: An example of the Zang-Hui of Shangri-La County', *Ethno-national Studies*, 4, pp. 58-65.

Blum, Susan (2001). *Portraits of 'Primitives': Ordering Human Kinds in the Chinese Nation*. Lanham, MD: Rowman & Littlefield.

Boum, Aomar (2011). 'Saharan Jewry: History, Memory and Imagined Identity', *The Journal of North African Studies*, 16(3), pp. 325-341.

Caffrey, Kevin (2004). 'Who "Who" is, and Other Local Poetics of National Policy: Yunnan Minzu Shibie and Hui in the Process', *China Information*, 18(2), pp. 243-274.

Caffrey, Kevin (2007). *China's Muslim Frontier: Empire, Nation, and Transformation in Yunnan*. PhD University of Chicago.

Dirlik, Arif (2003). 'Global Modernity? Modernity in an Age of Global Capitalism', *European Journal of Social Theory*, 6(3), pp. 275-292.

Fan, Ke (2003). 'Ups and Downs: Local Muslim History in South China', *Journal of Muslim Minority Affairs*, 23(1), pp. 63-87.

Fan, Ke (2012). 'Ethnic Configuration and State-Making: A Fujian Case', *Modern Asian Studies* 46(04), pp. 919-945.

Fei, Xiaotong (1978). *On the Social Transformation of China's Minority Nationalities* (Dui Zhongguo Shaoshu Minzu Shehui Gaige de Yixie Tihui). Peking: [s.n.].

Fei, Xiaotong (1989). 'Zhong Hua Min Zu Duo Yuan Yi Ti Ge Ju (Multiplex and Integrative Structure of the Chinese Nation)', in Fei, Xiaotong *et al.* (ed.), *Zhong Hua Min Zu Duo Yuan Yi Ti Ge Ju*. Beijing: Central University for Nationalities Publishing House.

Fiskesjö, Magnus (2006). 'Rescuing the Empire: Chinese Nation-Building in the Twentieth Century', *European Journal of East Asian Studies*, 5(1), pp. 15-44.

Gillette, Maris Boyd (2000). *Between Mecca and Beijing: Modernization and Consumption Among Urban Chinese Muslims*. Stanford, CA: Stanford University Press.

Gladney, Dru C. (2004). *Dislocating China: Reflections on Muslims, Minorities, and Other Subaltern Subjects*. Chicago, IL: The University of Chicago Press.

Gladney, Dru C. (1996). *Muslim Chinese: Ethnic Nationalism in the People's Republic*. Cambridge, MA: Harvard University Press.

Gladney, Dru C. (1998). *Ethnic Identity in China: the Making of a Muslim Minority Nationality*. Fort Worth, TX: Harcourt Brace College Publishers.

Hansen, Mette Halskov (1999). *Lessons in Being Chinese: Minority Education and Ethnic Identity in Southwest China*. Seattle, WA: University of Washington Press.

Harrell, Stevan, ed. (1995). *Cultural Encounters on China's Ethnic Frontiers*. Seattle, WA: University of Washington Press.

Harrell, Stevan (2001). *Ways of Being Ethnic in Southwest China*. Seattle, WA: University of Washington Press.

Hebdige, Dick (1990). 'Fax to the Future', *Marxism Today*, 20(1), pp. 18–23.

Hillman, Ben (2004). 'The Rise of the Community in Rural China: Village Politics, Cultural Identity and Religious Revival in a Hui Hamlet', *The China Journal*, (51), pp. 53.

Israeli, Raphael (2002). *Islam in China: Religion, Ethnicity, Culture, and Politics*. Lanham, MD: Lexington Books.

Jacka, Tamara (2005). *Rural Women in Urban China: Gender, Migration, and Social Change*. Armonk: M.E. Sharpe.

Jaschok, Maria, and Jingjun Shui (2000). *The History of Women's Mosques in Chinese Islam: A Mosque of their Own*. Richmond, Surrey: Curzon.

Jaschok, Maria (2012). *Women, Religion, and Space in China: Islamic Mosques & Daoist Temples, Catholic Convents & Chinese Virgins*. New York: Routledge.

Kipnis, Andrew (2007). 'Neoliberalism Reified: Suzhi Discourse and Tropes of Neoliberalism in the People's Republic of China', *Journal of the Royal Anthropological Institute*, 13(2), pp. 383–400.

Limbert, Mandana E. (2002). *Of Ties and Time: Sociality, Gender and Modernity in an Omani Town*. PhD University of Michigan.

Lin, Yaohua (1986). 'Zhongguo Xinan Diqu de Minzu Shibie (Ethnic Identification in the Southwestern Region of China)', in Yunnan sheng bianji zu, ed., *Yunnan Shaoshu Minzu Shehui Lishi Diaocha* (Collected Materials of Sociohistorical Investigations of Minority Nationalities in Yunnan). Kunming: Yunnan Renmin Chubanshe.

Lipman, Jonathan N. (1997). *Familiar Strangers: A History of Muslims in Northwest China*. Seattle, WA: University of Washington Press.

Litzinger, Ralph A. (2000). *Other Chinas: The Yao and the Politics of National Belonging*. Durham NC: Duke University Press.

Ma, Haiyun (2006). 'The Mythology of Prophet's Ambassadors in China: Histories of Sa'd Waqqas and Gess in Chinese Sources', *Journal of Muslim Minority Affairs*, 26(3), pp. 445–452.

Ma, Ping (2008). 'Le génocide de musulmans dans le village de Shadian au Yunnan', in Song Yongyi, ed., *Les massacres de la Révolution culturelle*. Paris: Buchet-Chastel.

Ma, Shaomei (1989). 'A Brief Account of the Shadian Incident', in Honghe City Shadian Hui Editorial Board, *Shadian Huizu Shiliao*, pp. 46–57.

Mahmood, Saba (2005). *Politics of Piety: The Islamic Revival and the Feminist Subject*. Princeton, NJ: Princeton University Press.

Mullaney, Thomas S. (2004). 'Ethnic Classification Writ Large: The 1954 Yunnan Province Ethnic Classification Project and Its Foundations in Republican-Era Taxonomic Thought', *China Information*, 18(2), pp. 207–241.

Mullaney, Thomas S. (2011). *Coming to Terms with the Nation: Ethnic Classification in Modern China*. Oakland, CA: University of California Press.

Mullaney, Thomas S., James P. Leibold, Stéphane Gros, and Eric Armand Vanden Bussche, eds, (2012). *Critical Han Studies: The History, Representation, and Identity of China's Majority*. Oakland, CA: University of California Press

Pan, Jiao (1997). 'The Maintenance of the LoLo Caste Idea in Socialist China', *Inner Asia Occasional Papers*, 2(1), pp. 108–27.

Pan, Jiao (2010). 'Deconstructing China's Ethnic Minorities', *Chinese Sociology & Anthropology*, 42(4), pp. 46–61.

Pigg, Stacy Leigh (1996). 'The Credible and the Credulous: The Question of "Villagers' Beliefs" in Nepal', *Cultural Anthropology*, 11(2), pp. 160–201.

Sautman, Barry (1997). 'Myths of Descent, Racial Nationalism and Ethnic Minorities in the People's Republic of China', in Frank Dikötter, ed., *The Construction of Racial Identities in China and Japan – Historical and Contemporary Perspectives*. London: Hurst & Company.

Schein, Louisa (2000). *Minority Rules : the Miao and the Feminine in China's Cultural Politics*. Durham, NC: Duke University Press.

Siu, Helen F. (2007). 'Grounding Displacement: Uncivil Urban Spaces in Postreform South China', *American Ethnologist*, 34(2), pp. 329–350.

Szerszynski, Bronislaw and John Urry (2002). 'Cultures of Cosmopolitanism', *The Sociological Review*, 50(4), pp. 461–481.

Tapp, Nicholas (2002). 'In Defence of the Archaic: A Reconsideration of the 1950s Ethnic Classification Project in China', *Asian Ethnicity*, 3(1), pp. 63–84.

Tapp, Nicholas (2003). *The Hmong of China: Context, Agency, and the Imaginary*. Leiden: Brill.

Tatlow, Didi Kirsten (2012). 'A Model of Inclusion for Muslim Women', *The New York Times*, October 9.

Tien, Ju-Kang (1981). *Moslem Rebellion in China: a Yunnan Controversy*. Canberra: Australian National University.

Wang, Jianping (1995). *Discrimination, Corruption and Moral Decline: the Historical Background of the Muslim Hui Uprising in Yunnan, China, 1856-1873*. Jerusalem: The Harry S. Truman Research Institute for the Advancement of Peace, The Hebrew University.

Wang, Jianping (1996). *Concord and Conflict: The Hui Communities of Yunnan Society in a Historical Perspective*. Lund: Studentlitteratur.

Wang, Jianping (2001). *Glossary of Chinese Islamic Terms*. Richmond: Curzon Press.

Williams, Raymond (1977). *Marxism and Literature*. Oxford; New York: Oxford University Press.

Yang, Bin (2008). 'Classification in to the Chinese National Family', in Bin Yang, *Between Winds and Clouds: The Making of Yunnan, Second Century BCE to Twentieth Century CE*. Gutenberg: Columbia University Press. Available at http://www.gutenberg-e.org/yang/index.html.

Yang, Zhaojun, ed. (1994). *Yunnan Huizu Shi* (A History of the Hui in Yunnan). Kunming: Minzu Chubanshe.

Zhang, Li (2006). 'Contesting Spatial Modernity in Late-Socialist China', *Current Anthropology*, 47(3), pp. 461.

Zhang, Li (2010). *In Search of Paradise: Middle-class Living in a Chinese Metropolis*. Ithaca NY: Cornell University Press.

Zhu, Yong (2005). *Kunming: Zuihou de Shuncheng Jie (Kunming: The Last Shuncheng Jie)*. Remin Gong'an (People's Public Security).

CHAPTER 9

Qingzhen: Embodiment of Islamic Knowledge and Lifestyle: A Case Study on Tongdao Street, Huimin District of Hohhot City

Liang Zhang

Yunnan University

A Reflection on *Qingzhen*: Learning about the 'Familiar Strangers'

The Hui are a famous ethnic minority currently boasting the widest distribution in China, with 31 province level regions inhabited by the Hui people. In a lot of provinces, most people of ethnic minority groups belong to the Hui. Besides, the Hui people also account for a large proportion of the urban population in China. According to the 2000 Census Data, 4.4471 million Hui people, or 45.30% of the Hui population, were living in urban areas, (SEAC, 2005) while 455.94 million people of 31 provincial administrative regions, or 36.09% of the total population, are urban residents (NBoS, 2002). Thus, the level of urbanization achieved by Hui is above the national average. The statistics on the Hui population in 183 megacities proves that Hui have done better than other China's ethnic minorities in terms of urbanization (Yang 2007: 121-128). Hui have participated in the social transformation aimed at modernization of China in its entirety (Yang 2007; Gillette 2000).

Hui have drawn attention from countless anthropologists. Moreover, daily life of the Hui people is frequently described in ethnographies focusing on urban society. The Hui are depicted as an 'ethnic minority' familiar to urban residents from various ethnic backgrounds in famous districts and big cities such as Cow Street of Beijing, (Gladney 1996; Liang 2006) Qijiawan of Nanjing (Bai 2005) and Lianhu District of Xi'an (Gillette 2000); the northwestern cities such as

Lanzhou, Yinchuan and Xining (Yang 2007); the central regions such as Zibo of Shandong (Li 1993) and Shenqiu County of Henan (Ni 1997); and the southern cities such as Guangzhou (Ma 2006) and Sanya (Pang 1992). The nationality is well known for faith in Islam shared by its members and its difference from neighboring ethnic groups in lifestyle. Therefore, 'Hui communities have a 'test-tube effect' unattainable for other ethnic groups. Hui people can be found in almost every city and county in Mainland China but are gathering in relatively small communities', therefore, 'Hui are in contact with other ethnic groups in different regions in a real sense, and hence the amazing 'test-tube' effect is produced. In other words, the nationality is serving as a window for us to examine the ethnic minority issues in China. (Zhang 2001:4).

Considering the intimate connection between Hui and other ethnic groups in China, studies on Hui can provide significant clues for understanding the relationship among the ethnic groups in our country as well as the inter-influence between multiethnic integration and the establishment of the modern nation-state. Hui have occupied a special position among Chinese ethnic groups, which represents the tension between one culture and an 'other culture' in the eyes of Westerners. Therefore, Jonathan N. Lipman dubbed Muslims living in Northwestern China as the 'familiar strangers' (Lipman 1997). Of course, such a nickname only depicts a specific group under given social circumstances from a historical perspective rather than the general nature of the whole nationality. Dru C. Gladney has clarified some misunderstandings about Chinese Muslims for Westerners (Newby 1988), based on which he analyzed the Islamic ideology and Muslims' socio-cultural practices after integrating them, breaking the traditional research patterns in which the 'religious ideology' or some 'folk phenomenon' is studied separately. Through investigation on the knowledge about *qingzhen*, which is embodied by the daily life of Muslims in Beijing (Gladney 1996: 9), Dru C. Gladney put forward that ethno-religious identity of Hui is centering on *qingzhen*. On that basis, he put forward a theory about the formation and identification of Chinese ethnic groups via a comparison of the socio-cultural practices that characterize four Hui communities in China.

Indeed, the Chinese word *qingzhen*, originally meaning 'being pure and natural', is completely native. It did not become the equivalent of 'Islamic' until the Ming and Qing Dynasties. The change in its meaning reflects the efforts made by some scholars of Islam in integrating Islamic ideology with the culture of the Han-Chinese-dominated society. Such a process is called 'sinicization of Islam' (Ma 2006: 252-261) or 'localization of Islam' (Yao 2006) by some researchers in this field. In terms of Muslims' daily life, *qingzhen* reflects not only the Islamic intellectuals' religious principle of 'interpreting Islamic classics in line with Confucianism' but also the lifestyle stuck to by Muslims embracing pureness and simplicity. Islamism has explicitly stipulated rules for Muslims' livelihood, education, marriage, household, social organization, rituals and celebrations, and Hui Muslims living in China have to abide by the doctrines and adjust their lifestyle. During interaction with surrounding ethnic groups, Hui have created a lifestyle covering Halal diet, clean life, ecclesiastical system based on the mosques as well as personal rituals and ceremonies, which are all depicted with the word *qingzhen* in China. Such a lifestyle highlighting immaculacy has been taken as a means of maintaining internal cohesion by the Hui Muslims.

While investigating Huimin District, Hohhot, the author found that *qingzhen* offers not only approaches to interpret the ethnic identity of Hui but also a key to understand the socio-cultural integration in a multiethnic society. Furthermore, the analysis on the knowledge about *qingzhen* is helpful in comprehending both the cultural traits of Hui communities and what is more important, the socio-cultural interactional mechanism in those localities. From an overall perspective on multiethnic integration, the paper focuses on local knowledge and the lifestyle of Hui in Huimin District cohabited by several ethnic groups, with the interactive relationship among ethnic groups in local society probed.

Knowledge and Lifestyle about *Qingzhen*: An Overview of Muslims in Tongdao Street

Tongdao Street: a Hui Community in a Multiethnic Society

Hohhot was jointly built by several ethnic groups such as Mongols, Han, Hui and Manchu. From the late 15th century to the 16th century, a short-term unification of Monan-Mongolia (the Mongolian region to the south of the Gobi Desert) had been achieved by Dayan Khan, who divided the area into Left Wing and Right Wing, each counting 30,000 households. None of Dayan Khan's sons survived. One of his grandsons occupied what we call Hohhot today, and his followers were named Turmot. From then on, the political situation here grew increasingly stable. During the reign of Altan Khan (1507--1582), that region saw a gradual revival and great development of husbandry, handicrafts, industry and commerce. Then the Hohhot City, whose name means 'Blue City' in Mongolian, was established for maintaining peace between the Ming Empire and Mongolia.

In the 8th year of the reign of Shenzong Emperor (1580), Ming Dynasty, the city was renamed 'Guihua' by the Ming Empire. Later, the Ming Dynasty collapsed and the Qing Dynasty was established. In a bid to enhance the military control over Inner Mongolia, the Qing Empire built a new city officially named 'Suiyuan' five miles northeast of Hohhot in the 4th year of the reign of Qianlong (1739). Then Suiyuan City and Guihua City were dubbed as 'New City' and 'Old City' respectively by local residents. The basic layout of modern Hohhot had been formed after the establishment of Suiyuan City. (Dai 1981; Rong and Rong 1981: 43-54).

In the history of Hohhot, the Hui people have been living with many other ethnic groups while gathering in their own communities. The Hui people began to migrate to Hohhot at least since the early days of the reign of Kangxi in the Qing Dynasty: some of them went on a military expeditions with other soldiers, came to the city and lived outside the north gate of Guihua City. In the 25th year of the reign of Qianlong (1760), 'Guihua Camp' was set north of Guihua City. As it was inhabited by a lot of officers and soldiers of Hui origin, the camp was turned into a Hui settlement. During the over 100 years from Qianlong's reign till the Revolution of 1911, some of the Hui living in the inland and northwestern regions had gradually migrated to Hohhot; in particular, numerous Hui people fled to avoid catastrophe after the Uprising of Hui People in Shanxi and Gansu during the reign of Tongzhi. During the early years of Guangxu's reign, the number of Hui people living in Hohhot had reached 3,000 to 4,000. In China's Republican Period, most of the Hui people settling in Hohhot were from Northwestern China (Editorial Committee at HDC, 1994: 15-94). Hence a decent-sized Hui community was formed in the northeastern corner of the Old-City District (which is near today's Tongdao Street), Hohhot, by 1950.

Since the 1950s, dwelling conditions of the Hui residents in Hohhot have been greatly improved following several tremendous social changes. With the increase of their population, they have lived far more dispersedly than before. By 1990, regions governed by sub-district offices of Tongdao Street and Huanhe Street in Huimin District of Hohhot have merged with the Hui community formed during the 1950s. Today, the Hui people here are still gathering in a compact community among other ethnic groups, despite the decrease in population proportion they account for compared with 40 years ago. In 1996, large-scale demolition and reconstruction in Huimin District began, with the establishment of 55 residential communities. The administrative division of Hohhot was adjusted in 2000, after which six sub-districts, namely, Tongdao Street, West Zhongshan

Road, Huanhe Street, West Xinhua Road, Guangming Road and West Hailar Road have been included in Huimin District, along with Youyouban Town. The administrative coverage of Huimin District has witnessed several changes since 1990, but Tongdao Street remains the most important Hui settlement in Hohhot. By 2004, four sub-districts, namely, Binhe Road, Yihe Alley, Youyi Alley and Kuanxiangzi Alley, have come under the administration of Tongdao Street Office, while the population structure remains relatively unchanged compared with 1990. That greatly differs from other regions in China, in which the massive urban reconstruction starting in the 1990s to a lesser or greater extent adversely influenced local Hui residents. For instance, most of the Hui in Nanjing had been forced to move from Qijiawan due to modern urban construction (Zhang and Bai, 2004); in Tianjin, a majority of Hui residents left the Hui community in the northwest corner of Hongqiao District which witnessed reconstruction at the turn of the century; in Beijing, the number of Hui households in Madian had been reduced from 400 to around 200 (Gillette 2000: 57-61); in Shanghai, a lot of Hui people moved from Fuyou Road and Xiaotaoyuan Street near Laobeimen to other districts such as Pudong due to the unforgiving demolition (Zhang and Bai 2004); in Yinchuan, the Hui people, who used to gather in clusters previously, live scattered now. In a word, it is rather rare now for the Hui people to cluster together in the same place and live with Han as the majority (Yang and Zhang 2008). Due to the nationwide urban renewal, the geographical communities that the Hui people's traditionally lived in are about to disappear (Zhou and Ma 2004). Therefore, a lot of scholars have voiced deep concern about the fate of Hui culture and ethnicity.

Tongdao Steet, in Huimin District of Hohhot, is still inhabited by several ethnic groups, with a lot of Hui people gathering here, though it has witnessed changes in administrative division and thorough reconstruction. According to an honored Muslim of the Small Mosque at Youyi Alley of Tongdao Street, most of the former Hui residents in Tongdao Street have moved back to where they were living, in which Hui leaders played an important role, coordinating between the superior authorities and the property developers and managing to persuade the residents to come back before the reconstruction was finished. Although the number of the Hui residents living in Tongdao Street is relatively small, this street is fully permeated with Islamic atmosphere. Besides, the *qingzhen* lifestyle adopted by Muslims here has also deeply impressed their non-Muslim neighbors, most of whom agreeing that these Muslims are "becoming more like Hui people". Gradually, more and more men wearing the *taqiyah* (white cap) and full beards, and women wear the *hijab* (scarf). Moreover, ceremonies held in the mosques become increasingly magnificent. Although residents from different ethnic backgrounds here have already got used to living with other ethnic groups and, in particular, to paying attention to the Muslim taboo stipulated by halal rules, they still clearly feel that their Hui neighbors' lifestyle has been focusing more on *qingzhen*.

Renewal of South and North Tongdao Roads was underway when I was conducting my first investigation on Tongdao Street in 2006. The 1150-meter-long street stretches in a south-north direction from the west end of West Zhongshan Road near the north gate of Old-City District to Xinhua Street. About RMB 65 million was invested in the reconstruction, with 50 million and 1,500 million spent on building construction and electric power engineering respectively. In terms of the design philosophy, "The new dominating style is borrowed from Islamic architecture in Central Asia as well as Turkey, with details blending Islamic cultural features of different periods and regions. At the same time, constructions at important sections, such as the triangle square in front of the Grand Mosque and surrounding buildings, the North Mosque, the north end of South Tongdao Road and the Hohhot Islamic Middle School, have their facades renewed. For exterior design, sequential features and continuity of streetscape have been taken into consideration, so these buildings are endowed with a strong Islamic flavor" (Hohhot Hui District News). After the reconstruction, buildings that had mixed styles in the past have gained a unified Arabic appearance; on the west side of Tongdao Street, the North Mosque, the only Arabic structure here before reconstruction, has perfectly mingled with surrounding buildings and become more eye-catching after being re-decorated. The sole architecture in Chinese style now is the Grand Mosque on the east side of the street. Indeed, such presentation of Hui ethnic culture led by local governments is not exclusive to Hohhot (Fan 2005). Leaving aside the factors about state-society relation behind these changes in architectural style, the uniqueness of Tongdao Street, where the Hui people are gathering, has been substantially enhanced via the massive infusion of Islamic features into the city landscape.

Mosques - the Basis of the Qingzhen Lifestyle

Mosques are playing a decisive role in the preservation of the *qingzhen* lifestyle of the Hui people living in Tongdao Street. In downtown Hohhot, the history of the Hui Muslims goes parallel with the construction history of mosques. In the early years of Kangxi's reign, the Qing Dynasty, some Hui people went on a military expeditions with other soldiers, came to Hohhot and settled outside the north gate of the Old City. Later they established a mosque which is the predecessor of today's Grand Mosque. The number of these Hui people remains unknown, and most of them became merchants. At the same time, some of the Hui people in Shanxi also travelled with the army to Hohhot for business. Hence several settlements were formed here. In the 15th year of Qianlong's reign (1750), 200 or 300 Hui soldiers escorting the 'Fragrant Concubine' to Beijing, as well as the girl's families, settled in Babai Village south of Hohhot before moving into the Old City. Besides, Hohhot was also inhabited by Hui from other places such as Beijing, Tianjin, Hebei, Shandong and Henan coming for trade or other reasons, who established both a new settlement along the west bank of Zhadagai River and the West Mosque. During China's Republican Period, the Ganningqing Mosque (today's North Mosque) was built for the Hui people moving in from Northwestern China (Rong and Rong1981). A total of nine mosques have been constructed since 1949.

By 2009, the city had 11 mosques, among which the Grand Mosque, the South Mosque and the East Mosque have been repaired and expanded with preservation of the original structures, and the North Mosque, the West Mosque, the Northeast Mosque and the Xincheng Mosque have been rebuilt, joined by the newly established Tuanjie Mosque, Northwest Mosque, Xianghe Mosque and Small Mosque. Eight of the 11 mosques are located in Huimin District, with two in New-City District and one in Yuquan District. All the mosques within Hohhot are administrated by democratic management committees in accordance with national laws and local situations. Serving as the keeper of a mosque, the director of such a committee is endowed with power over financial affairs and daily routines; the imams of the mosque are also selected by him. The director is not paid for his job, and money used to support the mosque comes from rental of properties owned by the mosque and the public's donations; resorting to other mosques is permitted in emergency. A notice board is set prominently in every mosque to inform of the donators' names and the donation amount that ranges from several yuan to several tens of thousands of yuan. Besides, items donated by Muslims are also clearly listed. A mosque's total expenditure is separated into an educational fund, a charity fund, the Imam's salary, bills for water, electricity, heating, cleaning and meal subsidy. The major duty of the director is to keep the account balanced for self-sufficiency. Some Muslims come voluntarily to assist the director in routine matters throughout the year, they are called *xianglao*. Besides, the mosque also employs some workers, usually Muslims, to deal with rough work and sundry duties, and have their wages paid on a monthly basis. Religious events are hosted by Imams who also play an important role in traditional ceremonies. For example, *salah* (prayer) and *udhiyah* (sacrifice) on Corban Festival are both directed by Imams.

There are four mosques within the administrative coverage of Tongdao Street: the Grand Mosque, the North Mosque, the Northeast Mosque and the Small Mosque. Resembling a traditional Chinese palace, the Grand Mosque is the oldest mosque in Hohhot. The Small Mosque, built in the early 1980s, features a distinct Arabic style, which is one of the typical characteristics of the mosques established recently in Hohhot. Situated at the south end of Tongdao Street, the Grand Mosque is surrounded by such shopping venues like Xianghe Market, Yiwu Commodity Market, Qiupeng Shopping Center and Jinqiao Shopping Mall, which constitute a Muslim commercial district with the Grand Mosque at its center. Featuring solid bricks and tiles, the Grand Mosque has an antique flavor. The whole complex of the mosque is arranged in a symmetrical fashion, with its central axis stretching in an east-west direction. The west-facing Salah Hall, the center of the complex, sits between the South and the North Lecture Halls. The North lecture hall is where imams give sermons to the *harifans* (students), while the South Lecture hall is used by the *harifans* for study and dormitory purposes. The women's bathroom and prayer hall are located to the north of Salah Hall, to the south stands a tablet recording the construction and expansion history of the mosque since the Ming and Qing Dynasties. The men's bathroom, the dining hall and the reception room are situated in the north, west and south of the backyard respectively. The Small Mosque is situated at Youyi Alley to the east of South Tongdao Street, 200 meters north of the Grand Mosque. Unlike the Grand Mosque which occupies a bustling section, the Small Mosque hides itself among residential communities. Covering an area of about 4,000 square meters, it is as huge as the Grand Mosque, despite its name. Comprised of three storied buildings and a row of single-storied houses, it has a four-storied east-facing Great Hall at its center. The hall, a concrete structure in Arabic style, has its entire surface covered with colorful tiles and embellished with green ones. To the northeast of the Great Hall is a two-storied building facing north in matching style. The building is divided into two sections: the second floor is women's prayer hall, while the eastern part of the first floor is the men's bathroom. To the east of the two-storied building lie four single-storey houses, which are used as the gatehouse, the accounting office, the democratic management committee office and the *harifans'* dining hall respectively. There is a four-storied versatile building to the southeast of the Great Hall, with a Moon-Enjoying Pavilion on either side. Generally speaking, all the mosques comprise the following structures: Salah Hall (usually the main body of the mosque), bathrooms, dining hall, lecture hall (or classrooms) and offices, regardless the layout adopted. The Salah Hall and bathrooms particularly offer Muslims in Hohhot the foundation for implementing the *qingzhen* lifestyle.

The word 'mosque' originating from Arabic means 'a venue for making a prayer'[1]. Obviously, a mosque is mainly used for performing *salah*. In Hohhot, male Muslims usually pray *salah* led by imams in group, while female Muslims are advised to pray at home individually. The Small Mosque has both a Male Salah Hall and a Female Salah Hall. The Great Hall of this mosque, which was re-decorated in 2008, features simple interior design. With an area of over 300 square meters, the hall is more than 20 meters in length and 10 meters in width. The structure is supported by square columns; with light coming in through the east, south and north windows, it appears wide and bright. The only ornaments on the walls of the hall are scriptures, lamps and fans. The hall can accommodate more than 1,000 people, but there aren't so many worshippers here at ordinary times. People persisting in performing *salah* at five different times throughout the day are mostly old Muslims, besides imams and *harifans*. Generally speaking, the number of Muslims praying in a mosque reaches its peak of the day at noon, namely, 300 or 400. However, the number often exceeds 1,000 on *jumah* (Friday), for which rugs are used in small mosques to offer extra room for praying.

Ritual cleanliness or ablution is required before *salah* prayer. In the Small Mosque, the cleaning rites are usually finished in the bathroom located at the first floor of the two-storied building to the northeast of the Great Hall. Having been rebuilt in 2001, the south-facing bathroom is well-equipped, wide and bright. In the room, there is a toilet at the north end, with shower enclosures arranged on either side. There are two annular pools in the middle and a row of pools on the far right. For most of the Muslims praying ordinary *salah*, only general cleanliness is required, while thorough ablution is performed by more people on Friday. Water is supplied in a unified manner via the water system monitored by a specially assigned person. Featuring a reasonable design, the device for general cleanliness contains a seat about 40 centimeters high, so the faucet is just facing the front of the user sitting here, and the lever is also within close reach. The drainage system is clean and unimpeded so as to prevent stagnant water in the basin. The thorough ablution has to be performed in the shower enclosure individually. Shower enclosures in the Small Mosque are very spacious and divided into two parts: the outer part is equipped with a wardrobe and clothes-hooks while the inner part is used to take a shower. Scriptures have to be recited during both cleaning and ablution, throughout which Chinese is permitted to be used though Arabic is the preferable option.

Having performed cleanling or ablution, Muslims who enter the hall earlier sit there, waiting for the beginning of *salah* prayer. Seats in the middle of the very front row are usually reserved to imams and *harifans*, while other Muslims, having no specific seats, select their places randomly. There are several benches covered with rugs on both sides of the hall, which are designed for Muslims with leg problems, who are unable to bow down and worship in a standing manner, they have to go through the ritual riding on the benches. *Salah* falls into several categories such as *salat al-faridah*, *salat al-sunnah*, *salat al-wajib* and *salat al-tatawwu*, among which *salat al-faridah* is compulsory for every Muslim. During *salah* prayer the following gestures are involved: raising hands, folding hands, standing to attention, bowing down, kowtowing and sitting on heels. The latecomer has to begin with raising hands and then follow others no matter which step is underway. *Salah* has to be performed in a rigorous and precise way, during which distraction is strictly prohibited, let alone looking around or whispering to each other.

Funerals for Muslims are very simple, in which mosques play an indispensible role. During investigation on the Small Mosque, I attended such a funeral. A non-native of Hui origin had passed away in Hohhot, and his body was carried to the Small Mosque by *xianglaos* and several *harifans* in a minibus. The next day he was bathed and wrapped in white cloth by an imam and *xianglaos* of the mosque before praying *salah* at noon. Then he was carried out of the great hall, to receive *janazah* (funeral rites) performed by the imam. All the *xianglaos* and *harifans* took off their shoes, lined up and raised their hands to pray for the decedent, who was transported in a minibus by mosque staff to the graveyard later. All people got out off the minibus upon arrival at the gate of the cemetery and walked about 300 meters before reaching the tomb. Cemeteries for Hui people have ready-made, north-south positioned graves which are about 1.8 meters long and 0.6 meters wide, with their depths ranging from 1.8 meters to 2 meters. A 0.5-square-meter opening leading to the coffin chamber can be found on the west side near the bottom of each grave. At first, two cemetery workers went down to clear up stones and weeds, while the decedent's family, wearing *taqiyah* or *hijab*, were watching from a distance in silence and the imam was reciting scriptures sitting on the ground. After clearing up the grave, the decedent was put into the grave carefully, and then the coffin-chamber opening was sealed off with mud bricks. Since it is a taboo to use burnt things in a Muslim's grave, the mud bricks were made in a special way. Finally, *harifans* filled the grave with soil piled nearby while other people led by the imam, were praying for the dead, which marked the end of the funeral. Muslims cannot live in a neighborhood without a mosque. The Small Mosque is a venue both for rituals and gatherings in the eyes of the worshipers frequenting here: in the mosque, they meet, exchange greetings and chat with their friends, and even business deals were sometimes made. Not only the old Muslims, but also young students in downtown Hohhot meet there; of course, the Hui university students are not allowed to come every day as *xianglaos* do due to the academic burden, so they can only participate in rituals at weekends. Worshippers coming to the Small Mosque multiply at Friday prayers; on such important festivals as Lesser Bairam, even the Hui residents who rarely go to a mosque would come to join the celebration.

In a word, mosques, sublime and sacred in the Muslims' heart, are essential for the Muslims' religious life as well as weddings, funerals and celebrations. It is through mosques that the Hui participate in such religious events such as *salah* prayer, fast and zakat donation, which is universal for Hui communities all over China. The Hui Muslims' pursuit of pureness has been presented by every detail of their mosques, which is reflected by the spatial structure and decoration of the Small Mosque; moreover, the Hui people also seek after the truest religious life by emphasizing precision in scripture-recitation and *salah* gestures. Hence with favorable conditions offered by mosques, a socio-cultural system centering on *qingzhen*, which covers the Hui people's everyday life in an all-around manner, is established, with the *qingzhen*-based religious ideology embodied in *qingzhen* lifestyle.

Dissemination of Knowledge about Qingzhen: Education on Traditional Islamic Culture

Knowledge about *qingzhen* is passed on via education on traditional Islamic culture. In Hohhot, the scripture-hall educational system initiated by Hu Dengzhou, a famous scholar of Islam in the Ming Dynasty, has still been used. A mosque enrolls several, or dozens of, *harifans* in accordance with its economic strength, in which the imams play a decisive role; these *harifans* go through elementary, secondary and higher education for studying Arabic and religious knowledge. Traditionally, the course duration was not specified, and there was no unified stipulation for graduation, with a harifan's academic accomplishment to be rated by the imam. Among all the mosques in Hohhot, the Grand Mosque boasted the largest enrollment and the most graduates before 1949, with some of its top *harifans* becoming imams (Rong and Rong 1981: 271). In the 1980s, Hohhot saw changes in the political situation: new ethnic and religious policies were implemented, the once shut-down mosques were all re-opened and rebuilt, and several new mosques were established. However, religious education had been suspended for nearly 30 years by then, which resulted in the failure to satisfy the demands from mosques nationwide for Islamic intellectuals who were in critical shortage at that time. Therefore, mosques in Hohhot have been paying special attention to religious education. I have conducted an investigation focusing on the Small Mosque.

Education on traditional Islamic culture in Hohhot has been re-energized since the establishment of the Small Mosque. Brilliant teaching results have been achieved by the mosque thanks to the application of a modern teaching methodology. By the fall term of 2013, the school attached to the Small Mosque had four male imams and about 80 *harifans*. The dean also gives lectures on *Qur'an* to the *harifans*. Classes aimed at first, second and third level education are set, which have 50, 18 and 13 students respectively. The school sticks to a four-year schedule, with Arabic, *Qur'an*, *Hadith* and *Shariah* as core courses; a Chinese language course is offered to Class Level I and Level II, and teachers teach Arabic with standard pronunciation. Four 40-minute classes before noon begin at 8 and end at about 11:50; while two afternoon classes last from 14:00 to 15:30. In the evening, time is spent on either individual study or *salah* prayer. There are two semesters in a year, which are scheduled in the same as ordinary schools. According to the regulations of the school, a student must at least complete junior secondary education, namely, national compulsory education, before becoming a harifan. There is no limitation on ethnic groups, which means opportunity to learn in that school is accessible to every academically qualified Muslim. At present, *harifans* in the Small Mosque all belong to the Hui nationality and most of them, aged between 15 and 21, have finished junior or senior secondary education. One third of the *harifans* are from Ningxia, and most of them came here following the dean, with some having been taught by the dean for years. In Hohhot, only one third of the *harifans* are locals, and the others are from northern provinces such as Shandong, Henan, Hebei, Gansu and Shanxi. *Harifans* need to buy the study materials themselves. Every class has a monitor and several 'student cadres' assisting the teachers in daily management of the class.

In the school attached to the Small Mosque, each class has specified its teaching objectives. Class Level I offers fundamental courses, for which it acts as the 'elementary school' in the traditional scripture-hall educational system. New *harifans* in this class differ greatly from one another in mastery of knowledge about their religion, with some of them even knowing nothing about Islam. Therefore, elementary education here focuses on building a solid foundation for deeply learning and using Arabic and, more importantly, inscribing into the learners' memory the six pillars of Islamic faith, namely, belief in Allah, belief in Allah's angels, belief in Allah's books, belief in the messengers of Allah, belief in the Last Day and belief in Qada and Qadar (predestination). *Harifans* in Class Level I can enjoy vivid lectures in which taboos related to the Islamic lifestyle are usually explained with modern scientific theories, such as "fast is beneficial for health as it helps cleaning up toxins in the body". Generally speaking, one year of study in this class helps a harifan build a solid faith in Islam even if he cannot pursue further education. The upgrade from Class Level I to Class Level II is only permitted for *harifans* who have passed a special examination for which a lot of them will fail. Of course, *harifans* that are fully equipped with solid background knowledge before entering the school are allowed to attend Class Level II directly. Those studying in Class Level II have got comprehensive understanding of fundamental knowledge about Islam and acquired certain Arabic reading and writing capabilities. However, they are still not sufficiently proficient to read and understand *Qur'an* and *Hadith* written in Arabic. Only the *harifans* who have studied in Class Level II for a year and passed the upgrade exam get access to Class Level III which requires the learners to master basic Islamic doctrines and the Arabic language.

The requirement to attain learning accomplishments for which a traditional learner would make over ten years of efforts, *harifans* in the Small Mosque are under tremendous pressure from both themselves and their demanding teachers, for whom they all study very hard. Most *harifans* in Class Level I and Level II hope to upgrade, and some third-level learners are seeking to study in Muslim countries. They have to stick to the schedule and join *salah* prayer on time, with Friday as the only day of rest. Teacher here pay much attention to physical exercise, so the school is equipped with table tennis equipment; every Saturday morning, the teachers let the *harifans* do workouts in the playground of a nearby college. There is also a women's school in the Small Mosque, of which the teaching mode is similar to that for the male *harifans*. Male and female *harifans* are isolated from each other by only a wall. Teachers in the women's school are female imams. At present, the mosque has 3 female imams and 30 female *harifans*.

Providing *harifans* with systematic courses is only one of the Small Mosque's educational functions. In recent years, the Small Mosque has launched three types of educational programs for common Muslims. Held at irregular intervals, the first type is designed for Muslim novices, most of whom were received after marrying a Muslim. Imams and *harifans* in Class Level III are selected for teaching. The second type is initiated for Muslim adults while the third, held during weekends and school vacations, is aimed at Muslim youths. In addition to imams of the Small Mosque, Muslim intellectuals from outside are also invited to teach here. I was told by imams and *xianglaos* that more and more young Muslims are coming to the lectures, which indirectly also influences their parents. For instance, in August 2006, some Hui mothers, who accompanied their children to attend the teaching program, replaced their improper dressing with long-sleeved shirts, long pants and *hijab* after several lectures.

The *qingzhen* lifestyle is promoted andIslamic knowledge is passed on via religious education carried out in the mosque. In Tongdao Street with its multiethnic context, education on traditional Islamic culture is of vital importance for preserving the *qingzhen* lifestyle typical for the Hui residents. According to a harifan in the Small Mosque, many harifan novices, having graduated from ordinary schools, behaved improperly because of lack of comprehension of Islam. However, study in the Small Mosque has helped them gain new understanding about themselves and Hui, after which they have influenced their families and friends with what they have learnt. Hence the *qingzhen* lifestyle is carried forward by young Muslims mastering knowledge about *qingzhen*, through which the future of Hui in Hohhot is seized by itself in a multiethnic society.

Promotion of the Lifestyle and Knowledge about Qingzhen in Tongdao Street

The *qingzhen* lifestyle demonstrates itself not only in the Hui people's religious life and education, but also in the interaction between residents of Tongdao Street from different ethnic backgrounds. In Hohhot, a city with several ethnic groups, the unique lifestyle of the Hui people has long been greatly familiar to residents of other ethnic origins, for whom respect for Hui food taboo has been integrated with their life. In the Qing Dynasty, even the government soldiers would cover sacrificial offerings containing pork with white cloth when passing by Huimin District (Tong, 1987: 113). Indeed, *qingzhen* has also a direct influence on the lifestyle shared by Hui and other non-Muslim ethnic groups in specific situations. Between the 19th and the 20th centuries, there had been a Halal meat store in Huimin District of Hohhot run by a person of Han origin. Wang

Wanjin, the owner of the meat store, came from Guo County, Shanxi Province (today's Yuanping City in Shanxi), to Hohhot at the end of the 19th century. At the beginning, he was hired by a Hui butcher to help with selling meat, during which he had not only learnt but also taken up the Hui lifestyle and faith. As a result, he never got addicted to cigarettes and alcohol while abstaining from pork. After he saved enough money, he opened his own halal meat shop, in which cows and sheep were slaughtered by imams and cleaned by Muslims in accordance to doctrines of the Hui. Hence he not only won recognition from the Hui residents, but also established close relationship with local mosques. Besides, Wang would make donations to the mosques on every Hui festival and borrow tableware from a mosque and invite Hui chefs for happy occasions. Wang's sons also opened halal meat shops in Huimin District after their father's death (Ma, 2001:12-14). In fact, non-Muslim residents have gained understanding of the *qingzhen* lifestyle during long-term cohabitation with the Hui people, though they might not get along with the Hui as well as the Wang's did. Pork was not sold to Hui communities in Hohhot even when the centrally-planned economic system was being implemented in China, with the non-Muslims neighboring the Hui also getting coupons for beef and button. (Wang, 2001:42)

At present, the *qingzhen* lifestyle has been integrated with social life of residents of different ethnic origins in Tongdao Street, Huimin District of Hohhot. In 'Qing Zhen Commercial District' with the Grand Mosque at its center, all the eateries around the mosque are Halal restaurants. Even the petty dealers selling sugar-roasted chestnuts and sunflower seeds are wearing *taqiyah*, a symbol of their nationality, and non-halal foods are banned from Jinqiao Shopping Mall. As this area has evolved into a commercial district specializing in halal foods, Hohhot citizens will not come here for non-halal items. The time-honored catering and food-processing businesses run by the Hui people have won a brilliant reputation. Among the Hui cuisines, meat and fried wheat foods are the most popular for their dainty taste, outstanding quality and reasonable price. Therefore, even people living far away from the Grand Mosque often come to 'Qing Zhen Commercial District' to purchase cooked foods. All the Halal eateries are fairly clean, regardless of their size. Highly competitive in catering industry, the Hui restaurants offer both unique ethnic cuisines and delicacies of Sichuan, Shandong, Jiangsu and Guangdong made from halal ingredients to satisfy a variety of tastes. In Hohhot, halal foods have been sold to places beyond Hui communities such as Tongdao Street, and *qingzhen* has become a brand shared by food-processing and catering industries run by Hui.

The *qingzhen* lifestyle has also been enhanced during the interaction between the Hui and their non-Muslim neighbors. Hohhot has seen a surge in immigrants over the last decade. For those having lived in inland and Han-dominated areas for years, dwelling in a multiethnic society brings along brand-new experiences, and they need some time to get familiar with the *qingzhen* lifestyle. When Wenzhou Pedestrian Street to the east of the Small Mosque was just established, a lot of non-native commercial tenants swarmed the shopping venue, most of whom were not Muslims. With commercial prosperity, both halal eateries and non-Muslim restaurants on that street flourished. Given their lack of experience with Muslims before, some non-Muslim chefs stewed pork outside their restaurants, which is extremely offensive to the Hui people. "We could smell stewed pork even at the gate of the mosque", said a *xianglao* of the Small Mosque. As a result, a conflict occurred between the Hui and the non-Muslims. After consultation of the local Hui residents, the district government made a decision: only retail business is permitted at Wenzhou Pedestrian Street. In this way, the Hui residents here guarded the *qingzhen* lifestyle successfully, and the non-Muslim immigrants also learnt about *qingzhen*. Under coordination of the local government, the balance between commercial activities and the ethnic lifestyle was achieved in a multiethnic society, and people gained more knowledge about *qingzhen*.

In Tongdao Street, understanding of *qingzhen* is also deepened via individual interaction, as in my personal case. I prepared simple gifts, Yili milk and 'Remill' Muslim pastries, for the imam before an interview. Since Yili is a famous Halal diary brand in China and 'Remill' pastries are also locally well-known, I thought these gifts were completely safe. However, the imam and his family were reluctant to accept them, because those pastries were sold in bulk without any packing, so they might be contaminated by impure things while being carried by me, a non-Muslim. Fortunately, the Imam forgave my ignorance after apology was made, and I also learnt more about *qingzhen*. It is through the long-term interaction between ethnic groups and individual residents that lifestyle and knowledge about *qingzhen* are promoted and accepted in Tongdao Street.

Inspiration from *Qingzhen*: Stepping Across the Ethnic Boundaries

Tongdao Street, Hohhot, a Hui community cohabited by several ethnic groups, is fully permeated with the *qingzhen* flavor. The Hui residents here are sticking to the *qingzhen* lifestyle which is understood and respected by their non-Muslim neighbors. *qingzhen* culture in Tongdao Street was built due to long-term multiethnic coexistence: the Hui residents here have been implementing and carrying forward the *qingzhen* lifestyle, which is sacred as well as practical, based on their mosques, and such a lifestyle embracing pureness has been widely accepted by the non-Muslims. As a result, socio-cultural features centering on the *qingzhen* lifestyle are formed. During the long-term cohabitation, Muslims and Non-Muslims in Hohhot have achieved positive interaction in their social life. At first, a body of knowledge favorable to both mutual development and ethnic identity preservation is built; secondly, local knowledge about the Hui has rooted in the Han-dominated society. On the one hand, the Hui, based on their faith in Islam, are learning about the social ideology and lifestyle of the Han while attempting to maintain their ethnic uniqueness and religious culture amid interaction between the two ethnic groups. On the other hand, the Hui have turned from non-natives to natives, during which Islamic culture interacts with Confucianism, Buddhism and Taoism prevailing among the Han people, and the Han citizens have also partially understood the Islamic lifestyle. Then the body of knowledge embodied by the terminology *qingzhen* grows out of the combination of Islamic faith and social ideology of Han. *Qingzhen* represents both the essence of the ethnic identity of the Hui but also the fundamental understanding about the Hui people by non-Muslims. Although more profound and extensive research on local knowledge about *qingzhen* via ethnographies is still required, *qingzhen*, the embodiment of Islamic knowledge and lifestyle discovered in local communities, has offered inspiration sufficient for my study of the Hui from an anthropological perspective.

Such a research on *qingzhen* in an overall context of multiethnic cohabitation is an attempt to step across the ethnic boundaries. The question "How have several ethnic groups constituted such a unified nation-state as China in a multiethnic context" has gone beyond the limits of anthropology and become a 'China problem' in the social sciences. Aiming at answering the question, Chinese scholars have explained and discussed research on western ethnic groups for years, with numerous achievements made in studies based on the 'ethnic group theory'. Dru made a breakthrough by integrating the ethnic group theory with Mainland China's ethnic policy so as to interpret how the Hui, one of the 56 ethnic groups in China, are being shaped under joint influence of national discourse and subjective identification. However, as said by a Hui scholar, "While studying an ethnic group and its culture unfamiliar to him, Dru might be under influence from his host culture, which would lead to some 'misunderstanding'" (Ma and Zhou, 2001). The author thinks that Dru's misunderstanding about China's ethnic groups is reflected by both his partial comprehension of relevant field materials and the fundamental mistake he has made in analyzing Hui in China based on a theory derived from Western society. Although he has fully learnt the influence of China's ethnic policy on society after 1949, he overlooked the long-term unification of our country amid multiethnic coexistence and over-emphasized heterogeneity of different ethnic groups. Fei Xiaotong has systematically elaborated about the basic nature of China's multiethnic society in his *The Pattern of Diversity in Unity of the Chinese Nation*. He has proved that unification of the Chinese Nation is the inevitable result in history by illustrating how "the diversity in unity featuring interaction and integration among different ethnic groups" (Fei, 1989:1) has been formed, with emphasis on the significance of the unified entity's subjective will for the Chinese Nation. Basically, the Chinese Nation is advancing towards unification, based on which ethnic diversity is effectively maintained. The *qingzhen* lifestyle adopted by the Hui people in Tongdao Street, Hohhot, results from their social practice for preserving and carrying forward their own culture, during which knowledge embodied by the term *qingzhen* is also shared by ethnic groups in a multiethnic society. Different ethnic groups in that street have been unified based on their common understanding of *qingzhen*, with the Hui Muslims' ethnic identity enhanced in the socio-cultural context. In a word, *qingzhen*, the embodiment of Islamic lifestyle and knowledge, survives on multiethnic coexistence rather than its own uniqueness. Such a perspective, namely, studying some kind of ethnic identity based on the whole picture of the community in which it shows up, can help us step across the invisible 'boundaries' between ethnic groups.

*This project (01CMZ005), under the subdivision 'Cultural Production and Ethnic Identification during Urbanization', has been supported by National Social Science Foundation. Special acknowledgement goes to Prof. Ma Guoqing in Sun Yat-Sen University, whose instruction in field investigation and paper-writing has been fairly helpful, as well as Tan Tongxue in Sun Yat-Sen University, Gao Peng in Yunnan University of Nationalities, Xu Shujing studying for her doctoral degree in history at Sun Yat-Sen University and Xia Zhongkio, a *xianglao* living in Huimin District of Hohhot, for their constructive assistance.

Notes

1 There is a debate on 'man mosque' (libasi) and 'woman mosque' (nusi). See Jaschok, Maria and Shui Jingjun (2000).

References

Bai, Youtao (2005). *Pan Gen Cao: Cheng Shi Xian Dai Hua Bei Jing Xia De Hui Zu She Qu (Hui Community Under Urbanization)*. Yinchuan: Ningxia Ren Min Chu Ban She.

Dai, Xueji (1981). *Hu He Hao Te Jian Shi (Brief History of Hohhot)*. Beijing: Commercial Press.

Editorial Committee at Huimin District Commission of Huhhot CPPCC, eds (1994). *Hu He Hao Te Hui Zu Shi (History of Huhhot Hui)*. Huhhot: Inner Mongolia People's Publishing House.

Fan, Ke (2005). "Zai Di Fang Hua' Yu Xiang Zheng Zi Ben ('Re-localization' and Symbolic Capital: Building Performance of a Muslim community in Fujian)', *Open Times*, 2, pp. 43-61.

Fei, Xiaotong (1989). 'Zhong Hua Min Zu Duo Yuan Yi Ti Ge Ju (Multiplex and Integrative Structure of the Chinese Nation)', in Fei, Xiaotong *et al.* (ed.), *Zhong Hua Min Zu Duo Yuan Yi Ti Ge Ju*. Beijing: Central University for Nationalities Publishing House.

Gillette, Maris Boyd (2000). *Between Mecca and Beijing: Modernization and Consumption among Urban Chinese Muslims*. Stanford, CA: Stanford University Press.

Gladney, Dru C. (1996). *Muslim Chinese: Ethnic Nationalism in the People's Republic*. Cambridge, MA: Harvard University Press.

Hohhot Hui District News. Available at http://huiminqu.nmgnews.com.cn/ [Accessed August, 24 2010].

Jaschok, Maria and Shui Jingjun (2000). *The History of Women's Mosques in Chinese Islam: A Mosque of their Own*. Richmond: Curzon. Revised for Chinese language edition: Zhongguo Qingzhen Nüsishi (2002). Beijing: Sanlian Chubanshe Harvard-Yenching Library.

Li, Bin (1993). 'Hui Zu Zai Cheng Shi Zhong De She Hui Wang Luo (Muslim social network in the city--studies on Zhangjiadian Zibo case)', *Ningxia social science*, 5, pp. 40-44.

Liang, Jingyu (2006). *Niu Jie: Yi Ge Cheng Shi Hui Zu She Qu De Bian Qain (Cow Street: Changes of a Urban Hui Community)*. Beijing: Zhong Yang Min Zu Da Xue Chu Ban She (Central University for Nationalities Publishing House).

Lipman, Jonathan N. (1997). *Familiar Strangers: A History of Muslims in Northwest China*. Seattle, WA: University of Washington Press.

Ma, Haiyun and Zhou, Chuanbin (2001). 'Yi Si Lan Jiao Zai Xi Bei Su Fei She Qu Fu Xing Shuo Zhi Yi (Queries on Islam's Revival in the Sufi Community at Northwest China)', *Ethnic Studies*, 5, pp. 34-40.

Ma, Qiang (2006). *Liu Dong De Jing Shen She Qu (The Floating Spirit Community – Anthropological Perspective Research of Guangzhou Musilim Zhemati)*. Beijing: China Social Science Press.

Ma, Qingcheng (2006). 'Jian Xi Zhong Guo Yi Si Lan De Min Zu Hua Ji Qi Zai Zhong Guo Wen Hua Zhong De Di Wei (The Nationalization of Chinese Islamic and Its Status in Chinese culture)', in Ma Qincheng, ed., *Hui Zu Li Shi Yu Wen Hua Ji Min Zu Xue Yan Jiu*. Beijing: Minzu University of China Press.

Ma, Xitian (2001). 'Min Zu Tuan Jie Yi Shi (Stories of Ethnic Unity)', in Editorial Committee at Huimin District Commission of Huhhot CPPCC (1994), *Hui Zu Shi Liao (History of Hui)*, Issue 4.

NBoS (National Bureau of Statistics of People's Republic of China) (2002). Available at http://www.stats.gov.cn/tjgb/rkpcgb/qgrkpcgb/t20020331_15434.htm [Accessed May 14, 2010].

Newby, L. J. (1988). 'The Pure and True Religion in China', *Third World Quarterly*, 10(2), pp. 923-947.

Ni, Shengzhang (1997). 'Development and Status of Yu Dong Huai Fang Hui (Development and Status of Hui at East Henan)', *Hui Studies*, 4, pp. 65-71.

Pang, Keng-Fong (1992). *The Dynamics of Gender, Ethnicity and State among the Austronesian-speaking Muslims (Hui-Utsat) of Hainan Island*. People's Republic of China, Unpublished doctoral dissertation, University of California, Los Angeles.

Rong, Xiang and Rong, Genglin (1981). *Tu Mo Te Yan Ge: Zheng Qiu Yi Jian Gao (Tumote's history)*. Tumote zuo qi: Bureau of Culture.

SEAC (State Ethnic Affairs Commission of the People's Republic of China) (2005). Available at http://www.seac.gov.cn/gjmw/ssmzx/2005 -08 -21/1176019928736444. htm [Accessed May 14, 2010].

Tong, Jingren (1987). *Hu He Hao Te Man Zu Jian Shi (History of Manchu at Hohhot)*. Hohhot: Hohhot Ethnic Affairs Commission.

Wang, Junmin (2001). *Qing Cheng Min Zu (Ethnic Groups in Qingcheng: the Evolution of Ethnic Relations in a Frontier City)*. Tianjin: Tianjin People's Publishing House.

Yang, Wenjiong (2007) *Hu Dong, Tiao Shi Yu Chong Gou (Interaction, Adaptation and Reconstruction)*. Beijing: Min Zu Chu Ban She (Ethnic Publishing House).

Yang, Wenjiong and Zhang, Rong (2008). 'Cheng Shi Hui Zu She Qu Jie Gou De Bian Qian Ji Qi Ying Xiang (Changes of Urban Muslim Community Structure and Its Cultural

Impacts)', *Journal of the Second Northwest University for Nationalities (Philosophy and Social Sciences Edition)*, 3, pp. 5-10.

Yao, Jide (2006). 'Hui Ru Dui Hua: Yun Nan Yi Si Lan Xue Pai Ge An De Li Shi Kao Cha (Dialogue Between Hui and Confucianism: A Historical Survey of the Yunnan Islamism Cases)', *Si Xiang Zhan Xian (Thinking)*, 5, pp. 37-42.

Zhang, Hongyan and Bai, Youtao (2004). 'Da Cheng Shi Hui Zu She Qu De She Hui Wen Hua Gong Neng (Social and Cultural Functions of Hui Community in Metropolitan: Survey of Qijiawan Hui Community in Nanjing)', *Ethnic studies*, 4, pp. 38-47.

Zhang, Zhongfu (2001). *Qing Dai Xi Bei Hui Min Shi Bian (The Incident of Northwestern Hui in Qing Dyanasty: Social Cultural Adaptation and Ethnic Identity Reflections)*. Taipei: Linking Publishing Company.

Zhou, Chuanbin and Ma, Xuefeng (2004). 'Du Shi Hui Zu She Hui Jie Gou De Fan Shi Wen Ti Tan Tao (Discussion on Paradigm of Urban Muslim Social Structure)', *Journal of Hui Muslim Minority Studies*, 3, pp. 33-38.

CHAPTER 10

Role of Ethnic Community of Hui Students in Internal Unity in the Context of Urbanization

Hacer Z. Gönül

Peking University

Introduction

Ethnic minorities are scattered over the entire territory and can be found in every province, autonomous region and municipality directly under the Central Government. In most county-level units there are at least two or more ethnic groups living together. Currently, over 50 million – accounting for half of the ethnic minority population - live in the border regions (Shen & Ou 2007: 19), while most of the Han reside in eastern or central China (Veeck, Pannell, Smith, & Huang 2007). Fifty-three nationalities have their own spoken languages, but the Hui speak Mandarin Chinese (Zhou 1999). Among the 55 minority groups in China there are ten ethnic minority groups who believe in Islam. Most Muslim populations live in northwestern China: Xinjiang, Gansu, Ningxia, Qinghai and Shaanxi. In Chinese governmental policies toward minority groups, *ronghe* (融合 meaning 'fusion', amalgamation), therefore, is frequently used to refer to the long historical disappearance of minority languages, cultures and knowledge (Mackerras 1994). Consequently *ronghe* is not a policy like multiculturalism. However, given the cultural differences between the majority Han and the ethnic minority groups, the PRC Government prefers the policy of *ronghe* (intermingling) instead of assimilation for its ethnic minority policy. "*Ronghe* (intermingling) differs from the Sinicization approach in the sense that it recognizes the cultural differences between the Han and ethnic minorities, while it does not enforce the compliance of the later to the former" (He 2005: 76).

Muslim Ethnic minorities had suffered in Ningxia during Cultural Revolution in the 1960s and 70s. But since the 1980s till today the Chinese government has been initiating policies of reform for opening up, which brought an upswing for the Hui Muslim Community. More than 400 mosques have been built and Islamic schools have produced 7,000 imams - or Islamic clerics known locally as *ahongs* (阿訇). The Hui, who constitute half of China's Muslim population, are scattered over 90 percent of cities and townships in China including our target area (Wuhan) (Israel 2002; Lynn 2004). The Hui have been afforded much more political and religious freedom by Beijing than any other Muslim ethnic group in China. Researchers say it is their friendly historical relation with the ethnic majority Han that is the distinguishing difference.

China has experienced a rapid urbanization and modernization since the 1990s. This aim started concurrently with the above-mentioned opening policy in 1980s. Although the Chinese government officially protects minority languages, culture, and knowledge through the Constitution of the People's Republic of China (CPRC) (1982) and the National Minorities Policy and its Practice in China (NMPPC) (2000), large gaps between laws and practices were reported (He 2005; Wang & Phillion 2009). Chinese language, culture, knowledge, and identity are imposed on minority groups through school education, media propaganda, and manipulation (Shih 2002). Minority culture and knowledge are underrepresented or misrepresented in school textbooks in China (Nima 2001; Qian 2007; Upton 1996; Wang & Phillion 2010). Minority culture, language, and knowledge are regarded as uncivilized, backward, and unscientific (Gladney 2004; Nima 2001; Schein 2000), and minority identity is also considered as less important than state identity (Qian 2007; Shih 2002). According to these constructed identities, the Han group is central, and minority groups are peripheral and remote. The Han group is civilized, and minority groups are uncivilized (Gladney 2004). Nonetheless, China has experienced its rapid urbanization and modernization since 1990s; hence the Hui minority has started to emphasize education for their next generation. Therefore, many Hui university students have started to move to metropolitan cities where Han culture dominates society. Consequently, they started to confront the new issues and difficulties in the process of embedding into such a heterogeneous society.

This research proposes to focus on these confrontations and adaptations they encountered and adaptations they adopted, as manifested in their activities, halal food, accommodations, communities, marriage etc. We tried to confirm or contradict the above-mentioned suppositions via quantitative scale inquiry of daily experiences, compatibility and religious inclination among the Hui ethnicity students in different universities of Wuhan. With anthropologic inquiry into the everyday life in university of Hui Muslim students, we seek to combine long-lasting anthropological interest in culture and religion with significant questions about the relationship between identity, the subject and contemporary religiosity to address three sets of questions.

First of all, we tried to examine both public and private practices of ethnical self-reform that Hui Muslims in university find important to cultivate modern forms of Muslim identity. Secondly, we placed these practices in the broader context of the sociocultural reality in universities and beyond to understand difficulties of presenting their own identity and citizenship, and new ideas for the methods of integration with the majority. Ultimately, we analysed how Hui students are situated in relation to urban life and how progress of modernization in China affected their own cultural values, which need to be protected.

To answer our questions, we first focused on their personal experiences, their daily activities and collective actions to expand various discourses, knowledge and commentaries, which they interpret in their own urban life. We paid more attention to Hui Muslim students and their relation to the Han majority, and the Chinese Muslim minorities from other places. This is done mainly, to examine how public social activities and interrelations, articulate discussions of difficulties or experiences relevant to contemporary Chinese society, such as urbanization, modernization and compatibility of Islam with the Chinese regime and also significant issue relevant to being Hui, as well as being Muslim minority and being Chinese Muslim.

Data Collection

Because of the time limitation, we used a quantitative questionnaire to get data out of our intended study. The close-ended questionnaire listed seventeen questions about their living experiences, interaction and compatibility in the Islamic context. The questionnaire was handed over to seventy Hui students on short notice. Sixty complete responses were sent back within the deadline so our sample size is sixty including ten face-to-face interviews. Seven universities of different fields were selected for data collection. Identity and personal information was not asked for as deemed unnecessary. One reason is the possible sensibility of the retrieved information on cultural and religious issues. Simple statistics was used to interpret the data and to make conclusions. We also participated in the mosque organizations and *xuexi ban*－学习班(study class/ group).

The following research questions guided our study:

1. Hui students' experiences in universities of Wuhan, P.R. China.
2. The perception and interaction of Hui minority students with Han students and teachers.
3. The awareness and compatibility of both cultures from an Islamic perspective.
4. The essence of the mosque in urban China to Hui student for protecting his or her culture.
5. How Hui students can protect their culture without loosing their identity in metropolitan city?

Here, it is important to remember that this analysis is based on two bodies of research in the fields of being Muslim in China and social identity theory. From among the many identity theories, we chose the Henri Tajfel and Turner's social identity theory because it offered three clear guidelines for exegesis of the Hui students' context in a heterogeneous urban society. Those three forms of explanation focus on culture, critical evaluation of the customs, and development of new contextual practices. (1979). It does so by focusing on theoretical perspectives aimed at applying critical understanding of the identity problem, intricately outlined by Tajfel (1979) to problematize binary divides between in-group (us) and out-group (them). Tajfel's theory of social identity focuses on comparisons people make between a dominant group and one's own ethnic minority group. Thus, discourse that features negative comparisons with other groups tends to adversely influence ethnic minority, social identity, contributing to an attitude of increasing dissatisfaction with one's social identity. As part of an identity issues process, we collected the main Hui students' cultural difficulties and needs which we interpreted as representative of their cultural themes. By researching the underlying meaning of those cultural expressions, we extracted the theme and clarified its meaning in light of the problems which they have to face. Then we chose the corresponding identity conflicts under the integration policy that addressed the same cultural meaning and dilemmas. In this way, the conflicts of being a minority in a multicultural state resonated with familiar, cultural and traditional themes without compromising the message or identity of either.

Results and Discussion

After the analysis of the results of interviews and questionnaires, we found out the following about Hui students' three main communities. First is life in the restaurants or canteens, second is the mosque and the last one is the most exclusive 'xuexi ban 学习班' which is basically called 'study class' or 'study group'.

Table 1: Experiences, interaction and compatibility of Hui students with Han Chinese students

Social Indicator	Always/ Agree	Mixed/ Sometimes	Never/ Disagree
Friendship level	39	02	9
Feelings at first interaction	29	8	13
Sharing joy/sadness	19	25	06
Sharing dormitory room	04	38	08
Getting invitations for get-togethers	26	12	12
Discriminatory behavior from faculty/administration	08	07	35
Master status as Hui	42	-	08
Participation in games and extra-curricular activities	36	04	10
Discussion of medical issues in hospital	20	07	23

Table 1 explains the experiences, interaction and compatibility of Hui students with Han students. The data collected in the table shows the remarks of sixty respondents on nine different scenarios. We detected mixed opinions but we feel confident enough to say that the living experience and interaction of Hui students with the majority Han students was predominantly compatible. Seventy-eight percent of the respondents were at ease to be friends with Han students whereas only sixteen percent of the population ever faced any sort of discriminatory behaviour. Along the same lines, responses for participation in games, feelings at first interaction and invitations for get-togethers from Han fellows were highly positive at the ratio of seventy-two, fifty-eight and fifty- two percent, respectively. The majority of the students were having mixed opinions towards sharing rooms, and feelings for non-Muslim Chinese friends. In addition, in the larger context of the Hui's social rivalry with the majority of the Han population, the term slightly ties in with the Hui's sense of ethnic superiority or assurance of ethnic pride of *qingzhen* '清真' ('pure and true enough'). The only contradictory evidence to our hypothesis was found in realms of master status as Hui students and discussion of medical issues with school hospital staff. This could be because of the sensitivity of religious issues in China and the medical issues of females.

Table 2: Awareness of Han students towards Islam and compatibility with Hui Muslim students

Social Indicator	Always/ Agree	Mixed/ Sometimes	Never/ disagree
Awareness about halal	03	-	47
Accompanying for meal	27	05	18
Gift exchange at Muslim festivals	01	-	49
Interest about Islamic knowledge	05	12	33
Attitude towards headscarf and beards	01	08	41
Criticism/scolding related to religion	22	16	12
Inviting Han to Muslim gatherings	05	25	20

Table 2 interprets the awareness of Han students of Islam and compatibility with Hui students. Most of the questions were replied negatively at a dominant ration. Ninety-four percent of the students knew nothing about halal food while ninety-eight percent of the Hui students did not get any gift on the religious festivals and occasions. Similarly, sixty-six percent of the Han students showed no interest in knowing more about Islam whereas eighty-two percent held a derogatory attitude towards Islamic symbols like beard and headscarf. Responses for other indicators were surely not that harsh but still clearly on negative lines. Contrary to positive response in terms of experiences, interaction and compatibility of Hui students with Han students, the Han students lacked knowledge and awareness about the religion of Islam and its practices and rituals. Additionally the compatibility level among the Hui and Han students from an Islamic perspective was also not found very positive in our study area. Knowledge about Islam was only very basic and primarily negative.

According to the interviewers, over sixty percent of the Hui students mentioned their own educational background being not as strong as the Han students. Particularly, north- western Hui families are still very conservative about female child education. Particularly, female Hui students stated the need for change and they also mentioned that change would start with their new and high-educated generation. Also, they mentioned that awareness of Islamic education is inadequate in many habits they have already taken, which aren't based on Islamic rules such as education in government kindergarten for pupils under 6 years old, boys and girls who use unseparated toilets in school, whereas in Islam toilet privacy is very important at all ages.

During the face-to-face interviews, we noticed that the ethnic communities have provided a convenient system for the Hui lifestyle, offering cohesion and a great confidence to find a free space to be what the Hui students want to do or discuss together their own issues. Thus, mosques and *qingzhen* ('清真' - halal) canteens or restaurants carry a very deep meaning among the Hui minority, particularly, in urban society. Basically, halal canteens and mosques function like centers for socio-religious activities, information networking and information transportation. Most of the Hui students who have participated in our research, mentioned that the mosques have educational programs, counselling, and community activities for the Hui minority in each city, which makes mosques and halal canteens integrated, fully functioning social centers. Thus, the mosques or masjids actually represent the real leadership in the Muslim communities.

The *xuexiban* (学习班 - study lesson/group) is the most intriguing part of our research. Over twenty-five percent participations are attending this learning lesson in each week. We have interviewed some of them personally and joined their class. We noticed that they gather together for acquiring Islamic knowledge or understand social problems and that they have the experience to discuss or share with one another. One of the participants prepares presentations or little stories that are linked with what they selected as a topic, and after that, they discuss these together. They told us that they need some kind of activities to remind themselves of who they are. Thirty percent of the Hui participants are afraid to assimilate and forget their own identity in city or university life. Ma Ping (Hui undergraduate student, 23 in CCNU) said "in daily life, nothing reminds us who we are or why we are supposed to be careful of what we eat or play with".

Finally, over fifty percent of the Hui students said that *xuexi ban* gives them self-confidence, and besides they don't need to fear loneliness anymore. Some of them said that because of *xuexi ban* they have learned many things about Islam and culture so they feel themselves improved a lot than before. Hathica (Hui undergraduate student, 23 in CCNU) said "after attending *xuexi ban,* I feel that I exist in the society and no longer neglected or ignored because I feel that I can express myself with great confidence which is given to me by my Hui sisters and brothers". In brief, the *xuexi ban* is supporting the Hui's spiritual and social needs especially, for Hui university students who live in cities.

Conclusion

Hui students' daily life experiences and religious compatibility in universities of Wuhan was inquired in this study. The day-to-day life was found compatible enough as no contradictory evidence was found during the investigation. On the other hand, no religious knowledge and a rather negative attitude was found among the Han students towards Hui, its symbols and practices.

Overall, after 30 years China implementing the policies of reform and opening up to the world, Chinese Muslims obtained opportunities to profit from this development. Hui Muslims tend to move to urban area for the pursuit of their career under the ongoing urbanization and modernization project. Thus, Hui students are confronted with several difficulties in daily life. If those cultural dilemmas, challenges and struggles which Hui students face in their daily life are being understood and can be solved properly, then Hui students will acculturate with urban life without losing their own identity.

References

Bauman, Zygmunt (2001). *The Individualized Society.* Cambridge: Policy Press.

Beck, Ulrich. (1992). *Risk Society: Towards a New Modernity.* (Mark Ritter, trans.). London: Sage Publications.

Gladney, Dru C. (2003). *Ethnic Identity in China: The Making of a Muslin Minority Nationality.* Thomson Custom Publishing.

Gladney, Dru C. (2004). *Dislocating China: Muslims, Minorities, and Other Subaltern Subjects.* C. Hurst & Co.

He, Baogang. (2005). 'Minority rights with Chinese characteristics', in Will Kymlicka and Baogang He, eds, *Multiculturalism in Asia*. Oxford: Oxford University Press, pp. 56-79.

Hsu, Francis L.K. (1948). *Under the Ancestor's Shadow: Kinship, Personality and Social Mobility in Village China*. New York: Columbia University Press.

Israeli, Raphael (2002). *Islam in China: Religion, ethnicity, culture, and politics*. Lanham, MD: Lexington Books.

Lynn, Aliya Ma (2004). *Muslims in China*. Indianapolis, IN: University of Indianapolis Press.

National Minorities Policy and Its Practice in China (2000). Available at http://news.xinhuanet. com/employment/2002-11/18/content_633175.htm. [Accessed January 2, 2007].

Nima, Badeng (2001). 'Problems related to bilingual education in Tibet', *Chinese Education & Society*, 34, pp. 91-102.

Qian, Minhui (2007). 'Discontinuity and reconstruction: The hidden curriculum in schoolroom instruction in minority-nationality areas', *Chinese Education and Society*, 40(2), pp. 60-76.

Schein, Louisa (2000). *Minority rules: The Miao and the Feminine in China's Cultural Politics*. Durham, NC: Duke University Press.

Shih, Chih-yu (2002). *Negotiating Ethnicity in China: Citizenship as a response to the state*. New York: Routledge.

Sun, Hongkai (2004). 'Theorizing over 40 years personal experiences with the creation and development of minority writing systems of China', in Minglang Zhou and Hongkai Sun, eds, *Language policy in the People's Republic of China: Theory and practice since 1949*. Boston: Kluwer Academic Publishers, pp. 179–199.

Upton, Janet L. (1996). 'Home on the grasslands? Tradition, modernity, and the negotiation of identity by Tibetan intellectuals in the PRC', in Melissa J. Brown, ed., *Negotiating Ethnicities in China and Taiwan*. Berkeley: Institute of East Asian studies, University of California, pp. 98-124.

Veeck, Gregory, Pannell, Clifton W., Smith, Christopher J., and Huang, Yougin (2007). *China's Geography: Globalization and the dynamics of political, economic, and social change*. Lanham, MD: Rowman & Littlefield.

Wang, Yuxiang and Phillion, Joann (2009). 'Minority language policy and practice in China: The need for multicultural education', *International Journal of Multicultural Education*, 11(1), pp. 1-14.

Wang, Yuxiang and Phillion, Joann (2010). 'Whose knowledge is valued? A critical study of knowledge in elementary school textbooks in China', *Intercultural Education*, 21(6), pp. 567-580.

Zang, Xiaowei (2003). 'Ethnic Differences in Neighboring Behavior in Urban China', *Social Focus*, 36, pp. 53-57.

Zhou, Minglang (1999). 'The official national language and language attitudes of three ethnic minority groups in China', *Language Problems and Language Planning*, 23(2), pp. 157-174.

Conclusion

CHAPTER II

Being Hui Muslim in China

Erkan Toğuşlu

KU Leuven

Hacer Z. Gönül

Peking University

Muslims in China have been studied and discussed in a variety of perspectives. Most of these studies have taken Sino-Muslims as a whole, which means that the Hui people as a national unique minority in China have been largely ignored. It is a fact that the Hui people share their religion, their historical roots and their traditions with other minorities such as the Uyghur, who mainly inhabit Xijiang Province. However, they have dispersed and are scattered across China (Pillsbury 1981a; 1981b). The Hui are the most widely distributed minority in China from the northwestern provinces of Xinjiang and Gansu to the southwestern province of Yunnan. Some of the Hui Muslim communities are spread over vast territories, whilst others live in concentrated individual communities in smaller areas.

The ability to adjust religious-political identity enables the study of citizenship rhetoric, community dynamics and institutional structures. The different dynamics between Muslims, non-Muslims and the state constitute the possible ways of pluralism and co-existence despite differences. In this book, we examine the specific strategies and policies developed by Muslims and by the authorities to negotiate the citizenship and integration models.

The aim of this book is to gather the views of scholars working in different disciplines on the Hui people in China in order to compare the similarities and differences of their practices in a very diverse society and state. In this book, the authors study the impact of ethnic-religious interactions and state integration positions and policies to grasp the increasing influence of the religious-collective-national expression of Muslims. We examine new patterns of expression and the interaction between religion and ethnicity of the Hui Muslims in China. The chapters investigate how the Hui encounter, accommodate and negotiate the different socio-political contexts in China. To achieve this, the authors seek to answer following questions in their respective chapters.

What does it mean to be Hui in modern China? How can you accommodate cultural-religious difference with national unity? What effect do institutions such as schools and mosques have on pupils' sense of belonging to the wider society? How far do their activities shape their identity? What kind of localized practices of Islam do Hui Muslims develop?

Hui Muslims in China are not well known in academia, in the international media, in domestic politics or in scholarly discussions. Even though the Hui are the second-largest minority in China, research about them and their way of life is rare and the majority of what few works there are on the Hui people in China are restricted to some specific research category. There is a notable lack of interest in Muslims in China with the exception of the Uyghur community. It has been more than thirty years since China began to reform and open up in 1978 and the trend of studying Islamic culture abroad is also attracting attention in Chinese academic circles. Nowadays more and more people have an intense interest in this field, but after a series of natural disasters which have brought terror and violence on the Chinese territory causing huge loss of civilian lives and property, the Chinese people have started to want to know what the Muslims' inner world is like, what the differences are between them and Han or other minority people, and what makes them different from other Chinese in their daily lives.

Chinese Islam is very diverse but various practices can be depicted as significant markers of Islam. Many scholars are beginning to study the multiple facets of Islam and Muslim practices in China to understand the increasing visibilities of Muslim communities. In order to map Chinese Islam, this volume also looks at contemporary works and studies (Gillette 2000; Gladney 1991 and 1998; Lipman 1997). From Broomhall's to Gladney's writings, these studies on Muslims in China, drawing on a number of issues and discussions on Islam, are prominent sources from which to analyse the origins and practices of the diverse Muslim populations in China (Israeli, 1994). A growing body of scholarship written by Western scholars and Chinese academics has fostered the formation of a Muslim ethnic identity, its differences from wider society and the implementation of Islam on Mainland China. A complex picture of Islam in China emerges as a result of interaction with other ethnic groups, Chinese culture and religion, political developments and transnational links with wider Islamic communities throughout the so-called Islamic world.

A comparison of the different ethnic groups in China, specifically Hui religious and ethnic practices, provides a guide for the analysis of different models. The chapters in this book look at the modes of organization of Muslims, the social-cultural and religious dynamics of their identity, and their relations with local-national governments and with non-Muslim communities.

To examine Muslims' ethnic-religious identifications in contemporary China, and to trace in which ways Muslims develop their religious and ethnic identity towards the wider society, the chapters broadly focus on three topics: (1) state policies towards the Hui community, (2) the interaction of Muslims with the local communities and the state, and (3) the localization of Muslims and Islam in China.

State Policies and the Hui

The Chinese government recognizes many ethnic and religious communities. The various ethnic nationalities form 'Chinese nationality'. The Hui are predominantly Mandarin Chinese-speaking Muslims in China's vast territory. With a population of over ten million, they are also one of the most numerous recognized ethnic groups in China. Of the 56 Chinese ethnic minorities, more than ten are Muslim. The Chinese Muslim population has reached more than twenty million and the Hui people are the largest Muslim group in China.

As the book's name suggests, the topic here is the Hui people in China, which means that not all Muslims or all people who believe in Islam in China are covered. The living conditions or other contemporary issues of people such as the Uyghur or people who converted to Islam in China are not explored specifically because even though they also obey the rules established by the Hui in politics, economy and culture, they also have to deal with complex situations, such as changes in ethnic policies from the central government and the enforcement of the policies by local government, to define their identity, interaction with non-Muslims or other people, or the influence of international culture. In order to explore this subject in depth, it is quite necessary to describe those ethnic groups and people. Such considerations, however, are beyond the scope of this small volume because of the lack of space and various other subjective and objective conditions.

Several major factors are emphasised in the process of maintaining relations between the state and Muslims in China. First, majority-minority relations take a role in shaping Muslims' identity and their religious understanding. The state has different policies to regulate all citizens regardless of whether they are from minority or majority ethnic groups. The scattered character of the Muslim population in diverse areas and cities across China tremendously changes the local-religious identity and the cultural habits of the Hui in China, and this is studied in the second and third parts of the book.

During the rule of the Kuomintang party under Chiang Kai-shek, five peoples of China were identified. Uyghurs were included in the Hui Muslim category. At that time before Mao Zedong, all Muslims formed a single ethnic entity (Gladney 1991). The Communist Party applied the same system as the Soviet Union used in Central Asia to classify people. The Party recognised fifty-six nationalities, among which the Uyghurs and eight other Muslim groups were counted separately, they were not in the general category of Hui. This categorisation reflects the policy of ethnic control and also the integration of Islam into China. As a religious policy, the association China Islamic Affairs Association (*Zhongguo Yisilanjiao Xiehui*) is responsible for the management of Islam. It is the representative body for Islamic practices. The association was founded in 1956 and works as a consultative organisation which makes recommendations to the government regarding the establishment of new mosques and Islamic schools. It plays a role in developing policies regarding Muslims' lives in China. By this means, religious practices have become domesticated and moderated in accordance with Chinese internal and external policies regarding Muslims.

The way that these policies are put into practice by Chinese government officials at different levels brings into question how applicable they are, taking into consideration the majority-minority and ethno-geographical framework. In the chapters by Glasserman and Holder, the successful Hui integration with the wider society is contrasted with that of another ethnic Muslim group, the Uyghurs. Ross Holder addresses the question of what role the state plays in the contrasting dynamic that exists between the state and these two disparate Chinese Muslim ethnic groups. As Holder explains, his chapter focuses on the relatively harmonious attitude of Hui Muslims and the positive role of the state. The interaction between the Hui and the state is regulated through state and municipal laws and policies. These regulations have affected the general minority-majority relations and other ethnic groups. So can the development of any successful policy between the Hui and the state be a model for other Muslim ethnic groups? Aaron Glasserman's chapter on the China Islamic Association (CIA) can be regarded as a policy to extend the model between the Hui and the state to other Muslim ethnic groups. In line with this policy, the CIA issues authoritative religious opinions that condemn separatism and religious extremism in Islamic terms.

In their dealings with Uyghur Muslims, the Hui claim a difference and regard themselves as the legitimate Chinese Muslims. In contrast with other Muslim peoples (Kazakhs, Kyrgyz, Uyghurs), they stress their attachment to China and they emphasise their Chinese identity, according to our personal observation and interviews with Hui individuals. This emphasis on difference may be the result of the Uyghur separatist movement which continues to influence much of the current debate on Muslims in China.

To depict the relations between state and the Hui, Gui Rong explores the community patterns (*jamaat*) and how collective features are employed in daily life. *Jamaat* practices such as *mawlid al-Nabi* celebrations and Arabic language classes supported by both rural and urban education departments are some of the elements by which it is possible to follow how the Hui's collective religious identity is reshaped and managed in diverse areas.

Hui and Han Inter-ethnic Exchanges and Relations

In the interactive process between Hui Muslims and the Han, there are many factors that have contributed to the Hui Muslim acculturation to Han culture. These factors include the special ethnic origin of the Hui Muslims, their geographical distribution interlocked with Han-inhabited areas, the imbalanced gender ratio when they moved into Han residential areas which caused frequent intermarriages with local Han women, and the adaptation to the larger socio-economic and political systems. In addition, for historical reasons, the places inhabited by Hui Muslims were located along communication routes and areas of strategic importance, and thus were those areas where Han culture was more preponderant and influential.

In a sense, the process of Hui acculturation is also a process of the re-elaboration of Han culture. This process is mainly achieved through participation in the Han-Chinese school education model, the imperceptible influence of daily life, and adherence to the cultural assimilation policy and through the adaptation process initiated by the Muslim intellectual elites (such as the *Yi ru shi jin* movement launched between the end of the Ming dynasty and the beginning of the Qing dynasty).

During the process of contact between the Hui and the main ethnic group – the Han, because of acculturation reasons, Han cultural factors seeped into Hui culture and the Hui developed important differences from the other Chinese Islamic ethnic groups. On the other hand, in order to avoid complete Hanification, the Hui further strengthened the Islamic elements of their culture, thus emphasizing the line of demarcation between them and the Han and the other non-Islamic ethnic groups.

Then, after having briefly examined the process of identification with Han culture, the chapter explores the process of the Hui's identification with Islamic culture. The spread and development of Islam in China has undergone three stages, the *Fan fang* stage, the Confucianism (Hanification) stage and the Hui Muslim stage.

The Hui have been regarded and accepted as Chinese Muslims or Sino-Muslims. This terminology, according to Gladney, is misleading since other ethnic Muslim communities are also Chinese (Gladney 1991).

The cultural resemblance of the Hui to the Han is one of the features of the Hui. They adapt many of their Islamic practices to Han ways of life. They share many cultural and folkloric affinities with Han Chinese, and religion is the only difference between the Hui and the Han, according to many Hui. They distinguish themselves from the other nationalities, and Islam serves as an identity marker. However, for Dillon, it is not possible to consider Muslims in China solely as a religious minority, which also counts for Hui (Dillon 1999).

The examples that Feng Yu gives in her chapter demonstrate how the Hui Chinese have adapted to Han culture while still maintaining their Islamic customs. Yu Feng casts doubts on the two main patterns – *assimilation* and *separation* – of interaction between the Hui and non-Hui by suggesting that the Hui's identity is multiple and dynamic. The Hui have been influenced by the majority Han culture and have adopted it in many areas, such as architecture, language and dress codes, as a consequence of the intermingling of the Hui with the Han Chinese. They are not totally isolated from the Hanus Mongolian and Tajik groups (Gladney 1991) and their identity is not considered a threat to the dominant Chinese culture. The Hui in this sense are unique among other recognised nationalities in China in that Islam is the sole criterion of ethnic identity, which represents the difference. Even so, some Han do not consider the Hui as a distinct ethnic group (Dillion 1999). The Parshi Dai ethnic group, a

Muslim ethnic group studied by Ma Chuang in this volume, demonstrates how the process of maintaining Islam defines their identity. They interact with the dominant Dai group and as a consequence of inter-marriage and social circles between Dai and Parshi Dai, their ethnic identities are expanded. The marriage strategies of the Parshi Dai people have changed over time in relation to the preservation of their ethnic identity. Chuang's chapter provides details about how Dai Hui marry with other Hui or non-Hui people and how they intermingle their Hui ethnic identity with non-Hui people.

Some Hui adopted Han names, wore Han clothes and some of them married people from the Han community, all of which can be seen as a process of acculturation which sustains the exchange between the Hui and the Han peoples. As a consequence of this acculturation and relationship, the Hui do not see themselves as apart from the Chinese people; however they insist on keeping many of their customs and traditions, especially religious ones. Among these practices, many Arabic words are preserved, particularly in religious life. It is interesting to see how the majority of Hui exchange their Chinese names for Islamic and Arabic ones. This multi-belonging and kind of hybridization has led to the localization of Muslims and Islam in China. The Hui acculturation process is studied in terms of religious synthesis as shown in Benite's excellent work on Confucian Sino-Islamic synthesis (Zvi Ben-Dor 2005). Muslim minorities have experienced the implication and influence of Confucian religious teachings in their writings (Murata and all 2009).

Does developing a localized version of Islam in the context of the Chinese and Islamic cultures result in a more accommodated religious identity within Chinese society or a more sectarian-fragmented Islam? This question is not directly addressed in this volume, but the third part, picking up the thread from the second part, deals with this question of local and trans-local practices of Islam in China.

Localization of Muslims and Islam

This part looks at the Muslim way of life and Muslim practices in different fields to understand how Islam is localized in different contexts. To do this, we have to analyse the circulation of narratives and trans-local practices among Muslims in China to determine whether they create new patterns or mixtures of their self-presentation and religious interpretation (Brose 2011). As Muslims are not a homogeneous group in China, ethnic-religious diversity enforces the diversification of Muslim identity and practices within various secular-national contexts. The aim is to observe the daily practices, narratives and strategies to figure out the dynamics through which Muslims formulate their self.

Islamic knowledge concerning Islamic history and rituals was translated into Chinese at the end of the Ming dynasty, in the late sixteenth century (Israeli 2002). This is a significant element for understanding how Islamic knowledge was localized and disseminated among Chinese people which resulted in conversions to Islam and the increase of the Chinese Muslim population. Does the dispersion of the Hui in China have an effect on their religiosity and national-religious attachment? Lesley Turnbull's chapter analyses this localization of Islam in China looking specifically at the practices of the Shadian people. The localization of Islamic practices and knowledge brings into question what exactly constitutes Islamic authenticity. What Turnbull argues in the chapter is very interesting because she shows that the degree of authenticity depends on its locally-defined and negotiated aspects. The chapter underlines the dichotomy between rural and urban areas as a means to unpack how place contributes to the Hui Islamic or ethnic identity and belonging. Muslims in Kunming and Shadian negotiate and redefine the notions of Islam and ethnicity. By negotiating Islam and ethnicity in defining their identity, the Hui give more place to religion. Gillette thinks that Xi'an, an ancient city in the center of China, is Arabized because of the increasing connection between China and the Middle East, whilst in Lesley Turnbull's investigation in Shadian, although the local Muslims emphasize the increasing connections, the connections have had no influence. Muslims in Shadian learn the essence of Islam by reading the *Qur'an*. Turnbull holds the idea that it is the interaction between different ethnic or cultural groups that causes the change rather than the significantly influential Islamic international power.

In Liang Zhang's chapter on Islamic courses given in mosques in Hohhot city, mosques are shown to be playing a decisive role in the preservation of Islamic identity and lifestyle of Hui living in Hohhot city. With Islamic rituals such as praying and ablutions, Qur'anic courses construct the ideal pious Muslim and also provide a distinction of identity based on that ideal. Weddings, funerals and celebrations are still taking place in mosques among the Hui community. So the mosque is central to the formation of Islamic identity, which follows Turnbull's argument, and it is the religion that shapes the authentic identity of the Hui. The systematic courses and religious education provided by mosques are vitally important for preserving Muslim purity. Many Hui form their Islamic lifestyle according the knowledge that they gain during their mosque classes. The rapid urbanization and modernization since the 1990s certainly created an upward mobility for the young Hui generation. Many Hui university students have started to move to metropolitan cities where society is mainly dominated by Han culture. Consequently, they started to be confronted by new issues and difficulties in the process of embedding into such a heterogeneous society (Zang 2007). Halal food, accommodation and marriage are some of the confrontations and adaptations that they face in their daily life. Gönül's chapter on Hui university students in Wuhan demonstrates the dilemmas and the challenges that have to be faced to maintain the religious identity of the Hui in urban areas. Coming from a rural area or from small-scale cities to metropolitan areas produces new lifestyles.

Territorial identification can dilute or strengthen the localization of Islamic practices. The mobility of Hui people in growing urban areas does not diminish the role of religious rituals and practices. At the same time, the opening up of China through trade has created links with the other Muslim countries and centres. The influence of the core lands of Islam and its teachings have developed a specific kind of Islam among the Hui people.

The idea that there is a strong link between territory and identity is not necessarily applicable to the Hui Muslims of China because of their non-attachment to any particular territory, as they are spread all over the country. It is also interesting to observe how territorial attachment has made a diversification in the moods, creeds and customs of the Hui in China. The Hui are going to an ethnic turn after the increase of trade ties and globalization (Ho 2013). It is also interesting to see how these translocal economical relations affect Hui ethnicity and religious identity.

Challenges

A lack of social cohesion among peoples of different ethnicities and religions has been identified in recent years in China. The recent development and concerns regarding Muslim extremism require more inquiry into relations between Muslims and non-Muslims in multi-cultural diverse societies (Gracie 2014). China has maintained and managed relatively well its racial and religious harmony in the face of rapid social change. There are risks as well as benefits linked to increasing ethnic, cultural and religious diversity. The core elements of a cohesive society, which are a sense of belonging, participation, inclusion, recognition, trust and social integration, are weakened by factors associated with social exclusion, discrimination and marginalization. Increasing the networks of relationships and trust between different social groups, tackling exclusion and marginalization, and fighting inequality are common denominators of a cohesive society.

In the last three decades, China's economic strength has surged, but have the citizens of the minorities benefited? Has the nation successfully delivered new wealth to them? Does religion impede the process? Can a devout ethnic group maintain its features when its members integrate into a modern, open and market-oriented society even though they have already taken advantage of minority nationality preferential policies? Questions such as these are the ones that challenge the existing relations between Hui, Han and the state.

Further Research

The major contributions in this volume give attention to Hui Muslims' relations with the state and other non-Muslim communities. The authors in this volume look at different aspect of Hui life in China, mainly in Yunnan province. There is a rapid growth of research on Muslims in China but little research has been conducted in English on Hui Muslims in China. In this regard, the present volume makes a valuable contribution to the study of Hui Muslims. The general point that the contributors found in this volume is that the interactions between Hui and non-Hui are fostered, which paradoxically goes hand in hand with the affirmation of Islamic recognition and visibility of Hui.

The public presence and visibility of Hui Muslim identity through mosques, Islamic scholars, halal food consumption does not create such controversies that we observe in Europe. However it is important to see new developments in terms of ethnic and religious relations, new emergence of Islamic authorities, the effect of transnational networks and activities and also the diversity of the Chinese Muslim population. Further research may provide tools to identify new patterns, challenges, and pitfalls of being Hui in contemporary China. The new researches are necessary on the implication of globalization, internet, media and transnational networks, potentially causing Sinicization of the Hui in China or Arabization of Islam, as part of the acculturation process. If you look at the religious landscape and architectural design of the mosques, one of the observations is that some are built in a traditional Chinese style with pagoda like temples; others imitate classical Islamic green tiled domes. Globalization, business and trade networks, as well as the rise of social media affect Muslim identity and appearance in public life.

Finally, we hope that this book can provide a forum for the dissemination and discussion of the latest research findings on topics related to questions of localization, ethnic and religious identity, and ethnic policies. Researchers from the fields of anthropology, sociology, political science, history and ethnology share their views and critical perspectives on these issues.

References

Gracie, Carrie (2014). 'The Knife attack that changed Kunming'. Available at http://www.bbc.com/news/world-asia-28305109 [accessed August 20, 2015].

Benite, Zvi Ben-Dor (2005). *The Dao of Muhammad: A Cultural History of Muslims in Late Imperial China*. Cambridge: Harvard University Asia Center.

Broomhall, Marshall (1910). *Islam in China: A Neglected Problem*. London Missionary Society, London.

Brose, Michael C. (2011), 'Globalization and the Chinese Muslim Community in Southwest China', *Asia Pacific: Perspectives*, 10(1), pp. 61-80.

Dillon, Michael (1999). *China's Muslim Hui Community: Migration, Settlement and Sects*. Richmond, Surrey: Curzon.

Gillette, Maris Boyd (2000). *Between Mecca and Beijing: Modernization and Consumption Among Urban Chinese Muslims*. Stanford, CA: Stanford University Press.

Gladney, Dru C. (1991). *Muslim Chinese: Ethnic Nationalism in the People's Republic*. Cambridge, MA, Harvard University Press.

Gracie, Carrie (2014). 'The Knife attack that changed Kunming'. Available at http://www.bbc.com/news/world-asia-28305109 [accessed August 20, 2015].

Ho, Wai-Yip (2013). 'Mobilizing the Muslim Minority for China's Development: Hui Muslims, Ethnic Relations and Sino-Arab Connections', *Journal of Comparative Asian Development*, 12(1), pp. 84-112.

Israeli, Raphael (1980). *Muslims in China: a Study in Cultural Confrontation*. London: Curzon.

Israeli, Raphael (1994). *Islam in China: a Critical Bibliography*. Greenwood Press, Westport.

Israeli, Raphael (2002). *Islam in China: Religion, Ethnicity, Culture and Politics*. Lanham and Oxford: Lexington Books.

Lipman, Jonathan N. (1996). 'Hyphenated Chinese: Sino-Muslim Identity in Modern China', in . Gail Hershatter, Emily Honing, Jonathan N. Lipman and Randall Stross, eds,

Remapping China: Fissures in Historical Terrain. Stanford, CA: Stanford University Press, pp. 97-112.

Murata, Sachiko, William C. Chittick, Tu Weiming (2009). *The Sage Learning of Liu Zhi: Islamic Thought in Confucian Terms.* Cambridge, MA: Harvard University Press.

Pillsbury, Barbara (1981a). 'Muslim History in China: A 1300-Year Chronology,' *Journal of Muslim Minority Affairs*, 3(2), pp. 10-29.

Pillsbury, Barbara (1981b). 'The Muslim Population of China: Clarifying the Questions of Size and Ethnicity,' *Journal of Muslim Minority Affairs*, 3(2), pp. 35-58.

Zang, Xiaowei (2007). *Ethnicity and urban life in China: a Comparative Study of Hui Muslims and Han Chinese.* London: Routledge.

Printed in the USA
CPSIA information can be obtained
at www.ICGtesting.com
CBHW080108210524
8864CB00004B/158

9 789462 700666